Praise for *The Big Book of HR*

"Gamlem and Mitchell have done a brilliant job of providing a roadmap for the secrets of successfully managing people in today's complex business environment. The authors understand the history and roots of the human resources profession as well as the importance of embracing change to meet the challenges of the present and the future. *The Big Book of HR* is comprehensive, yet concise and is an essential reference for every HR professional, manager and business owner."

—Mary Walter Arthur, SPHR, director, Talent Acquisition, Enviva Biomass

"I am pleased to see such a robust resource that will help guide human resource professionals in their human capital investment. This book provides a human capital framework for areas in selecting and retaining top talent, employee engagement programs, and total rewards. These types of programs will help drive the strategy and mission of the organization, lead to a highly engaged, committed workforce and significantly improve overall performance and profitability."

—Angela Galyean, vice president, Human Resources, Intelsat

"I am excited about this new edition of *The Big Book of HR*—a comprehensive HR management guidebook. Offering practical and useful tips to put knowledge into practice, this is a 'must have' for managers of all levels. I'm recommending it for use in my organization."

—Judy Perrault, CEO, Mindbank

"In this comprehensive book, the authors provide readers with a wealth of information, stories, resources, and discussion questions to guide you through the wonderful world of human resources. Mitchell and Gamlem are respected experts in HR and have generously shared their knowledge and experiences in this valuable new book."

—Sharon Armstrong, author of *The Essential Performance Review Handbook*
and *The Essential HR Handbook*

"To attain wisdom, you must first learn the language of your audience. Next you must walk in their shoes, cut down a few trees in the forest and blaze a new trail on your own. Finally, you need to simplify and just know where that 5-cent washer needs to go to keep the Rube Goldberg contraption running well. *The Big Book of HR*, like it's two authors, rises to and even transcends all three levels."

—Gerry Crispin, SPHR, co-founder, CareerXroads

"*The Big Book of HR* is a great HR reference book that covers virtually all areas of the human resources field—a one source of relevant information. The chapters include everything from the legal aspects of the employment relationship to the core function of HR which is attracting and developing talent for the organization. It is a practical guide which is easy to follow and provides solid recommendations on how to lead an HR organization for the benefit of the enterprise it supports. If I could only have one HR book on my shelf, this would be the one.

—Gus Siekierka, retired VP and chief HR officer, CSC

"HR Professionals: Buy it, read it, rely on it and you will never regret it! Although there are lots of books on HR, *The Big Book of HR* is best guide for an HR practitioner out there. Regardless if you are new to the profession or tenured, *The Big Book* will become a reference companion to your daily work. Throughout the book it is extremely clear that Mitchell and Gamlem are seasoned professionals in the industry. Their ability to break down the concepts and apply the to situations an HR professional will come across daily ensure that this book will be well worn and dog eared. I was very impressed by the way they conveyed 'insights' or 'things to be aware of' that most practitioners only learn through trial and error. I wish I had this book when I was starting out! The book also allows you to lean on leaders in the HR profession as if they were sitting in the desk beside you."

—Sarah Rajtick, principal, Rajtick Consulting

Revised and Updated Edition

The
Big Book
of HR

Barbara Mitchell and
Cornelia Gamlem

CAREER
PRESS
Wayne, NJ

THE BIG BOOK OF HR, REVISED AND UPDATED EDITION
Edited by Jodie Brandon
Typeset by Diana Ghazzawi
Original cover design by Rob Johnson/toprotype
Printed in the U.S.A.

To order this title, please call toll-free 1-800-CAREER-1 (NJ and Canada: 201-848-0310) to order using VISA or MasterCard, or for further information on books from Career Press.

The Career Press, Inc.
12 Parish Drive
Wayne, NJ 07470
www.careerpress.com

Library of Congress Cataloging-in-Publication Data

CIP Data Available Upon Request.

This book is dedicated to my family, who have encouraged me in this project and in so many other ways! Thanks for always being there.
—Barbara Mitchell

This book is dedicated to my parents, Vincent and Cornelia Gibaldi, who taught me the value of hard work and integrity. I wish they were here to share this milestone with me.
—Cornelia Gamlem

In memory of R. Gregory Green, SPHR, GPHR. Your leadership helped the HR profession soar to great heights.

During our journey in writing this book, we had many friends who helped us to bring it to completion.

We can never express enough gratitude to some special contributors: Susan Devereaux, who edited and formatted the manuscript for us. Susan's insights and great questions helped us write what we hope is a highly readable book. Our valued colleague and friend Mary Jane Sinclair, who shared her vast expertise and experience by writing a critical chapter about developing a salary structure for us. Another valued colleague and friend, Jennifer Whitcomb, who wrote the coaching chapter for us. A good friend and legal advisor, Robin McCune, who brought her years of experience practicing employment law to review and edit the legal landscape portions of this book.

Others who lent a hand along the way include Sharon Armstrong, Mary Walter Arthur, Leslie Borta, Angela Galyean, Becky Hadeed, Linda Keller, Gary Cluff, Gary Kushner, Suzanne Logan, Tom Murphy, Lance Richards, John White, and Melanie Young.

Thanks to our literary agent, Marilyn Allen, for her help and advice, and to everyone at Career Press for their support and their confidence in us!

Finally, a special thanks from Cornelia to Carl Gamlem and Erik Gamlem, who supported this effort in ways I cannot describe. And from Barbara, special thanks to the Mitchell family, Reebel family, Lohr family, Waites family, Parnaby family, Donegan family, and McGuire family for unconditional love and support always.

Contents

Disclaimer

The Big Book of HR is published only as an informational guide. The reader should keep in mind that although it is designed to provide accurate and current information on employment law compliance issues as of the date of publication, the information contained herein is general in nature and is not intended to be relied upon as legal advice. Laws and regulations are not static and they frequently change. Neither the information in this book, nor any information found on the Internet, should be a substitute for legal advice. The resolution of each circumstance encountered by readers should ultimately be determined on a case-by-case basis, depending upon the particular facts, and legal counsel should be sought as appropriate.

How to Use This Book

The Big Book of HR has 30 chapters and is organized into five sections. For the most part, each chapter deals with one topic or one function, and contains easy-to-follow text, lots of examples, tips, and sidebars to give you as much information as possible. The Appendix is filled with additional resources to help you design your own forms or processes.

Section One: Selecting and Assimilating New Employees (Chapters 1–12)

In this section, we discuss how you get started to determine what kind of employees and what number of employees your organization will need to meet your strategic goals and objectives. We look at the legal issues around the rights of employees before discussing the recruiting process, including where to find candidates, how to interview and select the best applicant, how to make a job offer, and then how to assimilate the new hires successfully into your organization.

Section Two: Employee Engagement and Retention (Chapters 13–16)

In this section, we explore the critical areas of how to engage your employees so that they are as productive as possible and, then, how to retain them for your organization. Both of these functions have major impact on your bottom line. We look at the issue of workplace flexibility and the role this plays in the retention process, and also give you information on how to craft rewards and recognition programs that will work for your organization.

Section Three: Total Rewards (Chapters 17–21)

In this section, we look at the legal issues around compensation, and introduce you to compensation and how critical it is to have a well-designed system that will work for your organization. We lead you through the steps to developing a compensation structure and then discuss the increasingly complex, but critical, area of employee benefits.

Section Four: Employee Development (Chapters 22–26)

In this section, we look at how critical it is to provide development opportunities for your employees and work through the process of determining what development is needed in your organization. We then look at the many ways to provide development, including training and mentoring, and also at the very positive impact that coaching can have in your employee development strategy. We discuss performance management strategy, including the appraisal process, the feedback process, and how to have the critical conversations so necessary to move employees toward reaching their full potential.

Section Five: Employee Relations (Chapters 27–30)

In this section, we look at the areas of employee and labor relations, risk management, conflict resolution, and ending the employment relationship. Each of these topics has huge impact in the lifecycle of employment.

Appendix: Additional Resources

This section has templates, charts, forms, and more to help your organization manage your human resources processes and maximize productivity.

SECTION 1

SELECTING AND ASSIMILATING NEW EMPLOYEES

1

Introduction to HR

Welcome to the updated version of *The Big Book of HR*. You may be an HR professional just starting out in your career, or a manager or a business owner without HR support who needs to gather information on how to hire, develop, or fire an employee. This book is intended for anyone who works with people and who wants to maximize the impact employees have to ensure the success of the organization. Although there are strong links between HR practices, this book is designed so that each chapter stands alone. Where it makes sense, we refer you to other chapters in the book for more information or to the Appendix, which is filled with forms and other valuable information you can use to supplement what you are already doing in your organization.

The HR profession has had many names—industrial relations, personnel, HR—and now some organizations have invented new names, such as Google, where HR is "people operations." HR used to be seen as only doing administrative work, but now HR (or whatever you call it in your organization) is actively involved in setting strategy around the people who do the work that move your organization toward the achievement of your mission, vision, and organizational goals. HR can and should serve as advisors to organizational leadership to develop strategic workforce plans that link to the organization's strategic plan to ensure that the right people are on board so that the firm can meet its objectives and fulfill its mission. HR partners with line management to provide development opportunities to maximize the potential of each and every employee. HR advises management on total rewards programs (compensation and benefits), and rewards and recognition programs designed to minimize costly employee turnover and to maximize employee engagement and retention.

In order to add real value to organizations, HR professionals must understand the business they are in—not just their part of the business. They need to also understand the economics of business—how the organization is funded if it is a non-profit or how it makes money if it is a for-profit organization. A fully functional HR professional, like any other businessperson, should be able to read and understand a profit and loss statement, create and manage to a budget, and understand profit centers. Too often, HR professionals limit themselves by not actively participating in discussions around marketing, finance, and the operations of the organization. They only speak up when the discussion gets around to topics like pay or benefits. The late Pam Farr, the brilliant and highly strategic HR executive at Marriott International, used to tell the story that she would time herself in senior leadership meetings. She would wait at least 20 minutes before bringing up an HR-related issue. All the while, she would be actively engaged in the marketing or finance discussions. This positioned her as a valued partner to the other executives, who saw her first as a business colleague and then as the HR leader she was.

To really set yourself apart as a HR professional, think about how you can add value to your organization. Can you:

- Actively participate with understanding in discussions around your organization's business objectives?
- Find a way to do something more efficiently than it is currently being done?
- Determine how people and processes can contribute to the bottom line?
- Partner with other leaders in your organization to maximize organizational efficiency?
- Think strategically by anticipating challenges and resolving potential problems?
- Ask the right questions to help your organization meet its goals and achieve its mission?
- Lead change initiatives when required?
- Communicate effectively in order to influence other leaders?
- Manage costs related to employees?
- Demonstrate your proficiency in HR related topics such as staffing, retention, HR analytics, compensation, benefits, total rewards, rewards and recognition, employee engagement, employee relations, employee development, leadership development, organizational development, labor relations, HRIS and more?
- Lead the organization in an ethical fashion and protect the organization?

There are several topics of general interest that impact everything else in HR and in business that we want to introduce you to before you look at specific HR functions that are discussed in greater detail in this book:

- Multiple generations in the workplace.
- Globalization.
- HR technology.
- HR analytics or people analytics.
- Organizational culture.

Multiple Generations in the Workplace

Because people are now living and working longer, we currently have five generations able to work simultaneously; and, we've become well aware of the issues of having several generations working together. The Millennial generation (Generation Y) is now the largest generation in the workplace since WWI Veterans and Baby Boomers. It is not unusual to have younger people managing older people, and this can lead to tension on both sides. Managers and HR professionals need to recognize this potential landmine and help employees acknowledge and appreciate that they each have a different set of skills and abilities that they bring to the workplace.

We've learned that the generations have both differences and similarities, and the most important thing to consider is how to maximize the similarities so that we can all work toward the mission of the organization. Organizations need to be aware of the makeup of their employee population and design strategies to attract and retain the talent needed—no matter what generation they come from!

According to Nicole Lipkin, author of *Y in the Workplace: Managing the "Me First" Generation*, "What we're witnessing is not a generational thing. Who doesn't want flexibility? Who doesn't want to understand the context for their work? Who doesn't want better work/life balance? The only difference is that Generation Y is finally saying what every other generation is thinking."[1]

There is a great deal of information available on the four generations including in *The Essential HR Handbook: A Quick and Handy Resource for Any Manager or HR Professional*.[2] Millennials and the iGen want a constant stream of feedback. They want to know how they are doing on every project every day. This is not a generation who will sit back and wait until their annual performance appraisal to hear what you think of them. And, they won't wait for you to give them feedback; they'll ask you up-front. According to an article in the *Harvard Business Review*, "Millennials view work as a key part of life, not as a separate activity that needs to be 'balanced' by it."[3] This translates into their need for finding work that excites them and where they can have friends at work. They also want to be able to learn new skills and connect to something that is meaningful to them personally.

This is a generation that is accustomed to being praised for anything they accomplish. Many of them have been serious over-achievers from a very early age and thrive on praise for a job well done. Millennials like to work in teams—they are used to working in teams—but they also can work alone. (Consider all the time they've spent playing video games while growing up!) They want to be recognized for good work and they respond well to being mentored.

Millennials love to try new ideas; accordingly use their enthusiasm to bring along some of your other employees who don't easily embrace change. Also, Millennials have been volunteering all their lives, so be sure your organization offers them opportunities to continue that passion.

Obviously, your organization needs to provide Millennials with state-of-the-art technology in order to really engage them in their work—or get them to help you find good technology solutions.

You need to be honest with them, starting with your website and continuing on through the hiring process and how you on-board them and, according to Bruce Tulgan in *Not Everyone Gets a Trophy: How to Manage Generation Y*, "There are few things Gen Yers are more sensitive to than false advertising. They will spread the word if they feel duped."[4]

The newest generation (iGen) are people who were born after 1995 and have been totally influenced by the rapid changes in our world. They tend to be tolerant, socially active, and committed to causes such as the environment. They have strong ties to their parents and have been raised in a media-saturated world. To say they are dependent on technology would be an understatement, so be sure your communication strategies include mobile applications because this is a generation that finds email too slow!

The impact the generational differences have on the workplace can be a challenge for managers and for HR, but as long as we acknowledge that each generation has distinct behavior, habits, expectations, and attitudes, and we understand those differences, HR can help organizations to smooth out the differences and use the strengths that each employee brings—whatever generation he or she belongs to. With the variety of multigenerational employees in today's workplace, organizations can achieve a strategic advantage by embracing the diversity the various generations bring to the workplace. HR professionals need to be innovative and develop novel solutions such as introducing reverse mentoring (where a younger employee mentors an older employee in the latest technology).

Globalization

The world and the business climate have experienced rapid globalization in recent decades, which now requires HR to shift perspectives in many ways, including recruiting globally and managing in different cultures. HR professionals or managers who work in global organizations must be highly flexible and adaptable to survive and thrive in the ever increasingly complex world we now work in. Working now requires a global mindset—an awareness of cultural differences and that doing business in other countries can be (and most likely is) significantly different from the way it is done in the United States or wherever your home country is. We need to learn local laws and regulations, and also learn how to influence and appreciate the culture in which we are working. As stated in *Managing Across Cultures*, "It simply can't be overstated: You will not succeed in global business today if you don't understand, appreciate, and know how to manage across cultures."[5]

To thrive in the global economy, we must all be highly flexible and must adapt to current situations, including when and how work is done, and the language in which it is conducted. A lot of issues around managing in a global economy result from the fact that many times we are managing people we can't see or perhaps have never met other than on Skype.

As Stephen Covey put it in *The 7 Habits of Highly Successful People*, "Seek first to understand, then to be understood."[6] It is essential that you understand your organization's culture as well as your headquarters' culture. Once you are clear on that, it is time to begin to understand cultures in other places and other businesses. It is not just the visible things such as business card protocol in Japan; it is the deeper issues of how people behave, and how they interact with others, according to Lance Richards, GPHR, SPHR, vice president of global workforce solutions at Kelly OCG.

Welcome to the 21st century, where we now all live in what has become a global village. The global economy touches every aspect of our lives and particularly our businesses. There was a time when global or international HR was a specialty that only impacted a few U.S. businesses, reports Melanie Young, GPHR, SPHR, vice president of the Global HR, Corporate and Global Business Group for Arror Electronics. Now it is a fact of life for most of us. Consider these interesting (and real) challenges:

- You work for a global organization and are asked to serve on a global task force with people from your own county, the country where your organization is headquartered in Europe, and others from South America and Asia. Your first challenge is to find a time when you can meet by teleconference or on Skype! There are huge cultural differences on the project team—different approaches to problem-solving. You learn quickly that you have to modify your communication style as you can't be too direct, and you certainly can't talk about how wonderful things are in your country because most everyone else feels that their way of doing things is right and has been working quite well!

- Working for the same global organization as in the previous point, you have the responsibility for designing a new performance management system that will be used around the world. Suddenly, you need to get up to speed on work councils in Europe and privacy laws in various countries. You learn that in some countries performance reviews can't be shared with anyone in the organization, including HR, and that some other countries require disclaimers that might be illegal in the United States.

- You are recruiting for a global organization and discover that their way of interviewing involves asking personal questions including age, marital status, religion, and other topics that are illegal in the United States. Your organization constructs a new job portal that asks candidates about their religion, race, nationality, age, and other such information.
- You are meeting with a group of global employees and tell what you think is a humorous story, and it is met with stony silence.
- Your organization is considering moving into other countries and you are on the planning team. You need to consider what kind of government exists in the potential locations and what the economy is like, as well as the size and skill level of the available labor pool. You then need to become fully knowledgeable in international, regional, and local laws that will impact your business. All this should be done before a final decision as to where to locate is made.
- You are sending some of your headquarters employees to work for an established period of time in another country. You need to prepare a compensation and benefits package that will work for your organization and the individual employee.

These are just a few examples of what HR professionals are dealing with in our global marketplace. They illustrate the complexity of the challenges HR is facing and will continue to face; therefore, HR professionals need to learn to think and operate differently.

According to Silvia Bagdadli, an associate professor of organization and human resource management at Bocconi University and the director of the executive master in strategic human resource management program at the SDA Bocconi School of Management in Milan, Italy, as reported in the May 2011 issue of *HR Magazine*, "Global HR professionals need to have several competencies: knowledge of HR strategies, models, methods and techniques; problem solving skills; people management skills; and, finally, the ability to adapt to international contexts."[7]

So what can HR professionals do to gain the experience needed to work in the global arena? Consider:

- Keeping up with international news and issues by reading publications that cover global issues, such as the *International Herald Tribune*, *New York Times*, *Washington Post*, and *Wall Street Journal*, and major business magazines, including *The Economist*, *Fortune*, *Forbes*, and the *Harvard Business Review*. Read daily newspapers from other countries online. (Many countries publish news in English, or Google has a translation service.)
- Networking with colleagues who have international background or experience. Consider asking one or more of these colleagues to serve as your mentor on global issues.
- Volunteering to serve on international task forces or committees to gain experience.
- Learning a foreign language either online or by taking classes.
- Taking an assignment in a less-desirable location to gain valuable experience with the hope of using that experience as a springboard to a better position someplace else in the world.
- Enrolling in a global HR master's program or taking international business classes.
- Taking advantage of global HR information on the Society for Human Resource Management (SHRM) website (*www.shrm.org*).

As you begin to work in other countries or with coworkers from other parts of the world, it is critical to understand that how we communicate is important for all aspects of working globally, because it impacts relationship-building, and is a key to how much influence and creditability you can gain. How you communicate with people from other countries can be more important than if you speak a common language. You'll want to be sure to share your message in a way that will acknowledge and show respect for the difference in culture or business environment. Without being condescending or patronizing, try to use simple words and concepts, brief sentences, and graphics to allow for consistent understanding. Using over-sophisticated language or overly complicated slides or templates may confuse your listeners and also come across as arrogant. Take the time before you meet or present to someone new or to an unknown group, to get to know enough about them to decide how and what to present.

Building relationships with people from other countries and cultures is done the same way you would if you wanted to get to know a coworker in your own country. Ask questions to get to know your fellow employees. If asked, participate in activities where you get to know the employees and how they spend their time outside of work. This will give you great insights into their culture. Whenever possible, involve people in what you are doing. For example, seek input on how they prefer to organize meetings, solicit ideas for the agenda, and ask who they suggest should be included in the meeting. If you are scheduling an international conference call, go with the time that works best for the majority of participants, even if this means an early or late call for you.

In most cultures, if you get a chance to meet face-to-face, food and the meal event is an important relationship-building step. Do your best by trying the local food. Most often they will serve dishes that are known to be acceptable to Americans unless you let them know you are willing to try something new.

HR Technology

One of the core competencies of an HR professional is the ability to understand how technology impacts current processes and how technology can be used to maximize efficiency while not damaging the strong interpersonal relationships required to do business. HR needs to look at the challenges of technology and the impact it has on the work we do. For example, who could have imagined the impact social media has had on recruiting? And what about the unique challenges we now face in managing people who don't work in the same place we do—maybe not even in the same country—and how we can keep connected using a wide variety of technological solutions.

We use technology to develop our employees by using virtual meeting software and other high-tech resources to keep employees up-to-date on new policies and procedures. We rely on intranets to share valuable information with our employees. Employees enroll and manage their benefits online. They make changes to their personal information such as marital status or benefits changes without HR having to fill out a form or enter data. We use technology to upload information to get employees on payroll, to make changes to deductions, or to enter paid time off information. We use technology to track applicants, capture EEO data, create skills inventories, and conduct background investigations on applicants. We rely more heavily on technology every day. Some forward-thinking organizations are even moving to paperless employee filing systems!

With our ever-increasing dependence on technology, it is important to be sure that privacy is maintained and that all employee data are kept secure. HR and IT can work to ensure critical data integrity is maintained. Therefore, HR needs to be able to have strong links with their technology partners in order to maximize the products used. An increasing number of firms specialize in technology products for HR, and SHRM is a good source for up-to-date information on new and innovative products. SHRM has a practice area around HR technology that can be found at *www. shrm.org.*

HR Analytics or People Analytics

Organizations need reliable data to make good decisions and HR needs to embrace analytics and do it as quickly as possible. Google has been a leader in this area. They've figured out that data can help assess the effectiveness of programs and processes, and most importantly, help organizations make better decisions about what is important both to the organization and to its people. It's about using data to drive everything related to your employees.

Organizations used to make decisions based on what we thought was the right thing to do—and that might have been based on research but most often was based on the latest trend or newest product out there! Now, we can use real data to make better decisions.

This trend has been difficult for a lot of HR professionals who don't feel comfortable with data. However, we need to get on board with analytics and understand that using data to make better decisions makes us more valuable to our organizations.

You will need to understand your own organization and how it operates in order to determine which analytics you need to study. Using data to make your point can be extremely powerful and make you a much more impactful HR leader.

Some of the data you need will be available from your HR systems; however, you may need to collect additional data using surveys or focus groups. Take the first step and learn what you already have available and then fill in the gaps.

Organizational Culture

It's extremely important that you understand your organization's culture and why it's critical to your success. It's amazing how many people think their organization doesn't have a culture. It does, and even if you're not aware of it, your employees know your organization's culture. Your culture is the unique set of values that define your organization, including how you:

- Lead and manage your employees.
- Are organized (lots of layers, flat, etc.).
- Communicate.
- Reward and recognize performance.
- Handle mistakes.
- Empower your people.
- Participate in your community.
- Encourage innovation.

Your culture is significant and impacts everything you do, including the ability to attract, engage, and retain the best available talent in your field; so, don't underestimate its importance. HR plays a part in developing and disseminating your culture to your employees.

Business only gets more complicated—doesn't seem to ever go the other way. Managing people is not an easy process, and we've tried to give you as many tips and suggestions as possible to help you do your best. Because things change so quickly, follow us on the web at *www.TheHRBigBook. com* for current information and a blog with updates on emerging HR trends and issues.

2

Workforce Planning...
Succession Planning

Great NHL hockey star Wayne Gretzky often said, "Good hockey players skate to where the puck is while *great* hockey players skate to where the puck is going." The same can be said of great organizations: You have to know where you're headed to be successful, and when it comes to your people, it's called workforce planning.

Any strategic business plan deals with resource requirements, and, just as financial requirements need to be addressed, a well-crafted strategic plan needs to ensure that the appropriate people with the right skills are available to accomplish plan goals and objectives. Smart organizations include HR in the organization's strategic planning process so that there is an easy transition from strategic planning to workforce planning. If you aren't included in your organization's strategic planning process, consider talking with your CEO or other key players in your organization to inform them of the value you bring to the strategic planning process. After all, the best strategic plan will be ineffective without the right people in the right places with the right skills to carry it out—or, as Jim Collins put it so well in *Good to Great*, "having the right people on the bus."[1]

If you are not successful in being included in the strategic planning process, you will need access to the plan to be able to do a workforce or HR plan that links to the strategic plan.

An increasing number of savvy organizations are seeing the value of a well-crafted workforce plan. The growing interest is being sparked by several factors, including talent shortages, an aging workforce facing retirement, and increased productivity that requires different skill sets. As more organizations include workforce planning in their business processes, the need for strong business analytics has emerged. Several companies provide technology solutions to help collect the required data. Some provide stand-alone analytic tools, including Kronos Inc., Vertrics, and Visier.

Workforce planning is the process an organization uses to analyze its current workforce in light of what is projected over the length of the strategic plan. Is the organization in growth mode, and, if so, what skills are needed to meet the demands of an expanded business and where will the new jobs be located? Is the organization going to need to downsize or outsource positions? If so, can any of the affected employees be trained to take on new responsibilities? These are just some of many issues included in a workforce plan. Workforce planning requires leadership, a clear vision, mission and strategic objectives, and the involvement of a significant number of participants including leaders and managers. It is an inclusive process that draws together finance, operations, human resources, marketing, and other key functions.

Workforce planning focuses on developing information that can help an organization make good decisions for both the short and long term with the realization that plans, no matter how well thought out, may need to be revised to meet the changing business climate. Therefore, plans need to be evaluated often and revised as needed.

In order to be successful, any workforce plan must be carefully grounded in the culture in which it will be utilized. In other words, there is no "cookie-cutter" approach to workforce planning; each one is unique.

A well-crafted workforce plan also provides managers with a better understanding of the strengths and weaknesses of their people. Workforce planning requires all participants to open their minds to the limitations and the possibilities and to consider issues around succession management (see "Succession Management as a Workforce Planning Tool," beginning on page 28).

Workforce planning allows the organization to build a longer-term context for short-term decision-making in an attempt to predict the future. It includes an inventory of all current and future positions, and focuses attention on positions that are key to the organization's success and/or positions that are hard to fill and, therefore, will take more time to recruit.

Some people see workforce planning as only a staffing tool for anticipating hiring needs, but it can also be a critical tool for determining employee development and succession needs. Successful organizations conduct regular and thorough workforce plans so that staffing needs can be measured, employee development needs can be assessed, and contingent workforce options can be utilized to create a fully functional workforce that is able to meet the organization's business requirements.

Tips for Effective Workforce Planning

- Designate a team lead from the HR department to manage the process.
- Find a senior executive to "champion" the process.
- Identify key stakeholders and involve them in the planning process.
- Coordinate the plan with the strategic plan, succession planning, and career development initiatives.
- Ensure workforce planning is an ongoing activity and evaluated frequently.

A strategic plan charts the future with broad mission-related targets and milestones; a workforce plan translates strategic thinking into concrete actions in the areas of workforce staffing and training needs. When an organization successfully aligns human resources activities with organization strategies, activities fit strategically and reinforce each other. This strategic fit produces consistency and ensures that HR-related activities will reinforce the organization's business strategy.

HR functions impacted by the strategic plan include:

- Staffing.
- Compensation.
- Retention.
- Succession management.
- Employee development.
- Management development.

Step-by-Step Process to Develop a Workforce Plan

Step 1: Analyze Current Workforce

This step looks at the current workforce—its skills and demographic makeup, including race, gender, and age. Age may be a particularly important factor to consider if the organization has a significant number of people moving toward retirement age who will need to be replaced. During this process, you will need to understand the skill sets of your current workforce. A current workforce or supply analysis also involves making projections of attrition (due to resignations, retirements, internal transfers, promotions, and involuntary terminations) over the planning period so that attrition is taken into consideration while looking at what the future needs will be in terms of the number of employees and the specific skills needed in order to achieve success.

> → See Chapter 30 (Ending the Employment Relationship) for information on tracking attrition.

When the current workforce analysis is complete, you will have a good understanding of your current workforce and its strengths and weaknesses.

Depending on the size of your organization, you may want to limit the number of levels you include in the current workforce analysis. Here are some ideas of what you might want to include in your current workforce analysis:

- List current employees and their skills/abilities/strengths.
- Look at who might retire or leave the organization and what gaps that creates.
- Review historic turnover (attrition) data.
- Are there any poor performers who need to be retrained or be terminated?
- How will the current workforce impact (positively or negatively) achieving stated goals and objectives as outlined in your strategic plan?

Step 2: Determine What Knowledge/Skills and Abilities Will Be Required to Achieve Business Objectives for the Next Year

The strategic plan may have outlined new products or services to be added. Consider what changes are anticipated over the next (insert the number of years in the plan) years related to:

- Mission and vision.
- Budget and economic forecasts.
- Competitive factors in your line of business.
- Labor force trends.
- Pending or existing government regulations.
- Innovations in technology.
- Outsourcing options.

- Strategic partner options.
- Potential mergers and/or acquisitions.
- New products.
- Expanding to new locations.

Consider:
- What are the key business goals and objectives for the next year?
- What are the key success factors for achieving these goals and objectives?
- What are the key work activities associated with these success factors, goals, and objectives?
- Are more employees needed to achieve the stated goals and objectives?
- What skills are needed to deliver these goals and objectives?
- Is the organization growing or downsizing?
- How is the business changing in relationship to:
  - ▷ Competition?
  - ▷ New projects that will require new skills?
  - ▷ New locations (domestic or global)?
  - ▷ Number of new projects or deliverables?

Step 3: Do a Gap Analysis

Determine the gaps that exist between what you have and what you need. Answer these questions:
- Can current employees be trained to take on new responsibilities? If not, how will you deal with them (transfer to other departments, demote, terminate)?
- Do you need to hire from the outside?
- If you need to hire, when does new staff need to be on board and trained?
- Is your organization doing what it needs to do to retain key employees?
- Is the organizational structure what it should be to accomplish the goals and objectives?

You now have a plan that should tell you when and how you need to add people or skills to meet your organization's strategic objectives.

Step 4: Implement the Workforce Plan

No plan is ever successful without an implementation phase to translate the actions into a workable schedule that includes well-defined objectives, specific and measurable workforce goals, and time tables and milestones. It involves dedicating time, energy, and resources to address the critical gaps or surpluses that exist within the organization, as related to the critical business issues identified in the strategic planning process.

A successful workforce plan requires the commitment and leadership of everyone in the organization, especially top management. Senior-level managers should lead the planning process, assure that workforce plans are aligned with the strategic direction of the business, and hold subordinate mangers accountable for carrying on the workforce plan.

During the implementation phase, the plan should be continually measured for its success in meeting both efficiency and effectiveness measurements. Look at the following:

- Do workload and/or workforce gaps still exist? And, if so, what should be corrected?
- Are the assumptions used to develop the plan still valid?
- Has organizational effectiveness increased?
- Do adequate staffing levels exist?

Successful workforce plans, like strategic plans, cannot be static; they must be constantly evaluated and adjusted as needed.

Checklist for Evaluating a Workforce Plan

- Is the plan based on the organization's strategic plan, and have you considered the mission, vision, and values?
- Was the plan evaluated on its impact on the current workforce, and will a proper diversity mix result from any proposed actions?
- Have you determined the number and skill set of employees who will be needed to address upcoming challenges?
- Was a gap analysis conducted to assess what is needed versus what you now have?
- Have strategies been identified to address the gaps between the projected supply and demand of required skills and available staff?
- Is there an action plan complete with responsible parties, due dates, and resources needed?
- Has the plan been communicated to appropriate stakeholders?
- Does the plan have the support of the organization's leadership?
- Is there a strategy to update the plan?

How to Get Buy-In for a Workforce Plan

It is critical to any organizational planning process that top management supports the process. Without that support, it will be difficult to conduct a workforce plan, and implementing it will be next to impossible. Some of the selling points to use are:

- A workforce plan is the logical next step after the strategic plan is developed.
- Organizations can't achieve their objectives without the right people in the right positions.
- A well-crafted workforce plan has the potential to save the organization time and money by laying out a logical way to hire, train, and develop employees. This is the one that usually gets their attention!

Succession Management as a Workforce Planning Tool

Another aspect of effective workforce planning is succession planning. Succession planning is used by organizations to identify and prepare employees who have the potential skills and abilities to move into key positions when the incumbent leaves the job. Having a succession plan generally ensures a smooth continuation of business when positions become vacant because of promotion, resignation, or transfer within the organization.

You've probably heard or read about the many highly visible examples of what happens when organizations don't have a succession plan. What happens when a senior executive is killed in a plane crash, or is indicted on a fraud charge, or has a serious illness and must step down? Who takes the place of that executive, and how quickly can that person be the leader the organization requires at that difficult time and into the future? This is why having a succession plan is critical to any organization's success.

It's not easy to get organizations to tackle the issue of succession planning. Some executives don't want to face the difficult discussions that must take place in the process; however, it is extremely important that this process takes place. In reality, the future of the business depends on it!

Most succession plans have historically focused only on high-level positions, but in recent years, more attention has been given to selecting successors for positions throughout the organization. This makes sense in the highly aggressive talent competition most organizations find themselves in. You have to know who your key players are at any level—and what positions you can't go long without having filled. These positions may be in sales, marketing, IT, or other places within the organization.

Multiple options exist to do succession planning, including highly sophisticated software models that collect data from performance reviews, employee development plans, courses taken, skills inventories, and recommendations for future development. Succession plans can also be done in an Excel spreadsheet or on paper. The method is not what's important; having one is the issue!

Not only does a succession plan help to facilitate a smooth transition, it can also be a retention tool for high performers who are slotted for higher-level positions by allowing them to know the organization values their skills and abilities and has plans for them if they stay with the organization.

Many organizations struggle with whether or not to tell an employee that he or she is slotted for a higher-level job in the succession plan. We've seen arguments on both sides; however, we believe the case for telling people is stronger than not telling them—and it may keep a superstar on board!

The downside of telling people where they stand in the succession plan is that you may lose someone who is unhappy about not being in line for the CEO's position or other high-level positions. We think that's a risk worth taking because this is most likely an employee who isn't clear about his or her strengths and weaknesses and would probably leave the organization no matter what.

Succession Planning Tips

- Train high-potential employees and provide them with coaching.

    → See Chapter 23 (Best Approaches to Developing Employees) and Chapter 24 (Coaching as a Development Strategy).

- Reward managers for developing their employees.
- Provide more than one way to succeed in your organization. Take the management track or remain an individual contributor; each adds value.
- Allow employees to move laterally—not just up in the organization—to gain valuable experiences.

Although executive support is a key to any program's success, it is vital to have that support for succession management. It seems like such a no-brainer that organizations should know who would fill key positions should the incumbent leave for any reason, but it is amazing how few organizations take the time to put a succession management system in place.

Organizations that create an effective succession management process:

♦   Quickly anticipate and fill succession gaps.
♦   Identify employees with high potential and actively plan their careers to develop "bench strength."
♦   Align their workforce planning with their business strategy so that as the organization grows and the strategy evolves, changes can be made quickly to recruiting and employee development practices.

Succession management is a comprehensive process that starts by identifying possible successors and a development plan for each person, and goes below the executive level to as deep into the organization as possible. The goal of an effective succession management system is to have a pipeline of highly developed leaders all across the organization who are prepared (or are preparing) to fill vacancies as they arise. It makes sense to make succession management an ongoing planning process whereby periodic discussions are held to assess talent and to determine development plans for those identified as high performers with the ability to move up the organization.

Succession management can be made too complicated by elaborate forms and processes. It can be as simple as a spreadsheet where you list your key players and who would replace them in case they leave for any reason. Then the process dominates the discussion rather than the focus being on the potential of employees under discussion. The most effective succession processes are flexible, open, inclusive, and owned by top management with HR support.

Key Recommendations for Succession Management[2]

♦   Understand what is unique about your organization.
♦   Recognize that subject matter experts have special challenges when it comes to succession management—it's not as easy to see where they might fit into other positions.
♦   Identify key positions and establish succession plans for key positions that identify at least one, and preferably more than one, potential successor.
♦   Create a detailed developmental plan for the targeted successors.
♦   Use leadership competency with caution; the future is imperfectly predicted.
♦   Refine your process over time recognizing that no succession management process is perfect.

If an organization has a board of directors, the board may take on the responsibility for succession planning for top executives. John Berry of PriceWaterhouseCoopers (PwC) Center for Board Governance suggests four key actions that a board can take in order to ensure qualified candidates are available when needed:

♦   Monitor career development plans for leading candidates.
♦   Help mitigate the effects of a "horse race" (when there are two or more candidates competing for the same position).

SECTION 1

- ◆ Get to know the leading candidates.
- ◆ Ensure that job criteria are continually updated.

Barry said, "Boards need to consider whether candidates are being effectively evaluated and coached and rotated to various positions within the company. Candidates should be given developmental assignments and attend educational programs to enhance necessary skills."[3]

Consider the story of the 2009 transition at Xerox when Anne Mulcahy was replaced by Ursula Burns as CEO, as reported in the *Harvard Business Review* in October 2010.[4]

Ms. Mulcahy tells how she identified Ms. Burns early in her career as someone with great potential. During the lead-up to Anne Mulcahy's stepping down, Ursula Burns was being prepared, behind the scenes, for taking on the role. Though this wasn't an easy process, the two women focused on issues that included the fact that it wasn't going to be easy for Ms. Mulcahy to step down and give up the power. However, they agreed that no matter what, they would put the company first.

Before the announcement was made, Ursula Burns was gaining valuable experience with the Board of Directors and she was also maturing as a leader.

One of the lessons learned, according to Ms. Mulcahy, is that leaders and boards need to start the succession planning discussions as early as possible so that people are prepared and the organization is ready to absorb the changes related to new leadership.

An integrated process that links succession planning with leadership development can provide a competitive advantage to forward thinking organizations. Incorporating succession management into the organization's culture helps to build strong leaders and can also be a recruitment and retention advantage. By providing an opportunity for employees to learn and grow, you are feeding a very significant need that most people have. Succession management is a huge investment in building a successful organization—one that can be sustained over time.

Discussion Questions

1. What role does HR play in the development of the organization's strategic plan?
2. What are some of the benefits of doing a workforce plan?
3. Name three to four HR functions impacted by a workforce plan.
4. List the steps to create a workforce plan.
5. Why is management support critical to successfully implementing a workforce plan?
6. How does succession management support the workforce planning process?
7. What are some of the issues created when an organization doesn't have a succession plan in place?
8. How can boards of directors participate in succession management?

3

The Legal Landscape of Employee Rights

"All may dismiss their employee(s) at will, be they many or few, for good cause, for no cause, or even for cause morally wrong, without thereby being guilty of legal wrong."

—*Payne v. Western and Arkansas Railroad Company*, 1894

Employment at Will

Since the last half of the 19th century, employment in the United States has been "at will," or terminable by either the employer or employee for any reason whatsoever. The employment-at-will doctrine avows that, when an employee does not have a written employment contract and the term of employment is of indefinite duration, the employer can terminate the employee for good cause, bad cause, or no cause at all.[1] At the same time employees are free to leave the employer at any time, with or without cause or notice.

The employment-at-will doctrine has eroded over time. With the advent of unions, collective bargaining agreements generally require just cause for adverse employment actions. Legislation at the federal and state levels contributed to the erosion by providing employee rights. Other exceptions to the doctrine arose from case law and include:

- The public policy exception, which prohibits employment termination or other adverse action for reasons such as the following:
  ▷ Exercising a legal right such as the right to report an unsafe working condition.
  ▷ Responding to a legal obligation such as jury duty or military reserve duty.
  ▷ Whistleblowing or discriminatory employer behavior.
- The implied contract exception, such as statements implying job security. The courts have found such statements as well as statements in policies and handbooks to be implied or sometimes even express contracts.
- The covenant of good faith and fair dealing, such as knowingly terminating someone near retirement where the action results in the denial of retirement benefits.

Selected laws focusing on employee rights and the major antidiscrimination laws are covered in this chapter. Other legal and regulatory issues affecting benefits, compensation, and employees' safety and security will be discussed in chapters 17, 20, and 29.

Recognize that laws and regulations are not static and frequently change. References to websites are provided so current information can be referenced. However, neither the information in this book, nor any information found on the Internet, should be a substitute for legal advice. Guidance should be sought for state-specific laws and regulations.

Theories of Discrimination

Understanding the theories of discrimination is important to understanding the anti-discrimination laws. Laws that protect employees' rights apply to the life cycle of the employment relationship—from sourcing and recruiting, to selection and hiring, to performance management, compensation, benefits, training, termination, and all other terms and conditions of employment.

There are two theories of discrimination:

- **Disparate treatment** is intentional discrimination. It involves all employment-related actions or decisions, such as hiring, salary, benefits, termination, and so forth, in which an employee is treated differently than another similarly situated employee or class because of a protected attribute (for example, but not limited to, race, color, religion, gender, national origin, age, or disability).

  Unfair treatment, or the perception of unfair treatment, may or may not be discriminatory. For example, an employee may perceive that a low performance rating or merit increase is unlawful discrimination. In fact, the employee may not be performing up to legitimate standards.

- **Disparate impact** generally occurs when a neutral policy inadvertently discriminates or has a discriminatory effect on a protected class or group of people covered by discrimination law. In the landmark Supreme Court case *Griggs v. Duke Power*, Willie Griggs was denied a promotion based on his lack of a high school diploma and the results of two pre-employment tests. The Court found that these requirements were not related to job success and had a negative impact on protected classes.

  Disparate impact differs from disparate treatment, in which the employment practice itself is discriminatory. It occurs when an employer engages in a practice that has the effect of excluding individuals because of a protected attribute regardless of the employer's intent. It applies to employment practices that are "facially neutral," meaning that the practice does not appear to be discriminatory on the surface and it is generally applied in an even-handed manner to all individuals.

  Inconsistent application of the organization's policies or the inconsistent treatment of individuals could result in disparate impact discrimination.

Non-Discrimination Laws

Title VII, Civil Rights Act of 1964 (Title VII)

Coverage: It is unlawful to discriminate on the basis of race, color, religion, national origin, and sex in all employment decisions and terms and conditions of employment.

Applicability: All employers with fifteen (15) or more employees.

Special Considerations:

- Prohibits retaliation.
- Prohibits sexual harassment.
- Allows for a Bona Fide Occupational Qualification (BFOQ). If gender, religion, or national origin is a BFOQ reasonably necessary to carrying out a particular job function in the normal operations of the business or enterprise, the factors may be used in employment practices. For example, being female can be a BFOQ for a women's bathing suit model.
- Covers *co-employment*, meaning not just the company's employees, but those workers from contract and temporary agencies. Both companies can be liable.
- Requires reasonable accommodation for all deeply held religious beliefs.

Remedies for violating the law can include payment of attorney's fees and other actual damages and injunctive relief such as:

- Back pay.
- Reinstatement.
- Remedial training.
- Remedial transfer.
- Remedial promotion.
- Requiring employers to take steps to prevent future discrimination.

Civil Rights Act of 1991

Title VII was amended in 1991 by expanding the remedies to include jury trials, and punitive and compensatory damages for intentional discrimination. Compensatory damages can include such out-of-pocket expenses as job search costs and medical expenses as well as emotional distress damages. These expanded remedies also apply to the Americans With Disabilities Act, which is discussed in this chapter.

Pregnancy Discrimination Act of 1978 (PDA)

This law amended Title VII to prohibit discrimination on the basis of pregnancy, childbirth, or related conditions. It requires employers to treat pregnancy the same as any other short-term disability.

Age Discrimination in Employment Act (ADEA)

Coverage: It is unlawful to discriminate on the basis of the employee being over the age of 40 in all employment decisions and terms and conditions of employment.

Applicability: All employers with twenty (20) or more employees.

Special Considerations:
- Discrimination can occur within the protected age group.
- Age can be a BFOQ in rare circumstances.
- Prohibits retaliation.

Remedies for violating the law are the same as Title VII, plus payment of:
- Liquidated or double damages for willful violations.
- Lost retirement benefits.

Americans With Disabilities Act (ADA) and the ADA Amendment Act (ADAAA)

Coverage: It is unlawful to discriminate against qualified individuals with physical or mental disabilities that substantially limit one or more major life activities in all employment decisions and terms and conditions of employment.

Applicability: All employers with fifteen (15) or more employees.

Remedies for violating the law are the same as Title VII.

Special Considerations and Key Points:
- Requires reasonable accommodation to allow covered individuals to perform the essential job functions unless it creates an undue hardship.
- The law prohibits discrimination only against those individuals qualified to perform a job's essential functions. There is no requirement for employers to lower their standards or to hire individuals who do not meet a position's minimum education, skill, and knowledge requirements.
- Discrimination would include, but not be limited to, questions about the nature of a disability during a job interview; failure or refusal to consider a request for accommodation of the disability; refusal to hire, demotion, placement on an involuntary leave, termination, harassment, denial of any other term, condition or privilege of employment.

> → Appendix: Definitions under the ADA.

A reasonable accommodation removes unnecessary barriers that prevent or restrict employment opportunities and enables a qualified individual with a disability to perform the essential functions of a job. Examples include:
- Part-time or modified work schedules.
- Job restructuring (task exchange).
- Reassignment to a vacant position (current employees only).
- Acquisition/modification of equipment or devices.
- Adjustment/modification of examinations, training, materials or policies.

It is *not* a reasonable accommodation to eliminate essential functions or duties of the position or to lower quantity or quality standards.

All requests for accommodation from applicants and employees must be considered. Failure to do so is discriminatory behavior and is actionable. Accommodation requests cannot be ignored or refused without proper consideration.

A Process for Accommodation

- Consider **and document** all requests.
  - ▷ Responsibility applies to applicants and employees alike. A current employee can develop a disability during the course of employment.
- Each request should be considered on a case-by-case basis.
- Evaluate all available options.
  - ▷ Evaluate the job's functions against the individual's qualifications during the selection process.
  - ▷ Identify barriers to job performance. Assess how they could be overcome through accommodation.
  - ▷ Consult with the individual to find out his or her specific abilities and limitations relating to the job's essential functions.
  - ▷ Several accommodations may be appropriate. Consider each accommodation's effectiveness, cost, impact on the work environment, timeliness, and resources available to implement and maintain it.
  - ▷ Consider the individual's preference. However, the employer is not required to implement the individual's choice. The option chosen should serve the needs of both the individual and the company.
- Document the possible accommodations considered and resources consulted.
- Document the interactive steps—discussions with the individual.

An undue hardship occurs when an accommodation would be unduly costly or disruptive, or fundamentally alter the nature or operation of the business. Determination of whether a particular accommodation will impose an undue hardship is on a case-by-case basis. Overall determination of significant cost depends on the size and nature of the business.

Genetic Information Nondiscrimination Act of 2008 (GINA)

Coverage: It is unlawful to discriminate on the basis of genetic information in all employment decisions and terms and conditions of employment.

Applicability: All employers with fifteen (15) or more employees.

Special Considerations:

- Prohibits retaliation.
- Restricts employers from requesting, requiring, or purchasing genetic information.
- Requires that genetic information be maintained as a confidential medical record, and places strict limits on disclosure of genetic information.
- Provides remedies for individuals whose genetic information is acquired, used, or disclosed in violation of its protections.

Remedies for violating the law are the same as Title VII.

    ➤   Appendix: Guidelines for Preventing Workplace Discrimination.

Equal Pay Act (EPA) and the Lilly Ledbetter Fair Pay Act of 2009

Both of these laws cover compensation only and are discussed in Chapter 17 (The Legal Landscape of Compensation).

Retaliation

Retaliation is a form of discrimination and all of the laws discussed in the previous section prohibit retaliation. An employer may not fire, demote, harass, or otherwise "retaliate" against an individual for filing a charge of discrimination, participating in a discrimination proceeding, or otherwise opposing discrimination. The Americans With Disabilities Act (ADA) also protects individuals from coercion, intimidation, threat, harassment, or interference in their exercise of their own rights or their encouragement of someone else's exercise of rights granted by the ADA.

Retaliation occurs when an employer takes an **adverse action** against a **covered individual** because he or she engaged in a **protected activity**.

- An adverse action is an action taken to try to keep someone from opposing a discriminatory practice, or from participating in an employment discrimination proceeding, such as termination, refusal to hire, and denial of promotion.
- Covered individuals are people who have opposed unlawful practices, participated in proceedings, or requested accommodations related to employment discrimination based on race, color, sex, religion, national origin, age, or disability. Individuals who have a close association with someone who has engaged in such protected activity also are covered individuals.
- A protected activity includes opposition to a practice believed to be unlawful or participation in an employment discrimination proceeding, such as complaining to anyone about alleged discrimination against oneself or others, threatening to file a charge of discrimination, or refusing to obey an order reasonably believed to be discriminatory.

> → Appendix: Guidelines for Avoiding Retaliation.

Equal Employment Opportunity Commission (EEOC)

The laws previously discussed are enforced by the EEOC. Employees may bring an individual charge of discrimination. The charge must be filed within 180 days of the discriminatory action, or 300 days in states that have a fair employment practice law and state agency. The employer has the opportunity to respond to the charge. The EEOC may attempt to settle or mediate. Potential outcomes include resolution, action based on a determination that discriminatory action took place, and dismissal on the basis of no reasonable cause of wrongful actions. The EEOC can bring a suit directly against the company if they believe there is a pattern or practice of discrimination. Suit would be brought in federal court.

The EEOC often issues enforcement guidance and policy statements. It also posts Q&As and Fact Sheets on them. This information is frequently updated and can be accessed on the EEOC website.

> → For additional information, visit *www.eeoc.gov/laws/guidance/enforcement_guidance.cfm*.

Reporting Requirements

Employers with more than 100 employees (and federal contractors with 50 or more employees) are required to collect and report demographic data about gender and race/ethnicity according to some type of job grouping of their workforces. This information is recorded on the EEO-1 report and filed annually.

→ For additional information about the EEO-1 report, visit *www.eeoc.gov/employers/reporting.cfm*.

Posting Requirements

Employers are required to post notices describing the federal laws prohibiting job discrimination. The EEOC's poster is available online and in various languages.

→ For additional information about the laws enforced by the EEOC and posting requirements, visit *www.eeoc.gov*.

Other Laws Affecting Employee Rights

Immigration Reform & Control Act (IRCA)

Coverage: Prohibits discrimination against job applicants on the basis of national origin and citizenship. It also establishes penalties for hiring individuals who do not have the right to work in the United States or who are here illegally.

Applicability: All employers with one (1) or more employees.

Special Considerations: Employers must verify that workers have the right to work in the United States. Within three days of hiring, the new employee and the employer must complete the Form I-9. This form verifies both identity and the employee's right to work in the United States. Employers are required to maintain these forms for a period of either three years after the date of hire or one year after employment is terminated, whichever is later. The form must be available for inspection by authorized U.S. government officials (e.g., Department of Homeland Security, Department of Justice).

Violation: Employers who knowingly hire someone who is not entitled to work in the United States face both civil and criminal penalties. Fines can also be imposed for recordkeeping violations.

E-Verify is an Internet-based system that allows businesses to determine the eligibility of their employees to work in the United States. It is an electronic program through which employers verify the employment eligibility of their employees after hire. Employers submit information taken from a new hire's Form I-9 to determine whether the information matches government records and whether the new hire is authorized to work in the United States. Government contractors must use E-Verify. Certain states have mandated its use. Many employers use it voluntarily because it provides a safe harbor and shows good intent.

→ For additional information on IRCA, Form I-9, and E-Verify, visit *www.uscis.gov/i-9* and *www.uscis.gov/I-9Central*.

Uniformed Services Employment & Reemployment Rights Act (USERRA)

Coverage: It is unlawful to discriminate on the basis of military obligation.
Applicability: Employers with one (1) or more employees.
Special Considerations:

- Requires job protected military leave for up to five years (extended in some circumstances).
- Requires that returning service members be reemployed in the job that they would have attained had they not been absent for military service.
- Requires oral or written notice of the need for leave.
- Gives employees on military leave the same non-seniority-based benefits and rights generally provided to other employees with similar seniority, status, and pay on other types of leave.
- Gives employees on military leave the same seniority-based benefits they would have received if they had not taken military leave.
- Requires that military leave not create a break in service for retirement plan purposes.
- Requires employers to give notice of rights and obligation under the law.

Remedies for violating the law include:

- Back pay.
- Lost benefits.
- Attorneys' fees.
- Double damages for willful violations.

> ➤ **USERRA is enforced by DOL Veterans Employment & Training Service. For additional information, including information on the posting requirement, visit** *www.dol.gov/vets/programs/userra/main.htm.*

Beyond the nondiscrimination laws, there are additional laws and regulations that protect employees' rights.

Consumer Credit Protection Act (CCPA)

The CCPA protects employees from discharge by their employers because their wages have been garnished for any one debt, and limits the amount of an employee's earnings that may be garnished in any one week.

> ➤ **The Wage and Hour Division (WHD) of the Department of Labor administers this Act. For additional information, visit** *www.dol.gov/whd/regs/compliance/whdfs30.htm.*

Employee Polygraph Protection Act

This law makes it unlawful for employers to use polygraphs or lie detectors in pre-employment and post-employment decisions excluding a few narrowly defined exceptions for "security-sensitive" positions. In addition, employers are required to display the EPPA poster in the workplace for their employees.

⇥   For additional information, visit *www.dol.gov/whd/polygraph*.

Fair Credit Reporting Act (FCRA)

This law protects the privacy of background information and ensures that information supplied is accurate. Employers that obtain consumer reports for applicants or employees through consumer reporting agencies and use such reports for employment purposes must notify the individual in advance in writing using a stand-alone format and get their written consent before obtaining consumer reports for applicants or employees. In addition, employers must notify employees and applicants:

- Before taking adverse action based on such reports.
- After adverse action is taken.
- When using investigative reports.

Employers are also required to a) disclose whether an adverse employment decision was influenced by a credit report; b) furnish the negative report and a summary of the FCRA rights to the applicant or employee; and c) afford the applicant or employee an opportunity to correct errors in the report.

⇥   Employers can find additional information at *business.ftc.gov/
       documents/bus08-using-consumer-reports-what-employers-need-know*.

Fair and Accurate Credit Transactions Act (FACT)

This law is an amendment to the FCRA. It provides relief to employers who use the services of a third party to conduct workplace investigations. It reversed the consent and disclosure requirements in the event that the investigation involves suspected workplace misconduct or violation of a law, regulation, or employer policy. Employers may now hire third parties to investigate workplace issues without first notifying the individual(s) being investigated and gaining consent.

National Labor Relations Act (NLRA)

A common misconception about the NLRA, or the Wagner Act, is that it only applies to those organizations whose employees are represented by unions. In fact, the rights granted under the NLRA apply to all workers, whether or not they are union members and whether or not union organizing activity has taken place. All employees are granted the following rights:

- To organize.
- To form, join, assist, and be represented by a union.
- To bargain collectively through representatives of their own choosing.
- To engage in concerted activity for the purpose of mutual aid and protection. The following is an example of a protected activity: After an employee in a non-unionized organization had consulted with his colleagues and they all agreed that he should speak on their behalf, the employee approaches his boss about certain working conditions. The employee and his colleagues were acting "in concert" and have the right to discuss terms and conditions of employment.

The NLRA prohibits employers from engaging in certain conduct, or unfair labor practices that would interfere in the employees' rights. Examples include:

- Employer-controlled or -dominated unions.
- Discriminating in the terms of employment to discourage union membership (for example, refusing to hire someone who has a history of union membership).
- Refusing to bargain in good faith.

    ➤   Employers can find additional information at the National Labor Relations Board website at *nlrb.gov*.

Discussion Questions

1. What can organizations do to assure that their managers understand the legal landscape of employee rights? What types of steps has your organization implemented and what has been the outcome?

2. With continued changes in the legal requirements, how does your organization stay informed and keep the management staff informed?

3. Do the managers in your organization understand that retaliation can be a cause of action in an EEOC complaint? If not, what steps can you take to assure that they avoid any actions that could be perceived as retaliatory?

4. What can organizations do to ensure that their managers are aware of employees' rights under the National Labor Relations Act as well as the organization's rights and responsibilities?

4

Strategic Recruitment

As Marcus Buckingham and Curt Coffman wrote in *First, Break All the Rules*, "Selecting for talent is the manager's first and most important responsibility. If he fails to find people with the talent he needs, then everything else he does to help them grow will be washed as sunshine on barren ground."[1] Approaching the staffing of your organization from a strategic perspective will enhance your opportunities to achieve your goals and objectives.

Now that your workforce planning process has ended, and you know the number of new hires you need and what skills your organization requires to move ahead, you need to determine the best sources for the new hires.

It once was simple: If you needed a new employee, you hired one. Now, many people don't want to actually work for you all the time; they want to be more in control of their own time and energy. Contingent workers can be consultants, independent/temporary contractors, seasonal workers, freelancers, temporary employees provided by an agency, on-call workers, or part-timers. Because of how quickly economic and competitive situations change today, you will most likely want to have a mix of all types of employees to have maximum flexibility and to get the best available talent.

Contingent workers come from many places, including from your current workforce. One source of part-time workers may be your employees who are reaching retirement age, but still have needed skills (and, most importantly, institutional knowledge) and would like to work fewer hours. Temporary workers can be hired to work in virtually every level of the organization, including at the executive level.

You may decide that you want to hire a consultant with a particular skill set to do a project or a series of projects for your organization. There is probably a consultant for any specific task you need. Your decision should be based on whether you have the talent in-house and/or the bandwidth to accomplish what you need or whether you need to retain an outside consultant.

HR plays a vital role in managing the flexible staffing process. First of all, HR must be involved in making the decision as to whether to bring on a full-time or part-time employee, or to use a temp or a contractor. If you decide to go outside your own organization, the next step is to find the appropriate firm to supply you with the quality of talent you require or to locate independent contractors for specific projects. The best way to find either a vendor or an independent contractor is by asking your personal network whom they recommend or by using a trusted resource that has provided your organization with high-quality talent in the past.

If you've decided to use an agency and have met with them and are confident that they can meet your requirements and checked their references, the next step is to draft a statement of work and a working agreement. Though we know that agreements do not guarantee understanding, an agreement that clearly outlines what each party is responsible for will make your life much easier in the long run. Your legal counsel should work with you to prepare the agreement, which can then be revised for future engagements. Firms you work with may have their own agreements, and it is perfectly acceptable to have their agreement reviewed by your attorney and modified for your situation rather than drafting your own.

→   Appendix: Sample Statement of Work and Consulting Agreement.

When you are working on the agreement is also the time to be negotiating rates. Whenever possible, ask for volume discounts or additional services. Be sure the agreement you negotiate protects your organization when it is time to end the relationship.

Options to Consider

Part-Time Employees

Part-time employees are employees of the organization (on the payroll) but work less than a full-time schedule. Some may work less than an eight-hour day for five days a week whereas others may work a restricted number of days. Part-time work can be effective when recruiting diverse workers, including students, parents of young children, older workers, and others who need or want to work but who do not want a full-time schedule. Part-time workers are subject to the same policies and procedures that a full-time employee must follow. Some organizations, including Starbucks, UPS, and Home Depot, provide benefits to part-time employees, and this trend has become very popular for organizations that need to compete in difficult labor markets. Some organizations also offer time off to part-timers, usually pro-rated by the hours they work.

Contract Workers and Consultants

There may be times when you need someone who has a specialized knowledge or expertise not currently found in your workforce. Independent contractors and consultants can be used to meet these special requirements. It is important to follow the Fair Labor Standards Act and the Internal Revenue Service regulations on who is and who is not a consultant. Classifying someone as an independent contractor should be made carefully, because these arrangements are closely monitored by the IRS.

Outsourcing

One way to handle new tasks or an increasing workload for some organizations is to consider outsourcing tasks or entire departments. Outsourcing became particularly popular recently in the human resources world, as well as for other functions such as IT and accounting. If your organization is considering outsourcing, it is extremely important to select the right firm and then to establish clear guidelines for the partnering relationship. The agreement between the two organizations should carefully lay out how you will communicate and what measurements will be applied to determine whether or not the outsourcing is successful. Many organizations find it highly cost-effective to outsource functions; others have found the cost savings are not worth the loss of control.

Temporary Staffers

Your organization may have a need to fill a job on a temporary basis—usually when filling in for an employee on leave or for a short-term project. Many excellent temporary agencies specialize in filling positions for short-term assignments, and they usually are able to fill them quickly. Develop relationships with a couple of agencies in your local market so that you are able to call them when you have a need. For example, if the CEO's assistant is in a car accident and calls to say she will be out the rest of the week, you have access to people who can get a replacement to your office in a matter of hours! Many of these firms also can supply other types of employees, including professionals, to fill in when needed for an assignment. Some organizations have guidelines as to how long a person can work for them as a temp. Consider the cost impact you will incur, because not only will you be paying for the temp's salary, you'll also pay a fee to the agency. Most agencies will work with you to come up with a way to hire the temp, based on performance.

On-Call Workers

Some organizations that have significant swings in the number of employees they need at a particular time use call-in workers. These are employees who have been fully trained for the job but who only work when needed—for example, seasonal workers in retail stores at holiday time or farm workers at harvest time.

Definitions of Each Type of Contingent Worker

- A contractor or consultant is an individual that contracts directly with the organization to perform services usually for a specific purpose where additional expertise is needed. Contractors may or may not work at the employer's site.
- A temporary staffer is an individual who comes to the employer through an agency specializing in providing workers for specific time periods.
- On-call workers are employees of the organization who are notified when their services are required. These workers are typically in high-volume organizations such as call centers.
- Part-time workers are employees of the organization who work less than a full-time schedule. Most organizations tie the definition of part-time to what is required for benefits. For example, if your benefit plan provides full benefits for employees working 30 or more hours per week, your definition of a part-time worker would be someone working less than 30 hours per week.

Pitfalls to Avoid

- Watch out for pre-printed or standard forms from agencies or others to be sure the form covers everything that concerns your particular situation.
- Any agreement you sign should be easily understood and as simple as possible.
- Run from any situation where you aren't able to at least attempt to negotiate price and terms.
- Consider including an alternative dispute resolution provision in any contract.
- Negotiate contract end terms up-front.
- Be sure there is a contract provision if you want to hire the temporary employee for your firm.
- Have any contract reviewed by your general counsel or outside attorney before signing.

Legal Issues With a Contingent Workforce

It is extremely important that you not assume that, just because you call someone a consultant, they won't be considered your employee by the IRS or the EEOC. If your organization misclassifies a worker, you can be required to pay back taxes and also to provide back benefits.

The EEOC has information on this subject that focuses on:

- What staffing companies need to know to avoid violations of all federal antidiscrimination laws.
- ADA information related to the types of questions that can be asked after an offer is made, and requirements and responsibilities for reasonable accommodation
- The allocation of responsibility between employers and staffing firms.

> For more information, go to *www.eeoc.gov* and review:

  ▷ EEOC Enforcement Guidance on the Application of the ADA to Contingent Workers Placed by Temporary Agencies and other Staffing Firms.

  ▷ EEOC Enforcement Guidance: Application of EEO Laws to Contingent Workers Placed by Temporary Employment Agencies and other Staffing Firms.

IRS Independent Contractor Test

The IRS formerly used what has become known as the "20 Factor" test to determine whether a worker is an employee or an independent contractor. The test was revised and the 20 factors consolidated into three main groups:

- Behavioral control.
- Financial control.
- Type of relationship of the parties.

Behavioral Control

Facts that show whether the business has the right to direct and control how the worker does the tasks for which the worker is hired include the type and degree of:

1. Instructions the business gives the worker. An employee is generally subject to the business's instructions about when, where, and how to work.
2. Training the business gives the worker. An employee may be trained to perform services in a particular manner while an independent contractor ordinarily uses their own methods.

Financial Control

Facts that show whether the business has a right to control the business aspects of the worker's job include:

1. The extent to which the worker has unreimbursed business expenses. Independent contractors are more likely to have unreimbursed expenses than are employees. Fixed ongoing costs that are incurred regardless of whether work is currently performed are especially important. However, employees may also have unreimbursed expenses.
2. The extent of the worker's investment. An employee usually has no investment in the work other than his or her own time. An independent contractor often has a significant investment in the facilities used to perform services for someone else. However, a significant investment is not necessary for independent contractor status.
3. The extent to which the worker makes services available to the public at large. An independent contractor is generally free to seek out business opportunities and often advertise, maintain a visible business location, and is available to work for others firms.
4. How the business pays the worker. An employee is generally guaranteed a regular wage amount for an hourly, weekly, or other period of time. This usually indicates that a worker is an employee, even if the wage is supplemented by commissions. An independent contractor is usually paid a flat fee for a project, although it is common for some professions, such as law, to pay contractors hourly.
5. The extent to which the worker can realize a profit or loss. Because an employer usually provides employees a workplace, tools, materials, equipment, and supplies needed to do the work, and generally pays the costs of doing business, employees do not have an opportunity to make a profit or suffer a loss. An independent contractor can make a profit or suffer a loss.

Type of Relationship of the Parties

Facts that show the parties' type of relationship include:

1. Written contracts describing the relationship the parties intend to create. This is the least critical of the criteria, because what the parties call the relationship is not as important as the nature of the underlying relationship. However, sometimes, a written contract can make a difference.
2. Whether the business provides the worker with employee-type benefits, such as insurance, a pension plan, or paid time off. The power to grant benefits carries with it the power to take them away, which is a power generally exercised by employers over employees. A true independent contractor will finance his/her benefits.

3. The permanency of the relationship. If the organization engages a worker with the expectation that the relationship will continue indefinitely, rather than for a specific project or period, this is generally considered evidence that the intent was to create an employer-employee relationship.

4. The extent to which services performed by the worker are a key aspect of the regular business of the organization. If a worker provides services that are a key aspect of the organization's regular business activity, it is more likely that the company will have the right to direct and control his/her activities.

This is a complex issue and we recommend that you consult a labor and employment attorney for advice on this topic.

> →   For more information, go to *irs.gov* and review IRS Publication 15-A, page 6.

Discussion Questions

1. When does it make sense for an organization to bring in a contractor or consultant?
2. What is the benefit to an organization to have some part-time workers?
3. What is the benefit to employees to have a part-time schedule?
4. Are part-time employees eligible for employee benefits?
5. How do you determine if someone is an employee or contractor?

5

Job Descriptions

This isn't nearly as dull and dry as it sounds. There are lots of good reasons why organizations invest the time to research and write job descriptions. An executive who recently completed a year-long process to finalize job descriptions for the more than 100 employees in a large medical practice is now seeing the value of job descriptions. She said, "Now we have a basis for our performance review process and a valuable tool that will help new hires become productive quicker. It took us a while to do it but it was worth the effort!"

Job descriptions start with a job analysis, which is a systematic study of positions in order to evaluate what activities a position should contain and how each position in the organization relates to other positions. A job analysis looks at what qualifications are necessary to succeed in the position and the conditions in which the job is performed. It is important to remember that a job analysis is about the job—not the person doing the job.

The best time to do a job analysis is before you have employees; however, that's not always possible. Ideally, start with an idea of what needs to be achieved, and then think about how that job would be accomplished.

There are three main elements included in a job analysis that are frequently abbreviated as KSAs:

- Knowledge—body of information necessary to perform the job.
- Skills—level of proficiency needed to perform the job.
- Abilities—capabilities necessary to perform the job.

Some of the information collected and analyzed in a job analysis includes:

- Job purpose.
- Work environment.
- Where in the organizational structure this position fits.
- Duties and responsibilities.
- KSAs required to succeed in this position.
- Performance criteria.

The information gathered in a job analysis is used in many HR-related activities, including:

- Recruiting.
- Developing a job description.
- Workforce planning.
- Training and employee development.
- Succession management.
- Organizational design and development.
- Leadership development.
- Performance management.
- Compensation management.
- Legal defense.
- Affirmative Action planning.
- Determining reasonable accommodation (ADA) issues.

Job Descriptions

A job description is a tool that describes the duties, tasks, responsibilities, and functions of a particular position. It outlines the purpose of the position, where it fits into the mission of the organization, the details of how work is to be accomplished, and the requirements necessary to do this particular job. It is not intended to be specific to the incumbent; it describes the job, not the employee who does the job. Every position in the organization should have a job description—even senior-level positions.

Job descriptions must be based on facts, so when developing them, it is best to start by gathering the information necessary to ensure the description is accurate.

One of the many ways organizations successfully use job descriptions is to on-board a new employee. A well-written job description is extremely valuable to anyone starting a new job—even when people get promoted or transferred within an organization. A job description is a road map as to what is expected and can be extremely helpful to anyone who wants to quickly become productive in a new position.

There are several types of data-gathering methods that can be used to generate the needed information to write a job description, including:

Questionnaire. Ask incumbents and managers to answer open-ended questions about the work. This is especially effective when there are a lot of jobs to be analyzed with minimal resources. If the questionnaire is crafted well, this can be your best method of getting the information you need. The questionnaire can be sent electronically with clear instructions as to why the information is being requested and with a reasonable deadline for completion. In today's busy world, some people may see this as an inconvenience, but if you're clear as to how it will be used and you don't make it too long, odds are most people will work with you on this.

Interviewing incumbents. Conduct face-to-face interviews, using predetermined questions, to gather information about knowledge, skills, and abilities needed to perform the position. This can be time-consuming and may create unrealistic expectations that the final description will include all their ideas; however, as opposed to using the questionnaire to gather the information, you'll be able to ask follow-up questions to enhance your learning.

Observation. Watch incumbents actually doing the job. This provides a realistic view of the daily tasks and responsibilities. This is also time-consuming and may alarm employees who think you are doing a time and motion study to determine which jobs are necessary, but if you set it up properly, you may be able to gather valuable information. You may also want to combine observation with the questionnaire described previously.

Work journal. Ask incumbents to record work including the frequency and timing of tasks. Information gathered is analyzed and translated into duties and responsibilities. This method, though it can be effective, collects data that is difficult to analyze because the person doing the job analysis has to interpret the information in the journal. If you use this method, consider also using the observation or interview methods in conjunction with the journal.

What to Include in Job Descriptions

Once the job analysis is completed on a position, the next step is to draft a job or position description that summarizes the most important functions of a job and includes a description of the work; a detailed task list; what knowledge, skills, and abilities (KSAs) are needed to perform this position; and the reporting structure. Job descriptions must include physical requirements for ADA compliance and should also include the Fair Labor Standards Act (FLSA) status of the position. At a minimum, a job description should include this information:

- Position title.
- Supervisor/manager.
- Geographic location of the position.
- Date prepared.
- FLSA status: exempt or non-exempt.
- Summary: a four- or five-sentence overview that states the purpose of the job, the results the incumbent is expected to achieve, and the degree of autonomy the incumbent has.
- Responsibilities or essential duties: tasks, duties, and responsibilities of the job and why the function is necessary, which will be useful for evaluating ADA compliance.
- Non-essential duties.
- Required skills and experience: education, years of experience, qualifications required.
- Desired, but not required, skills and experience.
- Managerial responsibilities, if applicable.
- Physical demands and work environment. Include any undesirable situations.
- Success factors: personal characteristics that will enable someone to be successful in this position.
- Statement such as "other duties as assigned" or "the organization has the right to modify this job description at any time."
- Signature of incumbent and date signed.

SECTION 1

Format for Job Descriptions

There is no legal definition of what a job description should contain or look like. Resources organizations can use to draft descriptions include the O*Net, the Occupational Information Network. Many trade associations or membership groups have sample job descriptions to be tailored to your organization. The Society for Human Resource Management (SHRM) has a toolkit to assist with preparing job descriptions that can be found at *www.shrm.org*.

There are common elements that a job description should include:

- **Summary**—a short paragraph that summarizes the purpose of the job and includes the primary responsibilities of that position, the results required for success, and what level of supervision the position is under.
- **Essential functions**—tasks, duties, and responsibilities of the position that should be listed in order of importance and may be weighted for performance management purposes. Should include a statement such as "other duties as assigned" to allow for management flexibility.

  ➔   See Chapter 25 (Performance Management).

- **Supervisory responsibilities.** Does this position supervise any functions, and, if so, which?
- **Working conditions**—type of working atmosphere. This is the place to list any unpleasant or dangerous conditions.
- **Minimum qualifications.** What is required to do this position (education, years of experience, certifications, knowledge, skills, and abilities)?
- **Success factors**—personal characteristics that will contribute to being able to succeed in this position.

Tips for Writing Job Descriptions

Job descriptions must be based on the specific duties and responsibilities actually performed:

- Accurately describe what the job does and title it appropriately.
- List FLSA status. (Is the position exempt or non-exempt?)
- Keep the summary brief.
- Be sure all functions are job-related.
- Include disclaimers such as "other duties as assigned" or "job description can be revised by management as needed."
- Use appropriate titles for the position and your organization.
- Don't use gender-specific titles such as "salesman" or "waitress."
- Use action verbs in the present tense.

- Only use explanatory phrases that add meaning or clarify the why, how, where, or frequency.
- Eliminate gender terminology by structuring sentences in a way that pronouns aren't needed or use neutral pronouns.
- Spell out acronyms wherever possible.

It is a common practice to include a phrase such as "other duties as assigned" in a job description. It is generally agreed that this is not sufficient for describing essential functions; you must spell them out.

It is critical that job descriptions be kept current and that every employee is given a copy. One way to ensure job descriptions are kept up-to-date is to require managers to review and update them at the time they do a performance review on that particular job.

➤ Appendix: Sample Job Descriptions.

Legal Implications of Job Descriptions

Federal regulations and guidance governing the Americans With Disabilities Act (ADA) do not require your organization to have job descriptions, but if you do have job descriptions, you should be aware that the ADA has a significant impact on format and content. Because the employment provisions of the ADA focus on essential functions, you must ensure that all essential functions are covered in a job description. A single job task may be essential, and if it is, it must be covered in the job description. Another requirement is that if you choose to describe non-essential functions of a particular job, you must distinguish them as non-essential. There are several ways to accomplish this:

- Indicate the time spent on each function to show that a non-essential part of the job requires a small percentage of the employee's time be spent on that function.
- Put asterisks around non-essential functions.
- List non-essential functions as a footnote.

Essential Job Functions

Because the Americans With Disabilities Act (ADA) uses "essential job function," it is important to define what an essential job function is in order to determine if a person can or cannot perform those functions.

Essential functions are distinguished from other non-essential or marginal functions that are part of the job but are incidental or ancillary to the purpose and nature of the job.

The ADA does not mandate that employers eliminate or lower valid job standards. All job applicants, whether disabled or not, should satisfy the skill requirements, experience, and education. The law does not suggest that employers ignore mental abilities, physical effort, psychomotor skills, and/or other job-related criteria required to perform the essential job functions. However, the ADA does require that employers look beyond the traditional means and manner of performance.

Be sure you can defend any statement you make regarding the essential job functions, as they are subject to scrutiny by federal compliance agencies.

Checklist for Determining Essential Job Functions[1]

- Does the job exist to do this function?
- How many times a day/week does the incumbent do this function?
- What are the minimum qualifications for this position?
- What critical skills are required?
- Do others doing this same function have these required skills?
- What equipment is used to do this function?
- Are there other employees who could do this function without harm to the organization?
- Would eliminating this function be detrimental to the organization?
- Did the previous incumbent perform this function?
- Is this function essential?

Job Analysis Questionnaire[2]

Purpose: To gather information about your job to prepare a formal job description

Directions: Answer all questions and return this questionnaire to your manager by (date)

1. List your major responsibilities. Prioritize each item by assigning a number to it. For example, assign the number "1" to the responsibility you consider the most important.
2. Why are these responsibilities important to your job?
3. What equipment and tools do you use in your job?
4. Describe some specific duties or tasks that you perform in your job. Next to each item, state how often you perform this duty or task.
5. What knowledge do you require to perform your job successfully?
6. What qualities are necessary to make you successful in your job?
7. What prior knowledge, skills, or abilities did you bring to your position that helped to make you successful in your job?
8. What level of education, training, or certification is needed to succeed in this position?

Discussion Questions

1. Name some of the HR functions that use information collected in a job analysis.
2. What are at least two ways to gather information to do a job analysis?
3. Why is it important to list essential job functions on a job description?
4. How can you ensure employees don't say, "It's not in my job description"?
5. What are some of the questions you would ask to gather information for a job description?

6

Determining Hiring Criteria

Gary Rogers, chairman and CEO of Dreyer's Grand Ice Cream, said it best: "You can't spend too much time on hiring smart. The alternative is to manage tough, which is much more time-consuming."[1]

Many organizations make hiring decisions quickly and without a lot of thought. Why? Because the work has to get done so let's just hire someone as fast as we can and hope we get the right person. Some people call this the "foggy mirror" method of hiring: All that matters is the applicant is breathing!

Taking a strategic approach to hiring may take a bit more time, but, in the long run, the time will be well spent if you get a hire who is successful. Hiring strategically involves knowing what will define success in the new hire—in other words, what skills, abilities, and qualities have other people who've succeeded in this position had, and what made them successful? You and anyone else who is part of the selection process will need to be trained in how to interview. You will need to define your culture and understand the qualities of a person who does well in your organization.

Hire for Culture

You need to understand your culture. In the wonderful book *Nuts: Southwest Airlines' Crazy Recipe for Business and Personal Success*,[2] the authors share stories of the beginning of Southwest Airlines. They've built a successful airline around their passion for "hiring for attitude and training for skill." By sticking with this philosophy, they have been able to create a sustaining culture in which flight attendants are encouraged to creatively give the FAA required briefing that, on most airlines, passengers totally ignore. On Southwest, you never know if you will hear it done in a song or a rap, or interspersed with funny comments. But passengers listen (and isn't that what the FAA wants them to do?) and passengers know immediately that this isn't a company that takes itself too seriously. (Southwest does hire its pilots and mechanics for their skill as well as their attitude.) They are right; it is easier to teach someone how to serve drinks from a rolling cart down a narrow isle than to teach him or her how to do that same job with a positive attitude and a smile!

So, how do you determine what your culture is? Here are some things to consider:

- What is the leadership style?
- Performance standards—how do you hold people accountable?
- How do you state your mission, vision, values?
- What is your work environment, formal or casual?
- What is your dress code, business or business casual with casual Fridays?
- How are mistakes handled in your organization? Are people encouraged to try?
- What is the prevailing management style?
- What qualities to you look for when hiring?

The Selection Process

Before you even start looking at resumes, it is a good idea to be clear about what you are really looking for. The first step is to review the job description and look at the knowledge, skills, and abilities needed to succeed in this position. HR and the hiring manager should carefully consider whether or not the skills are required, or, for the right person, you could do without one that is listed. Coming up with a list of required and preferred skills will help you search for candidates.

Another way of gathering valuable information prior to recruiting is to know what makes your "star" employees successful in a particular position. This can be done by interviewing each "star" and determining the background/skills/interests/abilities/education or whatever you find that makes each one particularly good at this position. You can take what you learn from these interviews to help you create your required/preferred skills list.

Sample Required/Desired Skills List for HR Manager position

Required:
- Bachelor's degree in business, human resources, or related field.
- PHR/SPHR certification.
- 6–8 years of progressive human resources experience.
- 2–3 years of HR management experience in an organization of 100 or more employees.

Desired:
- 2–3 years in a hospital setting.
- Experience with Taleo applicant tracking system.
- Experience with selecting Employee Assistance Program vendors.
- Bi-lingual (Spanish/English).

Reviewing Resumes

Set your Applicant Tracking System (ATS) to screen the resumes and online applications that include the key words you've selected as basic to your process or your HR team may pre-screen resumes for you. What you are looking for is relevant experience in the areas that are going to make the next person successful. Remember to only look for job-related experience and try to take out your biases. For example, if you went to the University of Michigan and really don't like anyone who went to Michigan State, try to put that rivalry aside if your perfect candidate happened to go to MSU!

How much time should you devote to reviewing a resume? That question is impossible to answer except to say this: Take enough time to get a sense that the person has the basic skills this position requires, and the necessary education, credentials, or certifications. Try to avoid coming up with arbitrary ways to exclude resumes, such as rejecting anyone who doesn't include a cover letter (unless you requested a cover letter in your job posting or the job requires someone who can write a well-crafted letter). Remember: Unless the job requires a degree from an Ivy League school, rejecting someone who went to your local state school is unacceptable; keep in mind the words *job related*.

When reviewing a resume or application, you should be looking for career progression and relevant achievements. A red flag would be a person who was a vice president two jobs ago and now is a manager in the same field for a smaller organization; usually a talented applicant's resume will show upward career progression. However, you may encounter really talented people who for personal reasons have taken lesser jobs simply to keep working. If you see something of value in the person's background, don't automatically disqualify the person because he or she has been unemployed or has taken lower-level positions. Do a phone screen and find out what his or her situation is, as this person may be that diamond in the rough!

There is a lot of discussion now about whether resumes are even relevant in the age of online applications. Many organizations don't require resumes but rely on their own online application. Your firm may still want to collect resumes; if not, be sure to let your senior managers know that many times online applications do not print well or may be formatted in an unusual manner. If a senior manager is expecting an application to resemble a resume, he or she may be disappointed and have a negative impression of the candidate—and you don't want that to happen.

Should you respond to every application/resume you receive? Well, if you've ever looked for a job, you most likely think the answer is yes. However, if you are in a busy HR department (or don't have an HR person), it can be a bit overwhelming to respond to everyone who applies to your firm. Many applicant tracking systems have an automatic feature that lets people know their resume/application was received. This is a great feature and helps to enhance your reputation as a good place to work. What we hear from applicants is they feel as if their resume/application goes into a black hole if they don't at least get an acknowledgment from the employer.

➔   See Chapter 10 (Making a Hiring Decision).

If you do a phone interview or an in-person interview, it is imperative that you let that people know whether they are being considered or not. You should not tell them why they are not being considered—just that they are not a candidate for this position—and thank them for their time and interest in your organization. Remember that every applicant is a potential customer, and how he or she is treated can really make a difference. Not only might the person be a customer, he or she might better fit a job you have available in the future or may know someone who would be a candidate. You want applicants to tell everyone they know that your organization, even though they didn't get the job, treated them with dignity and respect.

As you are reviewing resumes or applications, watch for these red flags. These may be areas you want to highlight so that when you are doing a phone screen with the candidate, you can get more information in order to evaluate the candidate's potential for the open position:

- No dates of employment (just organizations listed with job duties).
- Gaps in employment (unless they can be explained).
- Frequent job changes to positions of lesser responsibility.
- Lists of accomplishments that can't be linked to specific jobs.

Resume Gaffes

- "I have lurnt Word Perfect 6.0, computer and spreadsheet programs."
- "Very experienced with out house computers."
- "Received a plague for salesperson of the year."
- "To Home-ever it concerns…"

Resume Blunders[3]

- Candidate included a letter from his mother.
- Candidate used colored paper with glitter around the edges.
- Achievement listed as "nominated for prom queen."
- Candidate listed as hobbies "drugs and girls."

Discussion Questions

1. Why is understanding your organization's culture important in the hiring process?
2. Name three or four ways to determine organizational culture.
3. How can having a required/desired list help you make a good hire?
4. What should you look for when reviewing a resume or application?
5. Name two or three "red flags" on resumes.

7

Hire From Inside or Outside the Organization?

Jack Welch, former CEO of GE, said, "Great people, not great strategies, are what made it all work. We spent extraordinary time recruiting, training, developing and rewarding the best. Our reach and our success would have been limited without the best people stretching to become better."[1]

When a position becomes available either through growth or to replace an employee who is leaving for any reason, it is important to stop and determine exactly what is needed. If it is a replacement, it is common for managers to decide to hire someone with exactly the same skills that the previous employee had. It makes sense to, before you start recruiting, take the time to know what is needed for this position at this particular time. This is a perfect time to update job requirements or job duties, because things rarely stay the same in our fast-moving world. We recommend that you:

1. Review the current job description to determine if it accurately describes the position and if the requirements for success are as it is currently written. For example, you may decide that the job really doesn't require a four-year degree; so, you can move that requirement to the desired category. You also may decide that a job duty that performed by the former employee who held this job is now being done by another employee—so you can remove that job duty from this job description. Your goal is to have the description be as current as possible.

2. Look at the budget to see if there is money to fill this position at the current level or if other options should be considered, such as using a part-time employee or contractor to do the job.

3. Carefully evaluate if the position should be filled at all. Could the duties be shared by others in the department or eliminated altogether?

4. Will filling this position help your organization achieve its mission or contribute to growth in some way?

5. Is this the right time to fill this position?

If you decide that filling the job is the way to go, and the job description is approved or revised to reflect any changes in scope or requirements, then the next decision is whether to recruit internally or externally. Most organizations have internal job posting systems whereby your current staff is given the opportunity to "throw their hat in the ring" prior to the position being posted externally. If you don't currently have an internal job posting system, consider putting one in place.

"Any time a company has an opportunity, they should consider inside first," says Bill Greif, co-author of *No More Rotten Eggs: A Dozen Steps to Grade-AA Talent Management*. "They know the person and what they are capable of, so it reduces the risk and uncertainty of a new employee."[2]

Because we know that many people lie on resumes and, when you hire outside candidates, you must rely on what is on their resume/application, what you learn in an interview from how they respond to your questions and what you can glean from references—in other words, not much!

Promoting or transferring a current employee, whose skills are well known to you, can cost less and take less time than going outside to hire an unknown, but it is always a good decision to approach the situation strategically. Does it make sense this time to promote or transfer a current employee, or go outside the organization? And, of course, it is perfectly legitimate to do both; just be sure that you carefully consider both options and that, if you have a job posting policy that says that all jobs must be posted internally before any external recruiting can begin, you follow your policy.

Let's look at the advantages and disadvantages of internal or external recruiting.

Internal Transfer or Promotion

Advantages

- Provides career paths for current employees.
- Saves cost of ads, postings, and search fees.
- Boosts morale.
- Can create a "domino effect" that results in several internal moves, which can be highly motivational for current staff.
- Less on-boarding time/effort as the employee already knows the culture.
- You already know a lot about the employee: skill set, work ethic, career goals.

Disadvantages

- May not bring new ideas/new ways of doing things to the organization.
- May result in significant need for employee development.
- May pit employees against each other as one gets the promotion and another doesn't.

External Hire

Advantages

- Brings new ideas into the organization.
- May result in lower employee development need/costs.
- Brings new talent/competencies into organization.
- May bring competitive knowledge if new hire comes from a known competitor.
- May result in increasing organizational diversity (certainly of thought and experience, but perhaps in other ways as well).

Disadvantages

- Increased recruiting costs and lost productivity if the search takes a protracted amount of time.
- Decreased morale as current employees feel passed over for promotion.
- Increased on-boarding time as new hire learns the culture.
- You don't really know much about the applicant except what he/she's told you in the interview.

Job Posting Tips

- Do develop a well-crafted job posting policy and follow it for all open positions. If you make exceptions, be clear as to why.
- Do provide all pertinent information on the posting, including title, job grade, description of the job, and minimum qualifications, as well as what the process is for applying for open positions.
- Don't pick and choose which positions to post; be consistent. Some organizations post all positions below the vice president level whereas others post all positions in specific salary grades. Determine what works best for your organization and stick with it.
- Do allow enough time for internal applicants to apply before going outside for talent, but don't make the internal time frame so long that you delay your search if you need to go outside. Consider posting internally for five business days before posting externally—or some other time frame that meets your needs.
- Don't make it difficult for employees to find out where jobs are posted. Use your intranet or other widely used communication tools to get the word out when a position is open.
- Do have clear career paths or ladders or whatever you choose to call it, so that employees have a clear sense of where they would like to go in the organization, and what skills and abilities are needed to succeed at each level.
- Do encourage internal movement as a way to enhance employees' knowledge of the business as they read job postings and learn about what is required in positions and in other parts of the organization.
- Do build in ways to discourage managers from using the internal job posting system to get rid of non-performers in their department by requiring that internal applicants meet the hiring requirements for the position.
- Do use the job posting system to remind employees that they are responsible for developing their job skills so they are prepared for an internal opening.

Internal Hiring Process

Promoting from within is a selling point for many organizations, and it can be an effective retention tool, but in order for it to be truly effective, there has to be an established and followed policy. According to Maureen Henson, SPHR, vice president of HR at Henry Ford Bi-County Hospital in Warren, Michigan, "Internal recruitment provides a higher level of employee satisfaction."[3]

It is critical to have a well-crafted posting and application process, and to ensure that all employees know about the policy and how it works. Posting should focus on the skills and abilities you are seeking as defined in the job description, and it is quite important that you actually hire people with those skills and abilities to be sure your recruitment process is fair and legal.

And, if you use the same criteria for decision-making on inside and outside candidates—for example, you only interview people who have the minimum qualifications for the position—then you don't have to consider every inside applicant. Inside applicants must be treated carefully and must be informed about why they aren't being considered. You may want to also include in your policy a way to notify the person's supervisor if he or she won't be considered prior to telling the employee. Supervisors should be trained to encourage people who want to move up in the organization and to encourage them to develop the skills necessary for the next level. They should also be warned about "hoarding talent" and not holding back talented people. If a talented person thinks his or her career is being held up because a supervisor is afraid to lose him or her, the organization will be the loser as the employee will leave altogether.

If your organization has the ability to track skills of current employees, this is a great way to fill positions. When a position comes open, either because of a resignation or growth, you can go to your skills inventory and search for current employees who have those skills. If you don't already have a skills inventory, consider this story from a leading organization:

> A mid-sized government contracting firm in suburban Washington, DC, says, in our business, we need to submit candidates for proposals and sometimes we needed to move quickly. We didn't have a skills inventory of current employees, so it was decided the time had come to bite the bullet and develop one. We put a template together and asked each employee to complete it. We then scanned the completed templates and, just like that, we had our skills inventory. It made me wonder why we hadn't done it long ago! As we hire new employees or lose someone, we input their skills and abilities so the inventory is always up to date.

Whether you decide to go inside or outside your organization to fill an open position, keep in mind that your employees need to feel they were given a fair shot at the promotion/transfer and, if they weren't selected, where they fell short. When the employee who didn't get the new position knows what skills and abilities he or she must demonstrate to be considered next time, that person can work to develop that skill. Hopefully, your organization offers opportunities for development. Encourage your employees to take advantage of those opportunities to help them learn and grow their talents.

Discussion Questions

1. Name some of the things to consider before starting to recruit for an open position.
2. What are three or four advantages of promoting or transferring from within?
3. What are three or four disadvantages of promoting or transferring from within?
4. What are three or four advantages of hiring from the outside?
5. What are three or four disadvantages of hiring from the outside?
6. Why is it important to have an internal transfer policy, and how is it used?

8

Recruiting From Outside
of the Organization

Jim Collins wrote in his landmark book, *Good to Great*, "Those who build great companies understand the ultimate throttle on growth for any great company is not markets, or technology, or competition, or products. It is one thing above all others: the ability to get and keep enough of the right people."[1]

The challenge organizations face today is how to find the talented people who can take them to the next level of performance. If you've decided to go outside the organization to find a new hire, you will learn that most external recruiting today is done by using the Internet in some way—be it via social media sources such as Facebook or LinkedIn; using one of the many job boards, such as Indeed, ZipRecruiter, Craigslist, or Monster.com; or using the organization's own website. We will discuss each of these in detail, but it is also important to understand that the Internet is not the only way to find qualified applicants. It is important to "cast a wide net" to find the best and brightest to join your organization. Consider these sources in addition to the Internet (and we'll get to Internet recruiting as well!):

Networking. Other than employee referral programs and the Internet, networking is the best way to find good employees. Everyone in your organization should be attending networking events and be on the lookout for potential talent. You can set up a quick and easy way for your employees to feed the leads back to HR or hiring managers by putting a form to capture the referral contact information on your organization's intranet. It is highly recommended that you personally develop a strong network of colleagues that you notify of your job openings. They may be able to refer qualified candidates to you from their own network. They also may be able to pass along qualified applicants who applied for positions in their firm, but were not selected for reasons other than their qualifications.

New hires. Ask how they heard about your organization, and what websites or what sources they used to look for a job. These sources should move to the top of your list. Also ask new hires if they are aware of any colleagues from their previous employer who might be interested in making a change. This source is especially valuable if you have a vibrant employee referral program (ERP; see below).

Former employees. If you have a solid exiting process, you will have identified employees who voluntarily resigned from your organization. If those employees were solid performers and you'd like to have them back, keep in touch with them.

> ↪   See Chapter 30 (Ending the Employment Relationship).

It's a good business practice to keep in touch with former employees you'd like to have back and, when the time is right and there is an opening in the organization, you can re-recruit them. Former employees can bring a lot to the table. They already know your organization's culture and how you operate. You know them, and their skill set and work ethic. They may come back with increased ability or talent they have picked up at where they work now. Some organizations call these returning employees boomerangs!

Handle returning employees carefully. What will you do about breaks in service for your insurance programs or retirement programs? Don't overlook the morale impact on current staff if someone comes back to a higher position than what they had when they were here before. How will the current workforce who stayed with you react?

Retirees. It is increasingly difficult for retirees to survive without some income. Consider bringing them back to do special projects in their area of expertise or to work part-time for you. The benefits they bring are similar to those described in the discussion of former employees. This can be a very cost-effective method of getting high-quality talent for a reasonable price and no benefit costs.

Good employees who left for work/life balance issues and whose situations have changed. This may be a man or woman who left to take care of children or an aging parent. If you keep in touch with former employees, you may find this is a good pool of talent for your organization.

Laid-off employees. When your business picks up, contact them to see if they would come back to work for you again. Work with your legal counsel to review how and who you bring back so that you are not violating any laws or putting your organization at risk for legal action from those you don't bring back.

Applicants who weren't selected. They may be qualified for another opening, and, if you have an applicant tracking system, you can keep in touch with these people when the right opening presents itself—and no cost is involved. Keep in mind that these applicants must have had an excellent experience in your hiring process—even if they didn't get the job. If they don't think highly of your organization, they won't be interested when you contact them again.

Trade associations. Most trade associations maintain low- or no-cost job posting systems that are extremely valuable recruiting sources. The people who belong to those associations have the skills you need in your industry. Be sure your organization's reputation is excellent so that when applicants see your name, they want to apply.

Executive search or contingency agencies. There are many excellent firms you can pay to find talent for you. The best way to find the right search firm that will work best for you is through networking. Ask trusted colleagues what firms they use or have used.

State employment offices. All states have offices where you can (and if you are a government contractor you must) list open positions. Don't discount the referrals you can get from these offices. They do an excellent job of helping job-seekers link up with open positions.

Outplacement firms. Many firms will send out job openings to their clients who have been downsized from organizations. Maintaining good relationships with outplacement firms can be a good source for you—they may put your organization at the top of their list and steer their best candidates to you.

Radio/TV. Depending on your budget, you may want to investigate using these sources. Many organizations use radio in particular to drive applicants to their job postings on their website or to invite applicants to an event such as a job fair or open house.

Colleges/universities. These can be great sources for entry-level management positions or other positions within your organization. The key to a successful program is to invest time in establishing relationships with key placement officers and professors in your line of work. They will help lead you to the best talent available. On-campus recruiting is time- and labor-intensive, but can result in finding employees with valuable skill sets. Don't expect to show up once or twice a year on campus and walk away with the top students; it takes time and effort to establish a presence on campus, but the payoff can be huge. Also, post open positions with their career offices so that alumni have access to your openings.

Job fairs. Most major newspapers hold periodic job fairs. You pay a fee to have a table or booth where you give out information about your organization and collect resumes. There are other job fairs held around the country, and they can be a good way to collect information about available talent. However, they can be costly and time-consuming for a limited payoff. There are virtual job fairs in which applicants visit your company's booth virtually, and you have an opportunity to ask them questions about their skills and abilities. These can be cost-effective, but many recruiters still like to meet candidates face-to-face.

Consider holding your own job fair when you have a significant number of open positions. You'll need the support of hiring managers so that they attend and can interview candidates on the spot. This is an excellent way to also publicize your organization, as you'll want to advertise the job fair to get participants to attend. Some organizations also do invitation-only job fairs, where they select passive candidates and invite them to a special event.

Internships. Internships can be a real "win-win" for both your organization and the student, as you get a talented person to work for you and he/she gets experience they can use on resumes. Additionally, both parties get a chance to evaluate each other. It is critical that you offer interns meaningful work so that they gain experience and aren't just doing work no one else in the organization wants to do. Remember: They will be going back to campus and will tell everyone about their summer internship with your firm. You want them to have had a great experience!

Co-op programs. These are used primarily in technical fields where the student takes a semester off to gain work experience. As stated about interns, this is a great way to have talented students work for you while you evaluate whether you want to offer them a full-time job when they graduate.

Minority sources. There are many places you can post open positions to target specific minority groups.

> ➔   Appendix: Sources for Minority Applicants.

> ➔   You may also want to check the Department of Labor's Employment Resource Referral Directory on the DOL website at *www.dol.gov/ ofccp/ERRD/errsrvs.htm.*

Religious organizations. Many churches or other places of worship have job-seeking support groups and/or post jobs in their bulletins. For example, McLean Bible Church in suburban Washington, DC, hosts a weekly Career Network Night, at which attendees can have their resumes reviewed, practice interview skills, and meet with professional recruiters. This program is not focused on any religion and is open to all. It is a great place for local recruiting professionals to volunteer and to meet top-notch candidates in a relaxed setting. Check for similar programs in your area.

Retiring military. This can be an extremely good source for highly trained employees who have strong work ethics. And, hiring military retirees and those transitioning from the military can be a real source of pride for your current employees! There are several organizations you can contact for more information or to learn about their job fairs, including virtual job fairs. Check out organizations such as MOAA (*www.moaa.org*) and the Transition Assistance Program (TAP; *www.turbotap.org*). The TAP program was established as a partnership among the Departments of Defense, Veterans Affairs and Transportation, and the Department of Labor's Veterans' Employment and Training Service to give employment and training information to armed forces members within 180 days of separation or retirement.

Senior centers. Check with your local centers to see if they do job postings. Seniors, like retirees from your firm, come with great deal of experience and may be looking for ways to supplement their income or to add more purpose to their lives. Also check *www.aarp.org* for ideas on hiring and working with seniors.

Passive or non-active applicants. You should definitely focus some of your attention on finding candidates who aren't looking for a job. These might be people you've met at conferences or heard speak at networking events, and whose contact information you kept. They probably won't apply to a job announcement on an Internet site, so you will have to be creative to determine if they are interested and, if they aren't readily so, recruit them. LinkedIn is a great way to target passive candidates. Creativity and perseverance are the keys to recruiting passive job-seekers, but it may pay off with a great hire.

Employee referrals. One of the most effective ways to fill open positions is by having an employee referral program (ERP). Referred employees can be hired faster than those from other sources and usually at a lower cost. Referred employees usually stay longer than people from other sources and, because they already know someone at your organization, they typically on-board faster than others. New platforms exist, such as Sherpa.us, to help organizations design and manage effective employee referral programs. These platforms are cost effective and easy to incorporate into an existing ERP or to start one from scratch.

Employee Referral Program Basics

- Have clear policies and practices so that everyone understands how the program works.
- Post job openings, including required skills, education, etc.
- Develop a brand for the program and use it on all communications.
- Treat referred candidates with care.
- Communicate often with both the referring employee and the candidate.
- Recognize referring employee publicly.
- Pay referral fee quickly.
- Update the program often to keep it fresh and top-of-mind for employees.

Sample Employee Referral Program Design

- Hiring of referred employees must be within six months of the referral.
- Management, HR, and Business Unit Directors are excluded from receiving referral bonuses, but are encouraged to submit referrals anyway.
- Rewards are paid when referred employee has reached the 90-day mark.
- Fees are based on the position to be filled and change from time to time based on need.
- The first employee to refer a candidate will be the only referring employee eligible for payment.

EEO Staffing Issues to Consider

Being consistent in your staffing efforts is a primary defense for EEO discrimination complaints. As an example, if your internal transfer/job posting policy, says that all positions will be posted internally for five days prior to going to external sources, be sure that is what you always do.

⇥ See Chapter 7 (Hire From Inside or Outside the Organization?).

Global Staffing Challenges

Many organizations are now faced with being part of the global economy. Some U.S. firms have been acquired by international organizations; other U.S.–based companies do business all around the world. There are issues around work visas, relocation costs, different ways of doing business, language, and more that impact how global staffing is accomplished. As with so many things, there is no right way to do it, but it helps to understand the different types of international employees.

Some organizations use the term *international assignee* to refer to all employees asked to work outside of their home countries. Others use the following terms to categorize international employees:

- **Expatriates (or expats)**—people sent to work in a country other than that of their national origin. Typically, expats work for a specific period of time with the intent of returning to their home county. For example, an American employee of U.S. firm who accepts a four-year assignment in Spain is considered an expat.
- **Local nationals**—employees hired for a job in their own country. For example, a French national who is hired by an American organization for a job in Lyon, France, is considered a local national.
- **Inpatriates (or inpats)**—employees who are brought in to work in the headquarters country for a specified period of time. For example, a citizen of Scotland who has special technical skills required at the corporate headquarters of an American company is considered an inpat.
- **Third country nationals**—employees who are citizens of countries other than the organization's headquarters or the ones in which they work. For example, a Japanese national who works in Australia for a U.S. firm is considered a third country national.

"Assuming that you already have a solid understanding of how the laws work in your home country, state, or province, it is now time to start learning what is going on elsewhere," says Lance Richards, GPHR, SPHR, vice president of global workforce solutions at Kelly, OCG. "Certainly, obtain appropriate local legal counsel, but it is important to educate yourself as best you can. Remember: Employment laws and protections vary widely from country to country. In many countries, you are not so much employing people as you are marrying them."[2]

So whether you are recruiting internationally or locally, it is critical that you understand the issues, both legal and personal, around hiring people in different countries. This is a challenging area for HR and for mangers alike. The SHRM website (*www.shrm.org*) has a wealth of information on global challenges, says Melanie Young, GPHR, SPHR, vice president of Global HR, Corporate and Global Business Group at Arrow Electronics.

Insights Shared By Mary Walter Arthur, Sphr, Former Director of Talent Management of a Multi-National Firm[3]

This was a global organization and we posted all open positions, no matter where they were located in the world, or whether or not the position would be filled with an outside candidate or a current employee. Employees could post for any position and would be considered as long as they met minimum requirements. For example, an engineer in Sweden might see a position she is interested in, even if it happens to be in the U.S. She could apply for it but then it became interesting for us in HR. How would we weigh the costs of getting her global experience with the huge financial impact of moving her and her family to another country? How would we obtain the necessary visas, work permits, family housing, and travel costs, and still meet bottom-line objectives? And how would we ensure that the employee and her family would make a successful transition and be happy in their new country? Moving talent around is an excellent idea, but in reality it is not a simple process and is fraught with challenges.

Knowing When You Need Outside Help to Fill a Position

Many of us struggle with admitting we need help, although some of us are quick to pay an expert to do our recruiting for us. There is no exact answer to this question; it must be made on a case-by-case basis, and budget plays a big part in the decision. Possible times when you may want to engage an executive search firm or use a contingency agency for candidates might be:

◆ To hire a senior level executive.

◆ When you want to hire someone from a competing firm.

◆ When the pool of candidates is very small due to the requirements of very narrow skill sets.

◆ When you have a very short time to hire a lot of people (new contract, acquisition, new plant).

Carefully select a firm to work with by doing the following:

◆ Ask your professional network for recommendations.

◆ Meet with them to learn how they operate, what research capabilities they have, what successes they've had in your field, and to meet the team that will be assigned to your organization. You want a firm that will partner with you—not one that has a "cookie cutter" solution to what they think you need.

◆ Check references.

◆ Select your final candidates based on your research, meetings with them, and references.

◆ Make your selection, notify those who didn't get the work, and move forward.

◆ When you've selected your partner or partners, be honest about what you need them to do and the time frame you need them to deliver. Let them know how often you want updates on their progress and whether you want the updates via email or quick phone calls, or whatever works best for you and your schedule.

Using Social Media to Recruit

Using social media to recruit new hires is a highly effective method to attract qualified employees. Social networks help recruiters quickly identify and connect with people who qualify for open or future positions. And, for the most part, using social media for recruiting is free! You know the importance of your employment brand: It's critical to your ability to attract and retain top talent. Nothing provides a clearer picture of what your organization stands for than social media. The messages you send through these online networks can be extremely effective at engaging even passive job candidates.

According to Sherrie A. Madia, PhD, co-author of *The Social Media Survival Guide*[4] and director of communications at the Wharton School of Business at the University of Pennsylvania, the key to using social media to recruit is not to limit yourself to one network; effective talent sourcing is about "networking the networks" to provide ways for applicants across communities and platforms to find you and for you to find them. She says, "Researching blogs, niche communities, and groups within networks can give HR information to plant content seeds within these sites to attract more qualified applicants." To be able to compete, organizations should explore social media "as at least one component of the broader strategy," she says.

As you develop your social media recruiting strategy, be sure your organization's website is well-designed and colorful, and that your corporate jobs/careers page is lively, current, and easy for candidates to find. Take some time to look at other companies' careers or jobs pages on their websites and get ideas. At a minimum, include information such as:

- Corporate culture—what it's like to work at your organization.
- Open positions with complete descriptions of job content and job requirements.
- Employee benefits.
- Ways your organization contributes to your community, including any recognition you've received for your charity work or community activities.
- How to apply, including an online application that includes a digital signature.
- Links to your organization's Twitter, LinkedIn, and Facebook pages.

Savvy organizations include videos of actual employees in their work environment as part of their social media strategy. This is a great way to let potential job applicants know what it is like to work in your organization. Post new videos as often as possible to showcase what your organization does. The most powerful messages come from your current employees, so include informal interviews and testimonials. Include parts of presentations from the CEO on the future of the organization or from a town hall meeting to showcase how open and transparent you are. Whatever you decide to do, be sure it is an honest reflection of your organization—today's applicants can spot "spin" from a mile away!

Using Twitter to Recruit

Twitter is the most common network used by job seekers.
- Set up a separate organization career account.
- Be sure to tweet relevant information. If you don't, people won't follow you.

Twitter is amazingly easy to use and highly effective.
- Search for relevant people to follow by using the search tool. Many people will automatically follow you back.
- Be sure the link to your Twitter feed is visible on your job postings, your organization's career page, your email address, and any other place you advertise your open positions.
- Use hashtags when you Tweet. Hashtags allow tweets to be easily found. For example, add #jobs to the end of your Tweet because people will search #jobs and find your Tweet—and then may click on the job or follow you.
- Be sure to join "chats" related to your industry.

Using Facebook to Recruit

- Set up an organization career page separate from your business Facebook account that includes posts about what it's like to work at your organization and what type of candidates you're looking to add to your team.
- Include a link to your online application to make it easy for people to apply.

- Passive job seekers check out employer's pages to keep up-to-date on what's happening in organizations.
- Be sure your recruiters follow up quickly on any request from a potential applicant.
- Publicize your Facebook page wherever you post jobs or look for candidates.
- Respond to posts on your wall and formulate a policy on how to respond to negative comments. Don't ignore them. You can delete them, edit them, or respond to them, but you must do something!
- Encourage interaction among your followers by encouraging conversations. This take some work because you need a large number of people to create the community needed for this type of interaction, but it can pay off.
- Update frequently to keep in front of your competitors and top of mind!

Using LinkedIn to Recruit

LinkedIn is the social network used most often by recruiters to find talent—either active or passive job seekers.

- Create a company/organizational profile and ask your employees to use it.
- Expand your LinkedIn contacts as quickly as possible, remembering to link only to people you know and/or admire. Connect to other employees, customers, friends, colleagues, former coworkers, people you meet at networking events, people you interview for jobs, and family members. The more first-degree connections you have, the better!
- Use LinkedIn People Search to source candidates. This is a valuable way to find people with particular skill sets.
- Use the free job postings available and consider upgrading in order to have greater access to information/candidates.
- Join LinkedIn groups in your industry or where you want to source candidates.
- Use your status to alert your network when you have jobs open or to promote an event such as a job fair or open house you are hosting.

Once you have your accounts set up on the social networks, you can import your email contacts. These platforms make it easy to connect to your current email database, but be careful as some will literally include every person/organization to which you've ever sent an email.

Find the biggest influencers in your industry and follow them. The more you follow or connect with people, the more people will follow or connect with you.

Social Media Policy

Consider developing a social media policy or guidelines for your employees to follow to ensure consistency of message. It should:

- Link to your Code of Conduct and Privacy Policy.
- Say what is allowable. For example, can employees blog about their work as long as they don't disclose anything confidential, or is blogging prohibited in general?
- Describe the consequences. What happens if the organization doesn't like what an employee posts on a website?

- Update frequently. Technology changes so quickly, you need to have a procedure that looks at your policies often.
- Remind employees to be careful to only write about what they know, and to evaluate whether or not what they are posting will add value.
- Include contractors in your guidelines.

> → See Chapter 27 (Employee and Labor Relations) for additional information about social media policies.

Employment Branding

If your organization is going to compete for the best talent available, having an employment brand is important. Employment branding is the process of positioning your organization as an "employer of choice" in the marketplace and should encourage people to want to work for your firm.

You want to control what is written or said about your organization to the extent that is possible in today's media-driven world. This means you need to actively keep your website up to date with announcements of your successes, your new products, and your great employees. Being a good community citizen is another way to enhance your employment brand. Sponsor community events and provide opportunities for your staff to volunteer for their favorite cause. Apply for local and national awards. Many communities have "best places to work locally" programs. Find out what it takes to get on one of those lists. Remember that your employees will be contacted by the sponsors of those programs to verify if what you've said about your workplace is true, so be sure you can back up your claims of being "an employer of choice.

Elements of an Effective Employment Brand

- Creates a positive and compelling image of the organization that includes reputation and social involvement.
- Provides a clear description of what it is like to work at your organization.
- Links the brand to the organization's brand.
- Provides a sense of pride to current employees.
- Reinforces the organization's public image.

Your employment brand must be aligned with the organization's strategic plan, vision, mission, and values so that you create an image that attracts and retains the best talent available. The organization's value proposition is the foundation of employment branding. It must provide information for applicants who want to submit their resume/application and any inconsistencies between what is said about the organization and what is real can be deadly!

Your employment brand should be consistent with your organization's brand and reflected in everything you say and do on the job/career page on your website, job postings or ads, brochures, or any material used for recruiting purposes or for any employee communication. Consistency is the key to a successful employment brand!

Discussion Questions

1. How can your professional network help you with finding good sources for applicants?
2. When might you consider asking a former employee to return to work? What are some areas to consider if you re-hire a former employee?
3. Name three or four sources for applicants other than networking and the Internet. Which sources do you think would garner the best applicants for your organization and why?
4. Why is an employee referral program an effective way to measure morale?
5. When might it be a good time to use a recruitment agency?
6. What are some of the issues to consider when recruiting globally?
7. What are some of the ways to link your website to social media sites, and why is this an important step?
8. Discuss some of the benefits to the organization of having a well-defined employment brand.

9

The Interview

"In our business, people are intrinsic to the personality and style of our company. We believe hiring the right people is the key to our success," says Gordon Segal, founder and CEO of Crate and Barrel.[1]

Screening Applicants

Once you have selected the candidates who meet your minimum requirements from the applications/ resumes you've reviewed, the next logical step is to do a screening interview. We recommend that you email candidates to determine a convenient time for you to call them. Random calling can waste a lot of time, and you will have a better chance of getting good information from candidates if they are prepared for your call. However, before you make the first call, be sure you have a clear idea of what your requirements are and that you are prepared for the interviews. We recommend that you prepare some interview questions before making a phone call.

In place of a phone interview, many organizations are now using video screening interviews to help them decide which applicants to bring in for face-to-face interviews. There are a couple of ways to do this. One is to send a list of questions to the applicant and request that the person record the answers to the questions. The second approach is to set up a two-way video interview using Skype, Google Hangouts, Zoom, FaceTime, or other platforms that are easily accessible and free to both parties. Your Applicant Tracking System (ATS) may have video capabilities as well.

When you use video for interviews, keep these tips in mind:
- Prepare for the interview the same way you'd prepare for any interview.
- If you're doing a two-way video interview, keep the time zones in mind when scheduling.
- Always do a test of the equipment before going live.
- Be sure your setting looks professional (for example, clean off your desk).
- Have good lighting. Be sure your face isn't in the shadows and don't have light behind you.

- Ensure you won't be interrupted during the interview.
- Look at the camera and not the monitor. This will give the applicant the sense you're looking at him or her.
- Start with small talk.
- Smile from time to time.
- Pause to let applicant respond to your questions.
- Speak slowly and clearly.
- Avoid jokes or casual comments that might not translate.
- Dress as you would for any interview.
- Watch for energy, enthusiasm, and passion.

➔   Appendix: Sample Behavioral Interviewing Questions.

Pre–Phone or Video Interview Checklist

- Develop hiring criteria that accurately reflect the demands of the position.
- Develop a set of questions to yield information related to the job specifications.
- Review the resume to highlight areas that need clarification.
- Develop an interview plan that allots time to explore background and culture fit.
- Schedule a time that allows for no interruptions.

You can save yourself a lot of time using phone or video screening to learn more about selected applicants before bringing them in for face-to-face interviews. Schedule a time to call and allow 20–30 minutes for each interview.

During an interview, whether on the phone or via video, your objective is to determine if the person meets the minimum qualifications for the position and is in the salary range for your position. It is sometimes difficult to get candidates to discuss salary at this point, but do your best to get them to give you a range they are looking for. The screening interview provides you with information to help you decide whether it makes sense to bring the applicant in for a face-to-face interview. If the position pays $50,000 a year and the applicant is looking for $150,000, it probably doesn't make sense to move forward with another interview.

Although your intention should be to gather information from the applicant, you should also share some information about your organization and answer the applicant's questions. Don't, however, tell applicants what you are looking for; if you tell them your hiring criteria, they will feed you answers that they think you want to hear, and that is not a basis for a good hiring decision.

The Candidate Experience

Now that you've completed the screening interviews, you have your slate of candidates to bring in for face-to-face interviews. It's become increasingly important to focus attention on what's called "the candidate experience"—how the candidate is treated throughout the entire application process. Websites, such as Glassdoor, provide valuable information for applicants about what it's like to work for specific organizations. You'll want to ensure that what's out there online is as good as it possibly can be because applicants check out your reputation before they even check out the job specifics. Negative information can greatly impact your ability to attract the best talent available.

Keep in mind that every candidate should be treated like a VIP. Any applicant, whether or not you hire him or her, is a potential customer or client. You want all of these people to feel good about your organization and tell their friends and family how impressed they were with how they were treated. If a particular applicant isn't a candidate for this particular job, he or she might fit another position in your organization at a later date. And, keep in mind that in today's world of social networking, applicants share information with others, and you want to be sure your firm's reputation is excellent.

Make it as easy as possible for applicants to find openings in your organization. Keep the careers page on your organization's website up to date and filled with interesting information about your culture, mission, vision, values, and job openings. You want to immediately engage applicants and have them begin to imagine what it would be like to work for your organization! Be sure your online application is as easy as possible to complete. Consider applying for a job at your own organization to see what gaps in the process you spot, and then fix them immediately. Today's applicants will move on from your process if it is too difficult to complete.

Move as quickly as possible when you find a qualified applicant. Contact the applicant and let him or her know you're interested, and provide a sense of next steps. Schedule interviews in a timely manner; don't make someone wait weeks before you do a screening interview! You'll lose the candidate to your competition.

It isn't difficult to treat people well. "Say what you mean and do what you say" should be your mantra. If you say you are going to call an applicant at a specific time, do it. If you let an applicant know he or she will have your answer by Friday, call on Friday—or if you don't have the answer, email to say you haven't forgotten him or her, but the decision is taking a little longer than anticipated. Candidates expect frequent updates from recruiters, so keep in touch. Even a quick text message can make all the difference in the world to let someone know where he or she is in the process.

When the applicant arrives for the interview, be there to greet him or her or ensure that your receptionist (if you have one in this virtual age!) greets the applicant warmly, offers coffee or water, and lets him or her know where the restroom is. Don't keep an applicant waiting if at all possible. If your schedule is interrupted by an emergency meeting and the applicant is there, consider asking a colleague to meet with him or her, or have someone take the applicant on a tour of the offices while waiting for you. If you need to reschedule, do it as quickly as possible.

Greet the applicant warmly with a firm handshake and a welcome. Some organizations have welcome boards in their lobby, and it is a good touch to have the applicant's name on the board—which actually accomplishes two purposes: welcomes the applicant and alerts the rest of the office that you have an applicant coming in that day.

The Interview

As you are walking to your office or the conference room where you'll conduct the interview, use that time for small talk about the weather, traffic, the previous night's game, or some other topic you can both discuss. One innovative firm we know has an extensive art collection that links to their industry. This makes for an easy opening conversation while you are walking to the office—pointing out various pieces of art and why they were selected. Another firm we work with has won a lot of awards for its commitment to the community. This makes a great topic to share while getting the applicant to relax and lets the applicant gain some knowledge of the commitment the firm has made to its community.

Be sure the applicant has a glass of water or coffee before you start the interview. Let the applicant know the interview will be in three parts:

1. You will ask a series of questions to gather information about background and qualifications.
2. You will share information about the organization and this particular position.
3. You will respond to questions about the organization and the position.

Interviews are highly stressful events for nearly every applicant—and many interviewers don't enjoy them, either! Do your best to make the applicant comfortable so that your time together is profitable.

There is no hard and fast rule about how much time to spend in an interview, but the best estimate is 45 minutes to an hour for the first interview. This certainly depends on the level of the position. For example, for a senior executive position, you would most likely have a series of meetings/interviews, with at least one interview of two hours or more. This is because, at the more senior levels, your investment is larger, and it is more than critical that the applicant be able to fit the culture and that he or she has the skills to be productive quickly.

There is also no rule about how many interviews you should have before determining who your final candidate is, but try and make the process as simple and timely as possible. Today's applicants give up on organizations quickly if they think you're taking too long to make a decision. We recommend that, if your organization requires that many people interview each candidate, you do your best to minimize the number of times the applicant has to return for another interview. We've known organizations that have applicants come back five or six times to meet one person each time. How much better it would have been to have grouped those interviews into two half days or one full day? Remember, if you are doing multiple interviews in one day, to allow some time for the applicant to have a break!

If you plan to take notes during the interview (and you should!), let the applicant know your plan. There is nothing worse for an applicant to be responding to your question and suddenly you start writing things down. The applicant immediately wonders what he or she just said that was so important or that you didn't like. However, if you've already told the applicant you will be taking notes, it won't be such a surprise.

Interviewing takes a great deal of concentration. Therefore, we recommend you don't try to do too many interviews in one day so that you can easily focus on the applicant. You want to have as much good information as possible so that you can make a good hiring decision. While you are listening carefully, don't overlook non-verbal cues such as facial expressions, body language, gestures, and posture. For example, if you ask candidates what they are most proud of in their life, you would expect to see them smile and sit up as they talk about their accomplishments or about the pride they take in their children. You also should be aware if, while answering a question about a past position, they don't look you in the eye; that may be an indication that they are uncomfortable with the question or how they are answering it, and you will want to make a note to probe for more information on this later and when you are checking references.

It isn't easy to make a good hire, but it isn't impossible, either. You just need a plan and to be aware of some of the landmines that exist in the hiring process, such as *replicating the predecessor.* So many organizations don't take the time to understand the job itself and to think through the skills someone needs to be successful in that particular job. They merely start looking for someone "just like Sally." That's fine if Sally was promoted. But if she just resigned or was terminated, they often don't stop to think what it was that made Sally quit or what skills Sally didn't have that caused her to not be successful and, therefore, terminated. Take the time to really think through the position in question. What skills are needed? What personality traits would a successful person have?

Before you start the hiring process, consider:

- *Two years from now, how will we know if this person has succeeded? What measurements will we use?*
- *What do we expect him or her to accomplish in the first 90 days? First year?*
- *What help will the organization provide (mentor, executive coach, training, etc.)?*
- Before asking a question, consider:
    ▷ *What is the most likely response I will get to this question?*
    ▷ *Will that answer give me important information that will help me make a hiring decision? If the answer is no, don't ask the question!*

There are literally millions of books, websites, blogs, videos, and more that tell an applicant how to ace an interview. There are books on what are the most likely questions they will be asked and some even give the *answers* to those most frequently asked questions. Remember: You want to get more than prepared information from the candidate; you want to get the information you need to be able to make a good hiring decision.

Keep in mind that retention starts in the hiring process. You want to have applicants so excited about making the decision to join your organization that they just can't wait to get to work on their first day to be part of your team.

Because we know that today's applicants have a lot of tools at their disposal to help them convince you, the employer, that they are perfect for your open position, we recommend you consider using behavioral interviewing techniques that operate from the premise that past experience is the best predictor of future behavior. People demonstrate behavior patterns that are reliable and consistent predictors of future performance. The best way to assess a candidate's qualifications for a position is to use a simple, yet highly effective, method of asking questions. Rather than asking the traditional questions typically asked in interviews, you ask a series of well-planned questions to get the candidate to tell a story that illustrates his or her ability to perform the essential job functions and be successful in the position.

It all starts with understanding what skills and abilities are required to do this particular job, and you've done that when you developed the job description. Take the most important things a person needs to be able to do or be to succeed in this position and craft questions to get at that skill. For example, if the position requires a high degree of creativity, you might say,"*Tell me about your most creative work-related project.*"

What you are looking for is what is commonly called the STAR approach. You want the candidate to tell you about the **Situation** and to describe the **Tasks** involved in the approach, the **Actions** taken to complete the tasks, and the **Results** of the actions. Or:

S: Describe a **Situation** in which you demonstrated this behavior.

T: Explain the specific **Tasks** involved.

A: Explain the specific **Actions** you took to complete the tasks.

R: Describe the **Results** of your actions.

There is an easy formula for crafting behavioral interviewing questions. Start with phrases such as the following:

- *"Tell me about a time...."*
- *"Give me an example of when...."*
- *"Walk me through...."*
- *"Describe for me...."*

Once you've asked a behavioral question, you can continue to get more information with gentle probes to get the candidate to elaborate on what he or she has shared already. Here are some suggested probes:

- *"How did you do that?"*
- *"What did you do with the information?"*
- *"What did you learn from...?"*
- *"How did you handle...?"*
- *"How so?"*
- *"Tell me more about...."*

Using the behavioral interviewing techniques described here will allow you to gather a great deal of valuable information on the candidate in order to evaluate whether or not to continue the interview process. During the interview, be sure you ask enough questions to give you what you need to make a reasoned decision.

Spotting Potential Superstars in the Hiring Process

During the interview process, you want to be able to spot a superstar. Lisa Haneberg, VP and OD Practice Leader at MPI Consulting and author of "High Impact Middle Management," has developed eight key criteria that define star performers[2]:

1. They are well-rounded. In addition to strong technical expertise in their functional area, they also have a solid understanding of how business works—even if they are a rock star developer.

2. They get results. More than meeting performance expectations, they are known for getting results. And, more often than not, their approach to getting results is innovative.

3. They are builders. Whether they work inside a turnaround, a startup, or a mature organization, they are known for building the organization to make it stronger and more nimble.

4. They are flexible. In fact, you can put rock stars in charge of most any department and they will flourish.

5. They are open. Contrary to the stereotype that rock stars can be prima donnas, real rock stars are open to input from others, responsible to requests, as well as candid and assertive.

6. They keep their commitments. If they said it would be done on Monday, it is.

7. They are team catalysts. They know that no man is an island and that every rock star depends on a strong team. Rock stars do whatever it takes to build the team.

8. They are respected. Rock stars are respected by their peers and direct reports for the results they produce, as well as the way in which they get things done.

According to Doris Sims, author of *The 30-Minute Guide to Talent and Succession Management*, "[O]ne way to consider whether an individual is a star is to consider their ability and desire for focused development, challenging job assignments, and potential leadership career growth."[3]

Spotting stars during the hiring process could be considered an art versus a science. If the organization has determined what they consider a star to be, hiring managers can be trained to identify stars by asking certain questions during the hiring process. HR should document anything that might be meaningful, such as achievements/awards, patents, recognition, commendations, and so forth.

Referrals are a prime way to find star employees, especially when the referral is made by another star worker. A-listers like to work with others like them, and they tend to have contacts and acquaintances who are like them.

One pitfall of having stars spotted in the hiring process is that some managers may feel threatened by someone who has superior skills or expertise. They may think this person is too great: *"He knows more than I do." "We better not hire him because he might take my job."* Interviewers who are insecure in their own position may not point out superstars. Ways to reduce this are to have multiple interviewers and/or panel interviews.

Additional Interview Opinions

If the candidate has impressed you enough to continue the process, it is a good idea to put together a list of others in the organization you'd like him or her to meet. Include a representative list of people to also interview the candidate. Consider asking peers with whom the person will need to work on a frequent basis, and if he or she will be managing others, include some people who will be direct reports to the candidate. You may want to put together a half day of interviews, and then take the candidate and his or her potential direct reports to lunch so they can get to know each other. There is no magic number of required interviews to make a selection, but at least three to four other people should interview the candidate. Additionally, the hiring manager should interview the candidate for at least one hour to confirm impressions and get clarification on any issues resulting from the first interview. Many organizations require that the CEO or president interview all applicants or all applicants at a certain level. If this is the case in your organization, factor this in to your interview planning; senior leaders tend to have busy schedules, and you don't want to prolong the process and lose a good candidate due to scheduling issues.

When you are putting the schedule of interviews together, include topics on which you want each person to focus his or her time so that everyone doesn't ask the candidate the same questions. For example, if you are hiring a salesperson, you might ask one interviewer to focus on his or her ability to generate leads, another interviewer could focus on the candidate's communication skills, and a third interviewer might ask questions to get to the applicant's ability to work in a team atmosphere. Be sure each interviewer has a copy of the job description and any other information you think would help him or her conduct a good interview.

It helps if your organization has a Candidate Rating Form that everyone completes after an interview. These forms and comments will assist to the hiring manager in gathering the information needed to make a decision.

> ➔   Appendix: Sample Candidate Rating Form.

Certainly, you want to hire someone who will fit your culture and be able to do the job for which he or she is being hired. That is why we recommend that, to the extent possible, you get consensus on the final hiring decision, but if everyone doesn't agree and the hiring manager really wants this candidate, he or she should have the final say.

Panel interviews are very difficult to do well. It takes a great deal of coordination to put the panel together; arranging multiple schedules so that everyone is available at the same time is not easy. Panel interviews are also difficult for the applicant. They can feel like they are on the "firing lines" if people are shooting questions at them from all around the room.

If your organization does panel interviews, spend some extra time preparing the panel members for the process to ensure that the applicant feels as if he or she has had a fair chance to sell himself or herself. Also, be sure you inform the applicant well in advance that he or she will be interviewed by a panel of people so that he or she doesn't panic when entering the room for the interview.

Fair and Legal Interviews

Don't make any pre-employment inquiries regarding an applicant's:

+ Race.
+ Gender.
+ Color.
+ National origin.
+ Age.
+ Disability.
+ Veteran status.
+ Marital status.
+ Sexual orientation.
+ Religion.

Ask job-related questions and take good notes. Avoid writing things on resumes/applications that can be discriminatory. (For example, don't put "good looking blonde girl" on the application; applications can be subpoenaed!) It is essential that you know your state and local discrimination laws, as some individuals may be in a protected class even if they aren't in a federally protected class.

Now more than ever, it is important to conduct employment interviews within the law. The cost to defend a claim of employment discrimination can be hundreds of thousands of dollars; however, the cost to your organization's reputation can be even more damaging.

The most important thing to remember when asking a question is whether you can demonstrate a job-related reason for asking this particular question (whether on a job application or in an interview). The Equal Employment Opportunity Commission (EEOC) looks at both how the information is used and what the intent of the interviewer is when determining whether discrimination is an issue. Therefore, applicants should only be asked job-related questions; and before asking any question, it is a good idea to first determine whether the information is relevant to making a good decision on the qualifications, skills, and overall competence for the job in question.

However, there is something called *Bona Fide Occupational Qualifications*—a provision that permits discriminatory practices in employment if a person's "religion, sex, or national origin is a bona fide occupational qualification reasonably necessary to the normal operation of that particular business or enterprise."[4] To establish the defense of Bona Fide Occupational Qualification (BFOQ), you have the burden of proving that a particular class of employees would not be qualified. For example, if you are recruiting models for men's suits or swimwear, gender would be a bona fide occupational qualification reasonably necessary to the operation of the business. Typically, it is difficult for most employers that are not religious organizations to invoke the BFOQ defense as the parameters surrounding it are limited. Title VII does permit employers to hire and employ people on the basis of religion if religion is a "bona fide occupational qualification reasonably necessary to the normal operation of that particular business or enterprise."[5] Religious organizations do not normally have to use the BFOQ defense because the "religious organization" exception in Title VII permits them to prefer people from their own religion.

The EEOC provides this information to employers who are intent on avoiding racial discrimination in hiring and promotions: "Race or color should not be a factor or consideration in making employment decisions except in appropriate circumstances as set forth at Section 15-VI-C of the Compliance Manual section on race and color discrimination. Reasons for selection decisions should be well supported and based on the applicant's qualifications."[6]

➔   Appendix: Legal and Illegal Interview Questions.

The interview process can be time-consuming and uncomfortable, but there is no other way to find out whether or not the candidate is going to be right for your organization and this particular position. Although there is no fool-proof selection method, with careful preparation, good listening skills, and attention to detail you will be able to make informed selections.

Common Rating Errors When Interviewing

- **First impression**—making a quick decision based on how the applicant looks or dresses.
- **Contrast**—first candidate is weak, so second looks really good.
- **Blind spots**—overlooking potential areas for concern.
- **Halo effect**—candidate is strong in one dimension so you overlook other missing skill sets.
- **Pitchfork effect**—candidate has one minor flaw that you can't see past.
- **Presumptive qualification**—candidate went to your college, so he or she must be talented!

Discussion Questions

1. Why does it make sense to do a screening interview prior to bringing in a candidate for a face-to-face interview?
2. What information do you want to get from a screening interview?
3. Why does it make sense to set up an appointment for a screening interview?
4. Why should you not tell the applicant what your hiring criteria are in an interview?
5. What are some of the things to keep in mind when using video to screen applicants?
6. Why is the candidate experience significant?
7. Name two to three things that are important to consider prior to starting the interview process.
8. Describe the behavioral interviewing process. What do you want to get from the applicant in a behavioral interview and why?
9. Name three or four ways to spot superstars in interviews.

10

Making a Hiring Decision

George O'Leary was hired to fill the position of head football coach at Notre Dame. He described this as his "dream job," yet he resigned after only five days when it was uncovered that for years he had lied about his background. It turns out that he did not have a master's degree from New York University and he had not been a star college football player. If high-profile people lie about their background, you can be sure other people do as well.

According to Richard Paul and Michael Fox, attorneys who spoke at the 7th Annual Labor and Employment Law Advanced Practices Symposium in 2011, there are actually websites that show applicants how to lie on their resume because, as it says on one site, "Everyone else is doing it, shouldn't you?"

- 80 percent of resumes are misleading.
- 42 percent have major misrepresentations.
- 20 percent show unearned degrees.
- 30 percent show falsified employment dates.
- 25 percent list companies that don't exist.[1]

Hiring a new employee for your organization is a time-consuming, expensive, and highly impactful process, and you want to be sure you that applicants are who they say they are. Resumes, applications, and even interviews can give an incomplete picture of a candidate, so it is necessary to widen your quest for information on that person prior to having him/her join the organization. Reference- and background-checking is the next critical step in the hiring process.

Be sure your application (whether online or paper) has a statement that any false information on the application is grounds for rejection or termination, and that each application is signed by the candidate. This may prevent some candidates from falsifying information, but it isn't enough. You must check references and should consider some type of background checking to protect your organization.

Some organizations have HR do all the reference-checking. There's no reason HR shouldn't do them, but sometimes it makes sense to have the hiring manager do the reference check so that the

SECTION 1

manager can ask specific questions about the applicant's technical qualifications. If your organization uses hiring managers to do reference-checking, it is important that anyone who does a reference check be trained prior to making that first phone call. Training should include how to ask the right questions and the best way to approach a reference.

Checking references by phone allows you to ask follow-up questions to gather additional information. Trying to reach people by phone in today's busy work environment can be frustrating, so one tip is to email the reference to set up a time for a phone call. It is advisable to email the questions you will be asking in advance so that the reference can be prepared. You can gather information via email, but that doesn't allow you to ask follow-up questions.

Because most organizations now only release the absolute minimum information on previous employees (date of employment, title, and last salary if employee has signed a release), it can be frustrating to get useable information. This is where you should be creative and use your network or social media sites such as LinkedIn to gather information. Ask yourself who you know who worked for the organization in question, and contact that person to get what you need.

Here is where it gets tricky. We recommend that you don't give out information about past employees to people who contact you for a reference, so why would you think other organizations would give you the information you request on a prior employee? Most applicants will provide you a list of references for you to call whom they've asked to serve as a reference for them. These people will usually answer all your questions. (Just keep in mind that a person given to you by the candidate will not say anything remotely bad about the applicant.) If you have serious questions about the candidate's suitability for your position, that is where you will need to get creative and find other people to answer your questions.

LinkedIn is a great resource for finding names of people you know who work for (or who have worked for) the organizations your potential employee has listed as previous employers. Reach out to your network through LinkedIn and see what you can find out about the applicant that will help you make a final decision.

Should you believe references? If you are hiring a senior executive for your firm and rely on the references provided by the candidate, you are, in effect, taking the word of perfect strangers about something that may have tremendous financial impact on your organization. It is obvious that references provided by the candidate are nearly always going to say wonderful things about that person. Otherwise, why would the candidate give you that name?

When the candidate does not provide the number of references you've requested or when he or she takes a lot of time to give you the names/contact information, when references don't return calls, when references are from a long time ago, when references never worked directly for or with the applicant—all red flags.

→   Appendix: Reference Checking Template.

Here are some questions to ask if you're lucky enough to get someone to talk to you about a reference. Of course, you'll tailor the questions to fit the person with whom you're speaking. For example, if you're talking to someone who was the candidate's immediate supervisor, you'll ask questions different from the ones you'd ask of someone who was a peer or a direct report.

   ◆   How long have you been acquainted with the candidate?
   ◆   How long did you and the candidate work together?
   ◆   Confirm dates of employment shown on the resume/application.
   ◆   What were the job duties of the candidate when you worked together?

- Is the candidate eligible for rehire and if not, why?
- Describe the position for which you're hiring and ask: Can you comment on how well you think the candidate fits those criteria?
- Does the candidate have any developmental needs?
- End with this: Is there anything else you can tell me to help us make a good hiring decision?

Background Checks

There are many reasons for your organization to consider doing comprehensive background checking on potential employees, including increases in workplace violence, negligent hiring lawsuits, and dishonest employees. Before you take this on, consider this question: What should be verified?

Well, referring back to the George O'Leary story at the start of this chapter, education should be high on the list. Many organizations are now also checking criminal records and credit history. Be sure that you have job-related reasons for doing criminal or credit checks, and be sure to verify what the laws are in your state regarding using credit information as an employment-screening component. Some states have enacted laws restricting their use for employment related decisions. The EEOC, under Title VII, is closely monitoring how employers use criminal and credit checks to review the potentially discriminatory impact they have on particular applicants. The Commission has advised employers to consider the specific nature and gravity of the crime, the time elapsed since it was committed, and its relevance to the position in question when using a criminal background check in an employment decision. It has also carefully looked at the use of credit reports in the hiring process due to the potentially discriminatory effect aggregate race-related disparities in credit ratings can cause. If you are considering using credit checks, check with your state. Some states have recently enacted laws restricting or prohibiting employers from using credit checks in the employment process.

Before you put your background checking procedure in place, here are some tips:

- Check with your labor attorney to be sure what you are considering is fully compliant with all relevant laws and regulations.
- Determine what you want to accomplish.
- Document your procedure.
- Cover all employees with the policy—not just selected ones!
- Make sure your policy is defensible.

Once you know what information you want to have verified by an outside firm, develop a request for proposal to outline what you require. Ask your professional network for recommendations about firms they use, and send out RFPs to determine what each firm has to offer and their prices.

Making the Final Decision

This is where the "rubber meets the road," and now you must make a decision as to whether this person will meet your requirements and fit your organizational culture. If you've done your job up until now, you just need to trust your decision-making ability, and make the call and make the offer. This is where many managers become hesitant to make a decision. Though no one ever intentionally makes a wrong decision, waiting for the perfect candidate can have serious implications.

The most obvious one is that if you hesitate or take too long to make a decision, you stand to lose your best candidate. Applicants don't want to wait too long for offers (and there is no hard and fast rule as to what "too long" means), so work to ensure your hiring processes are as streamlined as possible and that everyone involved does their part in a timely manner. And, be sure you're keeping your candidates informed as you go through the decision process. Not only is this good business, applicants expect to hear from you often!

If you've done a very thorough series of interviews with your final candidate and have completed your due diligence by checking references and completing relevant background checks, it's time to make the job offer. Bringing a new hire into your organization is a big step and you want to be as sure as you can be that this person is going to be able to do the job and also be a good cultural fit with your organization. (See Chapter 14 of this book for more on culture and engagement).

This is an important decision you're making. Tony Hsieh, CEO of Zappos, estimates that bad hires have cost his company well more than 100 million dollars and the cost impact doesn't end when you get rid of the bad hire; it lingers for a long time and can have a huge negative impact on your organizational culture.[2]

>   See Chapter 11 (Making a Job Offer).

Once the selected applicant has accepted, there is one final action to be taken: to let those who were considered but not hired know of your decision.

Rejecting Applicants

Even though an applicant wasn't selected for the position, you want that person to feel as if he or she was treated fairly and have a positive impression of your organization; how you tell an applicant that he or she didn't get the job is important. A well-written rejection letter can actually increase your firm's standing in the marketplace. Rejection letters are so important that it's recommended that you not use a form letter. Instead, send a personalized letter. Some organizations actually offer help to candidates they reject—telling them what skills or experiences would make them a better applicant next time. Of course, you don't want to make any promises of future consideration; however, if someone has made it all the way to the end of your hiring process and lost out to someone just a little better qualified, why wouldn't you want to keep in touch with that person?

Discussion Questions

1. What are two to three reasons why it makes sense to check references prior to making a job offer?
2. Who should conduct the reference checks and why?
3. What is the best way to go about getting a reference?
4. Why is it a good idea to do background checks?
5. When and how should rejected applicants be notified of your decision not to hire them?

11

Making a Job Offer

John Armstrong, vice president of news at Contra Costa Newspapers, Inc., said, "To paraphrase Winston Churchill, never, never, never, never compromise. The bad hire was the third choice after two others were not hired. I compromised because the search was taking inordinately long. My experience reminded me that no hire is better than a bad hire."[1]

During the hiring process, the recruiter or hiring manager should have learned what it will take to get this candidate to say yes. If you are using an executive search consultant, he or she will work with you on developing an offer to meet the identified needs of the candidate. Some of the issues that may be important to a candidate include:

- Commute.
- Salary.
- Incentive compensation.
- Time off benefits.
- Flexible schedule.
- Opportunity for work/life balance.
- Health and other benefits.
- Ability to progress in the organization.
- Training and development opportunities.
- Availability of coaching and/or mentoring opportunities.

We highly recommend that the hiring manger make the verbal offer and then follow it up with a written offer letter, which should be emailed immediately and a hard copy sent via USPS. Some organizations ask HR to make the verbal offer and/or send the offer letter, but it is much more impactful if the hiring manager does it. The applicant really gets the impression he or she is valued, and it may make a difference in whether or not he or she accepts. Of course, HR can draft the letter and handle the logistics of sending it and tracking the response.

You may want to draft a form offer letter and have it reviewed by your labor attorney before use. It should:

- State your enthusiasm for this candidate to join your firm.
- Address all variables of the offer including:
  - ▷ Start date.
  - ▷ Starting salary.
  - ▷ Incentive compensation, if applicable.
  - ▷ Contingencies, such as the candidate's references must check out, or he or she must pass the drug screen.
  - ▷ Benefits summary (or use an attachment).
  - ▷ Reporting relationships.
  - ▷ Date offer expires (usually three to five days from date of offer).
  - ▷ Place for candidate to sign if he or she accepts.

Script for Making a Verbal Offer

"I am very pleased to offer you the job we discussed. We'd like you to start on Monday, the 3rd, at 9 a.m. for orientation with HR and some of our executive staff. Your salary will be $5,000.00 per month, and we are paid every two weeks. As we discussed in the interview, we have a complete benefits package, and I am sending you a letter today by email and U.S. mail that will outline the benefits and other details you will need to know. I hope you will accept this offer and I look forward to working with you. We will need a response from you by Thursday, (date), of this week either by phone or email, and then the signed acceptance of the offer letter can be forwarded to me. All these details are in the offer letter. Do you have any questions at this time? Again, I am very hopeful that you will say yes! Thank you."

Sample Offer Letter

Dear (first name of applicant):

This is to confirm the verbal offer made to you on (date) by (name of person who made the offer if it wasn't you). We are offering you the position of (title) at a salary of (always state salary in pay period amounts and, if necessary, what it is when annualized). We are paid every two weeks. We would like you to start on (date) and if that works for you, your first pay check will be issued on (date). You will be reporting to (name and title). This position is (state whether exempt or non-exempt).

Enclosed is a summary of our company's employee benefits. If you have questions on the benefits, please contact (name, phone, and email) in our HR department for additional information.

You will be entitled to (number of days) of paid time off. This includes any sick and vacation time. Your PTO accrues at the rate of (number) per pay period. [If your firm restricts PTO usage until after 90 days or whatever, state that here or say the new hire is able to use it as it accrues with management approval.]

This offer is contingent on the successful completion of a background check including a drug test, the signing of a confidentiality agreement and non-compete agreement (or whatever your firm requires), and compliance with the I-9 process within three days of starting employment with our organization. I've enclosed a list of approved documents that prove you have the right to work in the U.S., so please bring the appropriate documents with you on your first day of employment.

Your employment with (name of organization) is "at will," which allows the company to terminate your employment at any time, with or without cause, and gives you the right to resign at any time. We will discuss this with you at the new-hire orientation.

You will be scheduled for the new-hire orientation at (date and time). Please arrive no later than (time) on your start date for us to provide you with (list any security cards, badges, parking passes to be issued).

We are looking forward to working with you and hope you will accept this offer. Please sign the bottom of this letter and return as an email attachment to me at (email address) or fax confidentially to (fax number). This offer will expire on (date [usually three to four business days from date of verbal offer]).

Sincerely,
Name
Title

I hereby acknowledge that I have read this offer of employment and accept the terms and conditions as written.
Signature of Job Applicant   Date

Negotiating Do's and Don'ts

Today's applicants have access to a lot of salary information on the Internet, so be prepared to negotiate.

- Do know what the salary range for this position is and what your organization's policy is on where new hires should start in the range.
- Do know the absolute highest salary you can give and still be fair to the applicant and your current employees.
- Don't immediately think it is a negative if the applicant negotiates with you; it is expected.
- Do know if you have other qualified applicants so that, if you can't come to agreement, you have other options.
- Do think creatively if you can't get to the salary number the applicant wants. Consider:

  ▷ More paid time off (PTO).
  ▷ Flexible work schedule.
  ▷ Hiring bonus.
  ▷ Promise of an off-cycle performance review. (Don't promise an increase.)
  ▷ Health insurance subsidy.
  ▷ Health club membership.
  ▷ Additional perks (usually done at senior executive levels, and may include things such as company car, club membership, additional vacation time, first-class travel for business trips, etc.).

Legal Implications of Offer Letters/Employment Contracts

Legally binding contracts for employment can be created verbally or in writing. Organizations sometimes use written contracts to outline the terms of their agreement with the employee—especially for senior-level executives or for contractors. Any employment contract should be either written by or reviewed by your general counsel or outside attorney, but at a minimum, it should contain:

- Job duties and responsibilities.
- Compensation and benefits.
- Start date.
- End date (for a contract position).
- Confidentiality and non-disclosure requirements.
- Non-compete requirements.
- Resignation or termination provisions including severance pay, if applicable.

Please be aware that enforcement of individual employment contracts is generally a matter of state law, so contact your labor attorney for more information.

Relocation

It is increasingly difficult to relocate people today due to the realities of the real estate markets. You should develop a policy to cover relocation. To do so, answer these questions:

- Will you pay to move the employee's household goods from one location to your location?
- Will you include full packing services?
- Will you cover unpacking in the new location?
- Will you pay closing costs on the new home?
- Will you pay to relocate cars? Boats?
- How much temporary housing will you cover, and for how long?
- How many house-hunting trips will you cover, and for how many people (employee and spouse, or will children be included in one trip?)?
- If the employee's current home doesn't sell in a reasonable amount of time, will your firm purchase the house?
- If the employee needs a bridge loan, will you offer that or refer him or her to a local bank?
- If the employee resigns within a period of time (you determine how long), what percentage, if any, of moving costs will he or she be required to repay?

This is just a snippet of the issues around relocation, so approach it carefully and get advice from relocation specialists.

Discussion Questions

1. Who is recommended to make the job offer and why?
2. If a verbal offer is made, is it necessary to confirm in writing and why?
3. What are some of the topics a candidate may want to negotiate?
4. Name some of the areas where you may have some flexibility when making an offer.
5. At what level are employment contracts more common?

12

On-Boarding New Employees

"All the world's a stage, and all the men and women merely players; they have their entrances and exits." William Shakespeare probably didn't know how often those lines would be quoted (and not always on the stage), but these words certainly apply to the process of bringing new employees into your organization. Whether you call it new hire orientation or on-boarding, how you bring a new hire into your organization is critical to that person's success and his or her contribution to your growth and success. The goal of any on-boarding process is to ensure the new hire is as productive as possible in the shortest amount of time and knows he or she has made a great choice to join you.

According to the article "The Race for Talent: Retaining and Engaging Workers in the 21st Century" by Frank Finnegan, "Innovative employee on-boarding processes have more impact on both retention and engagement than tuition reimbursement and competitive vacation/holiday benefits."[1]

New employees are usually excited about the new job but don't have much of a clue as to what lies ahead of them. Most likely, they know a lot about your organization through their research and the interview process, but most of the time they were in interviews with your firm they were doing their best to "sell" their talents so that you would offer them a job. As their first day approaches, they are looking forward to working with and for you, but have a lot of questions and concerns. That's where a well-crafted on-boarding process can make or break the relationship.

As soon as the applicant accepts the job, the on-boarding process starts. Both HR and the hiring manger play a role here. HR should send the new hire paperwork, including information on benefit plans, and the hiring manager should consider sending a welcome letter or email as soon as the acceptance is received. There is a difficult time between the date the employee accepts and the start date he or she may still be getting offers from other organizations. You don't want the new hire to decide the other offer is better than yours, change his or her mind, and reject your offer; so, keep in touch. If you've already received a signed confidentiality agreement, include the new hire on department emails and send copies of company announcements and newsletters. It is ideal if the hiring manager calls the new hire at least once to welcome him or her and respond to any questions.

In the welcome letter, you can also include some information to help the new hire get connected with your organization, including:

- The latest employee newsletter.
- Recent press releases.
- Bios of company leadership.
- A list of items to bring to complete the I-9 process.
- An employee benefits summary and enrollment forms.
- A company t-shirt, pen, or other branded gift to link new hire to your organization.

Here are some ideas to welcome a new hire:

- Decorate his or her office with welcome signs, merchandize bearing the company logo, a plant, or flowers.
- Have a welcome coffee or lunch to introduce the new hire.
- Send a press release to local media.
- Announce the new hire on your website.
- Have the new hire participate in planning and executing an event in his or her first few months so the new hire gets a chance to bond. Assign him or her to a task force so he/she can get to work with others in your department quickly.

Although your business does not exist to create a social life for your employees, research has proven that having friends at work is a great on-boarding and retention tool. Buddy systems can be effective in some organizations. Ask for volunteers, and then carefully select people who you're sure will do a good job of welcoming a new hire and who will "sell" the good points of working for your organization. Consider having training for buddies and some sort of reward program for them if you don't compensate them. They can provide valuable assistance to a new hire; people are more comfortable asking questions of a peer than a manager.

Waterfilters.net has all new hires participate in their monthly "grill day"—a company-funded activity. New hires are paired with existing employees to plan the menu for the entire company. They shut down for an hour and all associates eat together.

Before the First Day

Carefully prepare for the new hire. There is nothing worse than a new employee arriving to find the manager has taken the day off or has done nothing to get ready for the new hire's first day! Not being prepared for a new hire sends a message that he or she isn't valued, and that's not the way you want to get started. Your organization probably has a process developed for on-boarding new hires that includes notifying your IT department to provide the new hire what he or she needs to be productive quickly.

Set up the work area. It is extremely impressive for a new hire to come in on Day 1 and have his or her work area (be it a cubicle, workstation, office, or whatever) ready, complete with the appropriate technology, paper, pens, paperclips, stapler, and/or whatever else will make him or her productive. If your organization has company mugs, pens, or other merchandise, have these available for the new hire, or be sure they are given out at orientation. If possible, have a welcome gift, such as a plant or book that would be useful for the new hire to read, already placed on the new hire's desk.

Here is a suggested list of items you should have prepared and ready for any new hire. Some of this may be covered in your orientation program, but be sure it is available at some point on Day 1:

- Payroll information (date of first check, regular pay schedule, payment process [i.e, direct deposit, hard check, etc.]).
- Instructions for how to set up computer and voice mail.
- Strategic plan, mission statement.
- Parking details.
- Building security processes (including keys, key cards, or whatever is used in your organization). Be sure to include details on what to do if the employee loses a key or key card and how to enter your facility after hours or on weekends.
- Emergency contact information for manager and others in department.
- Company disaster plan.
- Job description.
- Who to call for specific help with expense accounts, payroll, HR, administrative support, IT, reception, and so on.
- Employee handbook.
- Information on your employee referral program (if applicable).
- Neighborhood information (restaurants, dry cleaners, grocery stores, service stations, etc.).

Orientation Programs

Most organizations hold new-hire orientation as often as necessary. It is usually conducted by HR with assistance from other key players, including payroll, accounting, leadership, office administration, IT, and safety officers. However, research now shows that new hires prefer to get their information from their manager rather than from HR, so consider how you might make that happen. Orientation should be designed with new hires in mind. What do they need to know and when do they need to know it? The mistake most organizations make is to assume that the half day or whatever time they allot to orientation is all that is needed.

Consider how much information new hires can absorb at one time, and then think about how you might spread out your on-boarding activities to ensure that new hires get what they need. Some organizations consider the first year to be the on-boarding time period and spread out learning experiences throughout the year. This may be more than you can afford, but be careful not to assume that if HR does a quick benefits orientation and new hires fill out the payroll and benefits forms, they are up-to-date and can be productive.

Elements of a Formal Orientation Program

- **Organizational history.** This is where you reinforce the idea that they made a good decision to join your organization!
- **Bios of leaders, with photos if possible.** Or, have the leaders come to orientation to be introduced or have a video presentation to showcase the CEO and other leaders.
- **Overview of benefit programs.** New hires should already have had the benefits information sent to their home, so this can be just a quick summary.
- **Policies and procedures focused on the employee handbook,** with emphasis on EEO commitment, harassment, safety and security, disciplinary policies, time off policies, and other key policies specific to your organization. Each employee should receive a

hard copy of the handbook or a link to where they can retrieve it. Each employee must also sign a document that they have received and read the handbook. This document then goes into each employee's file.

- **Payroll procedures.** This is where employees fill out their W-4 and other tax forms, and payroll tells them how time is kept in the organization and their role in maintaining accurate pay records.
- **Employee referral program.** This is an ideal time to ask if they know of anyone who might be a good employee for your firm. It is ideal to have one of your star recruiters come in to orientation to let new hires know about the hard-to-fill positions and to explain the ERP.
- **Location-specific information,** such as emergency exits and procedures.
- **Department- or division-specific information.** This can be effective if your organization has a wide variety of positions. Ask the managers of divisions to come in to tell what they do, or split up the group and have new hires meet with their specific leader and then return to the group for the wrap-up.
- **Frequently asked questions.** Compile the list based on questions asked in previous orientation sessions, and keep adding to it.
- **Evaluation.** Ask "Did you get what you needed from today's session?" This information should be used to tweak the process to ensure success.
- **Tour of the facilities.** Ideally this should be done by the hiring manager so introductions can be performed.

Do's and Don'ts for New-Hire Orientation

- Don't overwhelm new hires and try to get everything done in one day.
- Don't hand out a lot of paper. Let them know where they can access information.
- Don't make everything so serious. Lighten up if you can.
- Do involve managers in the process.
- Don't have only one presenter. Vary the speakers to keep it lively.
- Do use technology. Show videos of organizational activities like the holiday party or a celebration for a new contract, and so forth.

The Manager's Role on Day 1

First, be available. It is amazing how many managers don't think about when a new hire will be joining them and take a day off or are on vacation, or assume that the new hire will be busy with other people so they book back-to-back meetings all day. What a mistake! The new hire really wants to spend quality time with his or her new manager and the first day is so important to that bonding experience. Yes, the new hire will probably be tied up in orientation for part of the day, but when he or she is finished, it would be great for the manager to take the new hire to lunch, either the two of them or with key members of the department. Managers need to make it comfortable for the new hire to ask questions and to get a sense of how things work in your organization.

SECTION 1

Checklist for Managers

- Does security know the new hire is starting?
- Does the employee know when and where to report on Day 1?
- Is the work area ready with computer, phone, supplies, and welcoming items? Is everything hooked up and ready to go?
- Does your staff know when the new hire is arriving?
- Do you have a plan for the first day and beyond?
- Does your schedule include time for the new hire?
- Does the new hire have a copy of his or her job description?
- Does the new hire have a copy of the organization's strategic plan and mission statement?
- Does the new hire know what to do in case of an emergency in the workplace (fire, bomb threat, and so on)?

30-Day, 60-Day, 90-Day Check-Ins

We recommend that you have a process for monitoring the progress of new hires for at least the first 90 days. This responsibility can be divided up between HR and the manager. The 30-day check-in can be done through the use of an On-Boarding Evaluation form (see page 100) whereby you ask the employee a series of questions. This can be done in person by HR or by asking the employee do a quick online survey. As with exit interview data, individual comments should be kept confidential, and HR should analyze any trends that emerge from the analysis.

Then, at or around the 60-day mark, the manager should do a brief check-in to see if there are any work issues. This gives the new hire time to get up to speed on job responsibilities. If the employee shares organizational issues, the manager should notify HR.

A great idea at 90 days is to do a one-page performance evaluation to let the employee know how he or she is doing and to raise any issues or concerns. If your organization doesn't do a 90-day evaluation, HR or the manager can do another quick check-in to see how the employee is progressing.

Each of these check-ins sends a clear message to the new hire that the organization is focused on helping him or her succeed.

When new employees at Northeast Delta Dental reach the 90-day mark, they sit down with HR VP Connie Roy-Czyzowski. They affectionately call it "20 Questions with Connie."[2]

Executive On-Boarding

It is even more critical that newly hired senior leaders have a smooth transition into your organization. Consider how long you searched for just the right person, and the time and money you expended to land just the right person at this particular time. Now the new leader is finally arriving to start work.

It is a common assumption that senior leaders don't need any special help to assimilate. After all, they are, in fact, senior leaders. They've worked in other organizations and they know their job; that is why they were hired. It is critical to put together a well-crafted process for on-boarding a new executive that will provide him/her with the information needed to be successful as quickly as possible. Think through how you will:

- Introduce the new executive to your existing staff.
- Announce the new executive to the business community.
- Provide a warm welcome.
- Integrate the new executive into your existing management/leadership team.
- Introduce the new executive to his or her direct reports.
- Orient the new leader to organizational policies and procedures.
- Get the new executive signed up for benefits.

Executive On-Boarding Checklist

Name: _____

Start Date: _____

Hiring Manager: _____

Activities prior to start:	Responsible Party	Date Completed
Welcome packet sent**	Hiring Manager	
New-hire checklist completed*	Hiring Manager	
Business cards ordered	Administration	
Supplies put in office	Administration	
Orientation scheduled	HR	
Comments:		
Return form to HR for filing.		

**Executive Welcome packet
*Checklist for Day 1 and First Week

- Letter from CEO.
- Gift with company logo for home (clock, coasters, or other small item to be a reminder to new executive and family).
- Book or DVD that is particularly meaningful to organization.
- Benefits enrollment information and forms.
- Parking information for Day 1.
- Schedule for first week.
- Bios of leadership team.

Name: _____

Start Date: _____

Hiring Manager: _____

Activities prior to start:	Responsible Party	Date Completed
Email announcement	Hiring Manager	
Name on welcome board in lobby	Administration	
Tour of offices/introductions	Hiring Manager	
Set goals for first week, month	Hiring Manager	
Benefits sign-up/orientation	HR	
Documents to payroll	HR	
I-9 completed and filed	HR	
Benefits enrollment follow-up scheduled	HR	
Keys (list numbers, if applicable)	Administration	
Security cards (list numbers, if applicable)	Administration	
Comments:		
Return form to HR for filing.		

SECTION 1

On-Boarding Evaluation (to be completed by new hire after 30 days)

Name: _____

Department: _____

Date of Hire: _____

We are very interested in improving our new-hire on-boarding process. Please complete these questions and return your comments to HR. Your individual comments will be kept confidential so please be as open and honest as possible so we can improve our process.

1. Please tell us how you felt when you received the offer to join our organization. What was it that made you accept the offer?

2. Tell us about the time between you accepted the offer and when you started. Did you begin to feel connected to our organization? Why or why not?

3. How about the Welcome Letter and information you received before you started? Was this valuable to you? Why or why not?

4. How was your first day on the job?

What could we have done better to make you feel part of the organization (if anything!)? Please be specific.

Please return this form to HR. Thank you for helping us improve our processes!

Announcement Email to Staff

It is my pleasure to announce that Joan Smith has joined our team today as a Project Manager and reports to me in my role as Vice President of the Midwestern Division. Joan is a graduate of the XYZ University and most recently was a PM for the Jones Company in Chicago. She brings over 10 years of experience and we look forward to her contributions to our growth. She will be located in the Arlington office, but will be visiting all accounts in the division over the next few months so you will all have an opportunity to meet her and welcome her to our team. Her direct dial number is 1–800–555–1212 and her email is jsmith@thecompany.com.

Sample Welcome Letter to New Hire

I am personally pleased that you have accepted the offer to join us on (date) as a Project Manager in our Arlington office. Please report to the office at 8:30 a.m. and give your name to the security guard on duty who will call me to come get you from the lobby. On your first day, please park in space 236 in the north parking structure. You will receive a parking card and a security badge on Day 1 along with parking instructions for the employee garage.

I am enclosing information on our benefits package and the enrollment forms. It will be most helpful if you read the benefits information prior to your first day and if you have questions, please call or email our benefits administrator, Sally Johnson, at 1–800–555–1213 or email her at sjohnson@thecompany.com. If possible, we would like you to complete the enrollment forms prior to your first day, but you will have a chance to review or complete them after your orientation.

Also enclosed is your schedule for the first week, which includes new-hire orientation and other events designed to provide you with a good introduction to The Company.

In order to complete the I-9 process, you must bring documents that prove your eligibility to work in the U.S. A list of approved documents is included in this packet. Please bring the required documents on your first day. If for some reason you can't supply the documents within three days of starting work, you will be terminated.

Please sign and return the enclosed Confidentiality and Non-Disclosure Form. You can mail them to me in a confidential envelope, fax directly to me, or send via email. Please return these signed documents no later than (date; three to five days from date of letter).

Here is a link (*www.thecompany.com/newsletters*) to some recent issues of our employee newsletter and recent press releases, which may help you get to know us better!

We are all looking forward to working with you, and I plan to call you on (day) the (date) at 3 p.m. to see what questions you may have. If this time or date isn't convenient, email me with alternative dates and times! I really want to connect this week!

Again, welcome to The Company. We look forward to the contributions you will make to our success.

Sincerely,
Name
Title

Discussion Questions

1. What are the two reasons to spend time to on-board new hires into any organization?
2. Name four to five things a new hire needs to know before Day 1.
3. Why is it important to keep in touch with a new hire between the time he or she accepts the job and when he or she starts?
4. What are some of the ways to keep in touch with a new hire?
5. Name four or five things a manager should do before a new hire starts.

SECTION 2

EMPLOYEE ENGAGEMENT AND RETENTION

13

Strategic Retention

"My job can be so exciting. I get to work with some of the brightest minds and most accomplished luminaries in technology, politics, and business. I am consistently humbled and feel lucky for the opportunities I get."

—Christopher Saccca, former head of special initiatives, Google, Inc.[1]

Not all of us can have the work environment of a Google—a firm that consistently makes the Fortune 100 Best Places to Work list, but, no matter what business you are in or how large or small your organization is, you can take action to retain your valued employees. It takes some effort, but the payoff is potentially huge!

Cost of Turnover

The cost impact of losing good employees can be high, and in more than just dollars. Consider the impact losing a valued employee has on his or her coworkers. Productivity will suffer as they adjust to a new team member. Think about the impact on your customers when you lose someone. If the terminated employee is in sales, consider the lost revenue. If you are a member-driven organization, consider the negative impact losing a key staffer may have on your valued members. Also consider the time investment of your managers, recruiters, and HR staff to recruit, orient, and train a new hire. Also, do not discount the impact that losing a valued employee has on the institutional knowledge of your organization!

Then, consider the cost to hire a new person and train the new hire to the level needed to be productive! This can have an enormous financial impact on your organization, so it makes sense to develop retention strategies to mitigate this potential loss or, to put it in more positive terms, it makes good economic and organizational sense to work to keep your good people. Although we know that it is impossible to keep people forever, why not make the effort to retain them as long as you can. Millennials, who now make up the largest segment of the U.S. workforce, are known for changing jobs frequently, but even they will stay with you if you give them a good reason to!

Turnover is especially difficult in smaller organizations, in which losing one person can severely impact productivity, culture, and institutional knowledge.

Research by SHRM shows that direct replacement costs (recruiting and training) can reach as high as 50–60 percent of an employee's annual salary and the total cost of turnover can range from 90–200 percent of annual salary.[2]

When looking at turnover, it is important to differentiate between turnover you can control (poor management, wages, benefits, working conditions, lack of development opportunities, inflexible scheduling, dress code, etc.) versus turnover you can't control (spouse gets transferred, employee returns to school to pursue graduate degree). Focus your attention on the turnover you can control, and try to learn as much as possible about why people leave your organization. Exit interviews can provide you with valuable information.

→   See Chapter 30 (Ending the Employment Relationship), for more information on exit interviews.

Strategic Retention

Originations invest a great deal of time and money to hire and develop their employees and, after all that effort, want to retain as many as possible. If you want to retain your talented employees, it is important that you approach it strategically. Retention starts very early in the relationship between the employer and employee. It starts even before there is a relationship; it starts from the time the prospective employee hears there is a job opening at your organization or selects your firm as a place he or she would like to know more about—just in case a job comes available.

It starts with how your employee brand is crafted and lived.

→   See Chapter 8 (Recruiting From Outside the Organization).

Prospective applicants learn about you from your website; from colleagues; from sites such as LinkedIn, where they may connect with someone who has or does work for your organization; and from sites like Glassdoor, where they can read reviews posted by your current or former employees. So, consistency is the key here to letting applicants know what your organization is all about, including your mission and your values, how you display those values in your advertising, and how you treat your employees. The applicant has already formed an opinion of your organization before ever completing your online application or sending in a resume—and you certainly want that impression to be favorable.

Though some managers resent sites like Glassdoor, try to approach their information with an open mind, and use what you see and hear posted about your firm to make positive changes. Don't ignore what's written about your organization either on social media or other online sites. Learn what you can and make needed changes.

The retention process continues during the selection process. How applicants are treated when they are going through the interview process gives them a sense of how they will be treated as employees; therefore, be sure every applicant is treated as a VIP. The increased focus on the candidate experience is extremely positive. Organizations are more aware than ever that applicants have choices and they want to work where they're valued and that starts in the hiring process, so be sure how your hiring process is as good as it possibly can be and never stop trying to improve it!

→   See Chapter 9 (The Interview).

Simple things can make all the difference, such as being warmly welcomed upon arrival and not being asked to wait for a long time before starting the interview. Were all of the applicant's questions answered? Did the interviewer get back to the applicant in the time frame that was promised? Did the applicant feel as if the interviewer gave the applicant a chance to tell his or her story?

The retention process continues during the offer/acceptance phase. How the offer is made can be significant. Did the hiring manager call to make the job offer, and did the manager convey enthusiasm for the applicant? Did the applicant receive a well-worded offer letter that contained the information needed to make a decision? After the acceptance was given, did the new hire receive calls, emails, or other information from the company between the time of acceptance and the start date?

The retention process begins in earnest when the employee arrives on Day 1. You want the new hire, from Day 1, to be so excited about what a great day the new hire had at his or her new job, and how happy the new hire is that he or she made the decision to join this great organization. These are the kinds of experiences that "glue" your employees to your organization.

> ➔ See Chapter 12 (On-Boarding New Employees), for information on putting together a process that will *wow* your new hires.

According to best-selling author Daniel Pink, the critical things organizations must do to keep current employees is tap the motivators that encourage them to stay engaged. Pink, during a presentation made at the SHRM 2011 Talent & Staffing Management Conference Exposition, said that "people can't be managed or incentivized to engagement; they have to get there on their own. So pay people enough to take money off the table. Instead, provide them with these three intrinsic motivators:

- Autonomy.
- Mastery.
- Purpose."[3]

> ➔ See Chapter 14 (Employee Engagement) for more on employee engagement.

Pink singled out companies including Netflix and Facebook as examples of organizations that give their employees a high degree of autonomy to do their jobs. Netflix's vacation policy is to give salaried employees as much time off as they want when they want it. Facebook lets its new hires interview teams and pick which ones they want to work on.

Pink said that employees are motivated to get better at what they do (mastery) through frequent feedback (especially Generation X employees and Millennials). He said, "Younger workers' lives have been rich with feedback, until they get to the office—a feedback desert."[4]

> ➔ See Chapter 25 (Performance Management), which discusses feedback.

He also reminded us to be sure our employees understand and are committed to our mission. This helps people understand where they fit and how the work they do matters. Pink said, "We want to learn, be engaged, and contribute."[5]

So, we need to hire good people and let them use their expertise to do what they were hired to do, provide them with development opportunities to increase their skills, and let them know where the work they do ties to our organization's mission. That is autonomy, mastery, and purpose!

SECTION 2

Finding out why employees stay can be even more important than all the time and energy that are put into finding out why people leave. Most organizations do some sort of exit interview when an employee leaves. Though these interviews can be informative, it is equally interesting to find out what it is about your organization that appeals to people. Why does one person stay while another quits? This information can be gathered in focus groups, individual interviews, from online interview using sites such as Survey Monkey (*www.surveymonkey.com*), or from information gathered in employee opinion surveys.

> ➤   See Chapter 14 (Employee Engagement).

You may discover that people stay with your organization because your organizational culture is strong, allows for a flexible schedule, and pays well. That information is helpful to you in several ways. First of all, you can talk about these issues in newsletters, on your intranet, and at all company meetings. In other words, build on what you now know resonates with your employees. You can also emphasize these positives in your job postings and on your website's careers page. If you find out that your employees particularly like your generous benefits package, this might not be the time to cut back on benefits; find another way to cut costs, if possible. Many people stay with organizations because of the mission. They believe in the cause the organization supports. Use this positively to continue to build your mission as another way to glue your employees to your organization. Some employees enjoy working for your organization because of your commitment to the community, so be sure you publicize your efforts on behalf of the community. People want to work someplace they can be proud of. This doesn't mean your organization has to be a "household name"—just that when your employees tell others where they work, they can say it with pride because your organization is well-respected.

One area to focus your attention on is your "superstar" employees. These are the people you couldn't run your organization without. These employees are not only valuable to your organization, but your competition would also love to steal them from you. So don't you want to know what is important to them and what keeps them motivated? Consider starting with your high-potential employees to gather retention information. What you learn from them may be applicable to others in the organization—and, if not, at least you know what is important to your stars so that you can design a strategy to keep the ones you can't survive without! Spend time with each of them to learn what is important to them at work and to assess what special skills and abilities they have that make them so good at what they do. You can build on what you learn to design a "stay" strategy for each person while using what you learn about their skills to help you develop others in your organization. And don't forget that talented people like to work with other talented people. Your outstanding employees will refer other good people to your organization!

We've all heard the phrase "People don't leave organizations. They leave managers." Although there are some that don't agree with that statement, it is true that managers have a tremendous impact on the people they supervise. A good manager can provide the encouragement, mentoring, and leadership to help an employee grow and reach his or her potential, whereas a manager who doesn't invest in his or her direct reports can drive people out of the organization. This is why management/leadership development is such a key retention tool.

Many organizations promote high performers to management positions without providing any training, coaching, or mentoring. They somehow believe that if someone was a good salesperson, he or she'll be a good manager. Well, maybe that will be true, but it would make more sense

to be sure the new manager has the skills he or she needs by providing her some basic training in areas such as:
- Interviewing.
- Motivation.
- Delegation.
- Time management.
- Conflict resolution.
- Performance management.
- Coaching.
- Counseling.

Because it is the first line supervisor who usually has the most contact with employees on a daily basis, providing them with the skills to really be successful managers should pay off in employee retention as well!

Keeping employees with your organization isn't a simple task, but it really isn't complicated, either. It comes down to forming connections:
- Employees need to connect to the organization.
- Employees need to connect to the work they do.
- Employees need to connect with each other.
- Employees need to connect with their manager.

People connect to the organization by believing in its mission, vision, and values. They connect to the work they do by understanding where their work fits in—and how it supports the organization's mission. They connect with each other to form teams and to pull together to get the work done as efficiently and accurately as possible. And they connect with their manager by being treated in a fair and equitable manner, and by knowing that their manager supports them and the work they do.

You won't know what matters to *your* employees until you ask them, but here are some things that research, including what Gallup did to create the Gallup 12,[6] says that organizations should do to retain employees. You will find many of these topics discussed elsewhere in this book:
- Hire carefully and for your culture.
- Be sure employees know what is expected of them.
- Provide opportunities for employees to learn and grow.
- Provide them with the tools they need to do the job.
- Provide a safe work environment.
- Provide clear and fair supervision.
- Communicate with candor and honesty.
- Celebrate successes and occasions.
- Have a pay program that is competitive and fair.
- Provide competitive benefits.
- Respect employees and celebrate their diversity.
- Acknowledge them as individuals.
- Provide constructive feedback.
- Reward employees frequently.
- Help employees build on their strengths.

- Solicit employee feedback on how you can help them do a better job.
- Create team-building opportunities.
- Address performance issues quickly.
- Provide a flexible environment.
- Prohibit discrimination of any kind.
- Listen carefully.
- Make work fun!

Realistic Job Preview

Realistic job preview is a way for applicants to know something about the job that's more than words on a page or verbal information from a hiring manager. It's real experience to get a sense of what the job entails. It can apply to all kinds of jobs where people have to deal with a lot of angry customers (call center for example) or where the work is repetitious (assembly line worker) or even a job like a receptionist in an office where the person has to be at the desk all the time, and be warm and friendly to *everyone* who calls or comes in the door.

If your turnover is high in the first 90 days, consider adding an element of realistic job preview to your staffing process. It can be in the form of a tour to see where the job is performed or a video clip the applicant sees early in the process that showcases each job.

Tips for Realistic Job Preview[7]

- Be totally honest about the job duties early in the process, including on the careers section of your website.
- Schedule the job preview early in the hiring process.
- Let applicants see where the work is being done.
- Involve current employees in the interviewing process, and let applicants ask them questions.
- Be honest about the turnover rate in the company.
- Consider online previews using videos on your website.

Follow-Up Exit Interviews

There is a growing trend around doing follow-up surveys several months after valued employees leave the organization, when the former employees may be more open and honest and provide information you can use. Most exit interviews are conducted on the employees' last day and they may feel self-conscious about saying anything negative. They may be worried that you won't release their last paycheck or give them a reference if they say anything about their manager. Doing a survey after a few months may net you better information. Asking for feedback after a short period of time (three to six months) also allows people to be a little more objective. They have, by that time, hopefully found a new position and may be able to share good insights about why they left and what they have found good in their new job. All of this information can help you as you develop your retention strategies. You may want to have an outside firm do these follow-up surveys, as people may be more open if they're talking with someone who doesn't work for your organization.

Information about why people leave can be valuable in planning a retention strategy—especially when coupled with the information about why people stay with your organization. For example, if you find that people stay because you offer great career opportunities, find ways to reinforce that upward mobility is encouraged. If you discover that people stay with you because you provide a flexible workplace that allows for work/life balance, be sure that you stay on the cutting edge and enhance your program when needed.

Targeted Retention Strategies

After you've collected data from exit interviews, focus groups, or interviews with your superstars, you may discover that some groups of employees have particular issues that need to be addressed as part of your retention strategy. For example, you might have a division or department that has higher turnover and, if you do employee opinion surveys, you may find those same employees report lower job satisfaction and less positive relationships with supervisors than workers in other divisions or locations. This information should lead you to design a retention strategy around supervisor training. A targeted retention strategy can be very cost-effective.

→   See Chapter 14 (Employee Engagement).

Re-Recruit Your Great Employees

Once you know what is important to your best employees, consider a strategy of re-recruiting them to your organization. Think about what you did to attract them to your organization. You probably met with them several times to find out about their background, their career goals, their interests, and their strengths.

Why not do the same thing now that they've proven to be excellent hired for your organization? Spend some time to find out how they are feeling about the work they are doing and about your firm. Find out if their expectations have been met. Ask about their career aspirations now; perhaps they've changed since you first met them in the job interview process.

Based on the answers you receive, put together a strategy to meet as many of their needs as possible. If you find out that they are interested in learning more about other parts of the business, consider a job rotation project, or getting them to serve on a task force or cross-functional team. Be as creative as possible. This kind of attention should go a long way toward retaining a valued employee.

If you find that your best employees are looking for more interaction with senior-level executives in your organization, consider something as simple as setting up a series of lunches with the CEO, COO, or other leaders where, in an informal setting, your great employees get a chance to learn from the leaders they admire. Additionally, your leadership gets a chance to see the talent you have in your department or division. This strategy can help as you work on your succession plan as well.

→   See Chapter 2 (Workforce Planning).

SECTION 2

Evaluate Retention Strategy Impact

Whatever retention strategies you come up with, build in an evaluation element so that you can see which strategies have the most impact to help you retain your best employees. You can use your employee opinion survey information, turnover data, and exit interviews as your measurement tools.

Retention and Engagement

There is an obvious link between engagement and retention. Strengthening employee engagement can help you retain talented employees. Engaged employees are satisfied with their jobs, enjoy their work, believe their job matters to the organization, take pride in the organization, and believe that their employer values the work they do. This is what it takes to retain employees in your organization. It isn't an easy task, but it's one with big payoff for you and your organization.

> →   See Chapter 14 (Employee Engagement).

Discussion Questions

1.   Other than financial costs, what are some of the costs of turnover to the organization?
2.   Describe the difference between controllable and uncontrollable turnover.
3.   Discuss some of the ways retention starts in the hiring process, in the acceptance phase, and in orientation.
4.   What are employees looking for from their work? How can you find out what matters to your employees?
5.   What role does the supervisor/manager play in retention?
6.   Name two to three ways to connect with your employees.
7.   How can realistic job preview help in retention?
8.   Discuss the link between employee engagement and retention.

14

Employee Engagement

In his book, *Employee Engagement 2.0*, Kevin Kruse says, "Employee engagement is the emotional commitment the employee has to the organization and its goals."[1]

How engaged is your workforce and why are organizations so focused on employee engagement? Leaders everywhere are focused on increasing the engagement of their employees. Increasingly we're seeing that employees, especially Millennials, get bored easily with their work and start looking for some new challenge to spark their interest. The Corporate Leadership Council says that engagement is employees' commitment to their organization, how hard they work, and how long they stay as a result of that commitment. They say that highly committed employees try 57 percent harder, perform 20 percent better, and are 87 percent less likely to leave than employees with low levels of commitment.[2]

According to the Society for Human Resource Management (SHRM), employees fall into three categories[3]:

- **Actively disengaged**—busy acting out their unhappiness and undermining what the organization is trying to accomplish.
- **Disengaged**—"sleepwalking" through their day and putting time, not passion, into work.
- **Engaged**—working with passion and feeling a real connection to the organization.

Disengagement costs the U.S. economy hundreds of billions of dollars in lost productivity annually. Employee engagement corresponds to the level of the staff members' commitment and connection to the organization they support. High levels of engagement have a direct impact on an organization's productivity, customer satisfaction, and shareholder value.

According to a survey conducted by the Boston Consulting Group and the World Federation of People Management Associations, enhancing employee engagement is one of the four critical HR topics to focus on at this time (the others are talent management, leadership development, and strategic workforce planning).[4]

What can organizations do to get employees engaged? Here are some ideas:

- Let employees know where the organization is headed and where they fit into the future plans.
- Hold firm to your values and create an ethical environment where people do what they commit to doing.
- Ensure pay and benefits are competitive and focused on what your workforce needs/wants at this time.
- Be open and transparent to your employees. Let them know when times are tough and what plans the organization has for moving ahead. Also, when things are good, let them know that as well! Share privileged information with your employees to let them feel as if they are a part of the team.
- Focus on employee career growth and development. Many development opportunities don't cost anything (such as mentoring).
- Recognize and reward top performers openly. Re-recruit your good people constantly by telling them how important they are to the organization. Maintain a positive work environment where people feel valued for their contributions as well as for who they are.
- Do things your employees can be proud of. Support local charities in your community or have a national cause you support. Involve your employees whenever possible in community-based activities. Ask your employees what causes they support and encourage them to volunteer. If possible, allow for volunteer work on company time.
- Provide management training to anyone who supervises people. Strong first-line supervisors are keys to maximizing employee engagement.
- Ensure employees have what they need to be successful.
- Review hiring practices to ensure new hires know a lot about the organization—what it does—so that they will come in with a recognized connection to the company and fit your organizational culture.
- Encourage employees to speak up and to share their ideas. Let them know it's okay to disagree with an idea or to propose an alternate way to do things.
- Continually reinforce your mission and vision so that your employees know what you stand for and why.
- Be enthusiastic about your work and your organization. Enthusiasm is contagious.
- Let people see you as a human being. Smile, laugh, and share positive stories so that your employees see you not just as the leader, but as someone to whom they can talk.
- Create an organization where employees feel they can have some sort of personal life. If possible, offer flexible schedules.
- Ask for feedback from your employees and listen carefully. Although there is no way you can make everyone happy or take every suggested action, you can let people know why you can't do something. Make sure it's a valid business reason!
- Encourage your employees to be healthy by allowing short breaks during the day. Offer healthy snacks at meetings and in your vending machines or cafeteria. Consider offering reduced memberships to local health clubs or, if possible, put one in at your location. Bring in stress-management courses for brown bag lunchtime programs to educate your staff. Consider holding some meetings outdoors in good weather and, when possible, do walking meetings for small groups.

- Have leaders available to connect with employees whenever possible. Invite employees to lunch or sit down with a group of employees in the break room from time to time to get to know them and, almost more importantly, have them get to know you.
- Let employees personalize their workspace. Sounds simple, but it can make a big difference if people are permitted to have personal items at work.
- Hold events for family and friends of your employees.

Employers can find out what issues are "top of mind" for their employees by doing a survey. Surveys can be simple and can be done by using online tools such as Survey Monkey to ask a few questions; however, we highly recommend you use an outside consultant to collect your survey responses to ensure confidentiality.

One thing you must take into consideration when doing any employee survey: If you aren't prepared to deal with the results, don't do a survey. If employees take the time to respond, they expect to know the results of the survey. This is not to say you have to take action on every suggestion made, but you should be prepared to put action teams together to deal with the information collected and then to report back to the employees about what will (or will not) be done based on this information. It is perfectly acceptable to let employees know that a suggestion will not be acted upon because of business pressures or the cost to implement. It is not acceptable to ignore the suggestion. When doing employee surveys, carefully worded questions are critical to the success of the survey. Be careful when collecting demographic information—especially if you are a small company—as the responses may allow you to pinpoint whose questionnaire you are reading. If possible, collect data on location, department, gender, and age if you think there may be issues at particular locations or with specific groups of people.

Employee engagement should be measured annually in order to be able to adjust strategies or implement new programs. Include questions that are asked every year in order to have a baseline for comparison purposes.

It comes as no surprise that engagement starts off strong in new hires and then can taper off—so managers should pay particular attention to keeping in touch with long-time workers. Not all employees are the same or have the same work drivers, so it is extremely important that managers be trained to listen carefully and communicate often.

Managers play a huge role in driving engagement. Employees are looking for mangers who:

- Accept responsibility for success or failure (and don't assign blame but work to correct if there is a problem).
- Accurately evaluate performance and potential.
- Are able to adapt to change and help their employees also adapt.
- Care about their employees as individuals.
- Clearly communicate performance expectations.
- Defend their staff to the leadership, if necessary. (Stand behind them; do not blame them.)
- Work to find solutions together.
- Are friendly and approachable.
- Are open to new ideas.
- Value work/life balance.
- Work harder than they expect their employees to work. (In other words, they don't ask employees to do something they wouldn't do themselves.)

The leadership of any organization also plays an important role in driving engagement. Employees are looking for leaders who:

- Care deeply about their employees.
- Celebrate wins and learn from losses.
- Create an atmosphere of trust and accountability.
- Are open to new ideas.
- Make employee development a priority.
- Model the organization's vision, mission, and values.
- Provide the tools necessary for employees to succeed.
- Think strategically.
- Communicate often and well.
- Are visible to employees.

Training, learning, and development are also critical to employee engagement. Creating learning opportunities does not mean the organization has to spend huge amounts of money on training or development. Some low- or no-cost ideas include:

- Mentoring.
- Cross-training.
- Task force participation, where employees get access to working with executives or people from other departments.
- Lateral moves.

Sample Employee Satisfaction Survey Questions

To honor our commitment to our valued employees, we are asking for your opinions and candid feedback. We will be using your feedback to learn and develop action plans for improvement. Your individual responses will be completely confidential and the results are being analyzed by an outside consultant so that all information will remain private.

Please tell us how you feel about each statement below using a scale of 1 to 10, where 1 means you totally disagree with this statement and 10 means you totally agree (you can use any number between 1 and 10):

1.	My compensation package (salary and benefits) is competitive with jobs in my field.	
2.	My incentives are aligned with company goals.	
3.	I understand my benefits.	
4.	I am satisfied with my benefits.	
5.	Our leadership has a clear vision for our future.	
6.	My manager keeps me informed of changes in the company.	
7.	My manager is open to ideas from me and others.	
8.	I can have open and honest conversations with my manger.	
9.	I have confidence in the leadership of my company.	
10.	I am proud to work for my company.	

11.	This is an enjoyable place to work.	
12.	I have what I need to do my work.	
13.	My salary is fair for my responsibilities.	
14.	I know what is expected of me at work.	
15.	I receive recognition for my work.	
16.	I plan to leave this company within 6–12 months.	
17.	My coworkers are good to work with.	
18.	I can develop my skills here.	
19.	I have received the training I need to do a good job.	
20.	I get timely feedback on my performance.	
21.	I have had annual performance reviews.	
22.	The company's advancement policies are fair.	
23.	The company fosters teamwork and collaboration.	
24.	This company hires only the best available employees.	
25.	This company allows me to have good work/life balance.	
26.	My job is not unreasonably stressful.	
27.	I think I can make a contribution here.	
28.	I have friends at work.	
29.	I hope to be here for a long time.	
30.	Everyone, no matter what their background or origin, is welcome here.	

Please comment on any topic above or respond to any question we didn't ask. (Allow space for typed comments).

Note: In order to be able to fully analyze survey data, you may want to consider asking some demographic questions. Then, if there is an issue with a particular manager or location, you will be able to tackle it specifically. You don't want to ever identify individual comments; therefore if a manager has less than seven direct reports, you would want to not ask his or her people to state their location. Use good judgment when crafting questions or find a consultant who specializes in employee surveys. Here are some examples of possible demographic questions:

- How long have you worked for the company?
- What age group are you in? (List in 10-year increments.)
- What is your gender?
- What division do you work in? (List divisions or departments.)

Wal-Mart[5]

According to Georgia Sherrill, PHR, Wal-Mart's senior HR director of integration, "there are six dimensions that aid in improving engagement. They are:

1. People, specifically senior leaders who model world-class behavior such as listening, calling people by name, communicating and recognizing people.
2. Work that creates a connection to the organization and resources available to support tasks.
3. Total remuneration and recognition programs that attract employees. Pay scales must be consistent, and pay levels must be competitive in the market to make an employer credible. A one-size-fits-all approach does not apply when it comes to pay.
4. Opportunities that include career development and training.
5. Quality of life issues that include benefits and work schedules.
6. Company practices such as diversity, sustainability, company reputation and performance management which must be perceived as fair and based on goals that align with those of the company."

When Wal-Mart conducted an employee survey in 2010, 402,000 out of 450,000 employees participated in the survey. This greatly helped them determine where to focus attention to maximize engagement.

Sherrill also recommends using a British definition of employee engagement: "Engaged employees are so emotionally and intellectually committed to their jobs that they want to give discretionary effort."

Wal-Mart, like any successful organization, wants to maximize the number of engaged workers to drive business results. The behaviors they want to see exhibited include:

*   Say—when employees consistently speak positively about the organizations with coworkers, potential employees and customers.
*   Stay—when employees have an intense desire to be part of the organization.
*   Strive—when employees exhibit the extra effort and engagement that contributes to business success.

Discussion Questions

1. What is your definition of employee engagement?
2. What percentage of your workforce do you think falls into the three categories (actively disengaged, disengaged, or engaged)?
3. Why is having an engaged workforce important to any organization?
4. How much revenue is lost to disengaged workers in the United States annually?
5. Name four things that organizations can do to increase employee engagement.
6. How often should employee engagement be measured?
7. Name some of the things managers can do to impact engagement.
8. What is the role of the leadership in engagement?

15

Workplace Flexibility

In November 2014, then–Vice President Joe Biden wrote the following memo:

To My Wonderful Staff,

I would like to take a moment and make something clear to everyone. I do not expect, nor do I want, any of you to miss or sacrifice important family obligations for work. Family obligations include, but are not limited to, family birthdays, anniversaries, weddings, any religious ceremonies, such as first communions and bar mitzvahs, graduations, and times of need, such as an illness or a loss in the family. This is very important to me. In fact, I will go so far as to say that if I find out that you are working with me while missing important family responsibilities, it will disappoint me greatly. This has been an unwritten rule since my days in the Senate. Thank you all for the hard work.

Sincerely, Joe[1]

When we were an agrarian society, the lines around home and work were nonexistent. People worked and lived on their farms, and there were no schedules. Nature often dictated when tasks were done. During the Industrial Revolution, workers moved from the farm to the factory. Laws and rules evolved to regulate work and work schedules. Now the Information Age is transforming the way we work. Workers are moving from the office back home, and the lines between work and home are getting blurred. We've come full circle.

As technology has made it easier to work remotely, workplace flexibility is becoming a reality for organizations. In today's competitive environment, flexibility and a culture that encourages balance between personal and business obligations are advantages in attracting and retaining the best employees. Smart organizations recognize that allowing employees some flexibility increases their loyalty to the company and is a good retention strategy.

Often thought of as a way to address the needs of employees with young children, workplace flexibility benefits can provide all employees the flexibility to successfully work and manage their personal lives. Gen Xers and Millennials have a very strong work ethic, but they want more balance—and not just the women. Members of these generations have been using technology for years and do not want to be chained to a desk and desktop computer.[2]

Flexible Work Arrangements

According to a report by WorldatWork issued in 2015, the prevalence of flexible work arrangements (FWAs) continues within organizations, although the types of programs offered vary with telework on an ad-hoc basis, and some type of flex-time or part-time schedules among the most popular. Other programs include:

- Compressed workweek schedules, such as a 4/10 schedule (working four, 10-hour days with one weekday off) or a 9/80 schedule (working nine, nine-hour days over a two-week period, with one weekday every other week off).
- Flex-time with core work hours. Employees can vary their start and stop times, but must be present during core hours every day.
- Part-time schedules, with or without benefits, including non-traditional part-time work, such as one week on/one week off.
- Telework on a regular monthly (at least one day per month) or regular weekly (at least one day per week) basis, but not full-time.
- Telework on a full-time basis.
- Shift flexibility, whereby employees coordinate with coworkers to adjust their schedules by trading shifts.
- Phased retirement.
- Job sharing, in which two employees share the responsibilities, accountability, and compensation of one full-time job.
- Phased return from leave.
- Career on/off ramps.
- A combination of programs tailored to fit an employee's needs.[3]

Many of these programs, such as phased return from leave, job sharing, or career on/off ramps, are designed to help employees transition their return to work after a major life event. Alternative location arrangements, in which employees work part-time in one location and part-time in a second location, have also been cited as a means of addressing commuting and congestion issues in communities.

Capital One's Flexible Work Solutions allows employees to work in the same office every day, work from home one or two days a week, or work entirely from home, getting all the technology needed to be productive wherever they work. Open workspaces in office buildings allow employees to plug in their laptops and work there.[4]

Sara Lee Corporation offers a multitude of flexible work options, including one called Returnships, which is aimed at midcareer professionals who have been out of the workforce for a number of years. It offers them the chance to retool and retrain with an eye toward a permanent and probably flexible job.[5]

Delta Airlines' customer service agents enjoy a generous shift-swapping policy that allows employees to complete unlimited shift swaps with no minimum hours worked.[6]

An alternative location arrangement that appeals to older workers is snow bird programs. Pharmacists at CVS may work in Florida for the winter months (for the same organization) and return to their previous job locations up north during the summer months.[7]

In order to address the loss employees' of institutional knowledge, Dow Chemical introduced scheduling options for those transitioning into retirement. People can move to a part-time, telecommuting, or job-sharing schedule with no loss of benefits and no increase in medical premiums.[8]

Implementing Flexible Work Arrangements

Flexible work arrangements can indeed meet the needs of today's changing workforce. However, before implementing any of these programs, make sure they are a good fit for your organization.

- Make sure that the program or programs you want to introduce align with your organization's culture, mission, and vision.
- Understand the needs of your organization to determine if using FWAs could help meet your goals while meeting your employees' needs. For example, would FWAs address the need to reduce operating costs, especially those associated with office space and energy efficiency, and provide effective recruitment and retention tools?
- Determine if the type of work performed by an employee or group of employees is suitable for flexibility.
- Determine if FWAs are appropriate throughout the organization or just in certain parts. If they are not appropriate organization-wide, consider how distinctions can be made.
- Obtain top management support by providing corroborating facts showing how FWAs that are effectively implemented can increase not just morale and employee engagement, but productivity and return on investment.
- Engage middle management in the design and implementation. Line managers must have an understanding of their organization's FWA policy and program for it to be effective. Ensuring their involvement will help them to understand the needs of the employees they manage.
- Survey your employees to understand the types of programs that will meet their needs. Engage them in the design and implementation process.
- Research what other employers in your industry and in your geographic location are doing, but recognize that there is not one solution that will be right for all employers.
- Design ways to measure the success of your programs early in the process. This will help to show their value and success. Measurements can be simple, easy-to-administer tools such as employee surveys that measure participation and satisfaction.
- Train line managers and supervisors. When they need them, employees will most likely learn about these programs from their manager rather than from other sources such as human resources, their employee handbook, formal communications, or coworkers.

SECTION 2

The Legal Landscape

Because many of the flexible work arrangements involve changes to work schedules or working from alternative locations, it is important to make sure they comply with the laws and regulations discussed throughout this book. Most importantly, assure that you are in compliance with the Fair Labor Standards Act (FLSA), the Family Medical Leave Act (FMLA), and the Occupational Safety and Health Act (OSHA). Other applicable laws include the Americans With Disabilities Act (ADA) and non-discrimination requirements of federal and state civil rights laws with regard to how these programs are implemented. Assure that all employees have access to these programs on the basis of relevant business reasons. Finally, make sure that you understand the applicable state workers' compensation programs for all of your organization's locations.

> Treehouse LLC of Portland, Oregon, challenges the belief that working longer hours equals creating more value. The company is closed every Friday. Employees work a 32-hour work week Monday through Thursday and are expected to spend Fridays at home, with their families, having fun, and doing anything other than work. To its CEO, Ryan Carson, who considers it working smarter, it has been a life-changing, valuable experience that allows him to spend more time with his family. Carson is building a culture that will last and it's helping the company with recruitment and employee retention.[9]

Telecommuting

Telecommuting, sometimes referred to as distributed work, mobile work, or remote work, is on the rise. Advances in technology, especially the introduction of mobile computing devices and cloud-based storage, make it possible for employees to work from different places and under different arrangements. Working from home either intermittently or regularly under a formal arrangement is becoming typical, as is working remotely from a different geographic location, satellite office, or other work center. Global Workforce Analytics' research finds that:

- Fifty percent of the U.S. workforce holds a job that is compatible with at least partial telework and approximately 20–25 percent of the workforce teleworks at some frequency.
- Eighty to 90 percent of the U.S. workforce would like to telework at least part-time, with two to three days a week as an ideal balance between concentrative work (at home) and collaborative work (at the office).
- Fortune 1000 companies around the globe are revamping their physical space because employees are already mobile.
- There is a return on investment for organizations who adopt telework: a savings of up to $11,000 per person per year for the company and between $2,000 and $7,000 a year for the telecommuter.[10]

Approach telecommuting as a business strategy. In addition to considering it as a retention tool for existing employees, it's also a way to attract top talent, regardless of where they live.

Organizations are beginning to view it as a business imperative required to stay competitive in the modern workforce.[11]

There are issues that companies need to consider when integrating telecommuting, whether it's on an intermittent or regular basis. Two of the first considerations should be the suitability of the position and the individual employee. In today's knowledge economy, many jobs are a natural fit for telecommuting. Is the nature of the work independent, or does it require constant, personal interaction with others? Does the work require a great deal of concentration? How will results be measured? In determining which employees make good candidates for telecommuting, consider characteristics such as their self-motivation, performance, organization and time-management skills, and their familiarity with the job and work. Their tenure with the company, though an important consideration, should not be the overriding factor.

There may be resistance from line managers concerned about supervising and controlling the work of a remote employee. Managers and other team members need to know how to communicate and collaborate with a virtual employee, and the employee needs to know this as well. Make sure everyone involved, most especially line managers, know how to use the right technologies and tools to facilitate all interaction with virtual employees and other team members. Finally, managers must communicate expectations, and be comfortable empowering and trusting their employees to achieve the required results rather than focusing on the time spent "working."

Employees should also be aware of the challenges present when they work from home. Traditional challenges for the employee working from home may include:

- Isolation and lack of interaction, and the perceived lack of the ability to collaborate with team members. This is why it's important to make sure that both the job/position and the person are suited for telecommuting. Processes should be in place for regular check-in meetings, whether these meetings are in-person or through technology.
- Household distractions and reduced living space. These could be factors for employees who telecommute on a regular basis. Although dedicated work space has been a standard requirement for telecommuting, more portable computing devices allow for more fluid working space both inside and outside the office.
- A lack of support services (but these can be addressed through portals to the organization's internal services). Technical support may be a consideration and this is why it's imperative to have IT involved from the beginning.
- The perceived hindrance of career advancement. This makes it important to provide training to employees about career management and progressing through the company as a virtual employee.

Technology provides the framework that allows employees to work remotely. It's critical that IT understand the business requirements and HR, along with other business leaders must understand the technical needs, the current resources and the limitations of technology. Technology needs integrated hardware, software, and security. It's important to determine and set guidelines regarding:

- What equipment the employer will provide and maintain.
- What equipment, if any, the employee will provide and maintain.
- The appropriate use of employer-provided equipment and software, making employees aware they are to be used only for work-related purposes.

SECTION 2

- Placing controls to prevent uploading of unauthorized programs (for example, virus programs).
- Maintaining an inventory of employer-provided equipment.
- Ensuring the protection (physical security) of employer-provided equipment.
- Providing technical support for installation and maintenance of equipment and software.

Cybersecurity is critical in today's environment, and organizations should be mindful of the security of their data which workers are accessing outside of the secure office environment. The portability of equipment makes it easy for all employees, not just those who work remotely, to do so in public places using their work devices to communicate via unsecured public networks. Safeguards should be in place against potential breaches. These include:

- Password-protecting all business devices.
- Making sure that all data going out from those devices is encrypted.
- Keeping a current inventory of all devices and making sure each has its GPS tracking turned on.
- Installing technology to remotely wipe data from a lost or stolen device.[12]

Risk management is a key consideration, especially for regular telecommuting arrangements. Be sure that the appropriate staff members from your organization are consulted, and discuss the following with them:

- How will the organization determine regular hours of work? It may dictate whether an injury is compensable under workers' compensation.
- What procedures will be in place for reporting work-related injuries?
- How will the organization monitor the effects of overwork and isolation, which could lead to stress-related illness, burnout, and reduced productivity?
- Will the organization provide training in ergonomics, equipment use, and safety? If the employer provides the equipment, there is more certainty that it is ergonomically correct.
- Will the organization be involved in setting up the home office and workstation?
- Will the organization consider conducting home inspections to ensure safety standards are met?

Also consider posting safety notices on the intranet. Discuss insurance and liability with your insurance broker or risk-management department. Be sure you understand:

- What your general liability will cover.
- What the employee's homeowner's, renters', and automobile liability will cover.
- Who will be responsible for injuries to third parties (for example, if the employee is having a meeting at his or her home or is driving a client in his or her car).
- Who will be responsible for equipment losses and damages.

→   Appendix: Template for a Telecommuting Agreement.

Implementing a Telecommuting Program

Telecommuting programs are a type of flexible work arrangement, and there are some additional considerations for employers:

- Develop a telecommuting policy (or guidelines) and a telecommuting agreement. They should discuss eligibility, guidelines for equipment, work space at home, IT, security, and risk management. Expectations and objectives should also be included. Additionally, include provisions for ending the telecommuting arrangement.
- Set goals, objectives, and measurements tied to the organization's business case for the program, such as reduced operating costs, energy efficiency and environmental sustainability, competitive advantage, recruitment, and retention.
- Pilot the program. Strategically choose one part of the organization in which the program is likely to enjoy success and start there. Use the pilot program to develop metrics and gather lessons learned. Make any necessary adjustments before expanding the program to the entire organization.
- Develop a communication strategy. For the program to be effective, managers, employees, and applicants need to know about it. Use a wide range of communication media such as brochures, job aids, frequently asked questions, intranet pages dedicated to telework, and blogs. In addition to advertising the program, discuss the value it brings to the organization and the employee, as well as the lessons learned during the pilot program.
- Provide training. Both managers and employees need to understand the goals of the program, the criteria for eligibility, the roles and responsibilities of the manager and employee, the support that is available, and the expectations. You can use customized instructor-led or online training, as well as the communication tools discussed in the previous point.

Discussion Questions

1. Changing weather patterns, higher energy costs, traffic, and other external factors may be drivers for organizations to consider flexible work arrangements. What types of creative approaches do you think organizations could use to address these external factors?
2. What flexible work arrangements, if any, has your organization implemented? What lessons have you learned during the implementation process? What adjustments have you made?
3. One of the myths about flexible work arrangements is that they are designed to address the needs of working mothers. What other segments of the workforce are requesting and benefiting from flexibility, and how can their needs be met?
4. Other than recruitment and retention, what benefits can an organization derive from flexible work arrangements?
5. What measures has your organization made to address cybersecurity? Namely, what have you done to protect mobile computing devices and the information communicated through them?

16

Rewards and Recognition

Ken Blanchard, co-author of *The One Minute Manager*, said, "If there is one thing I've learned in my life, it is the fact that everyone wants to be appreciated. That goes for managers as well as employees, parents as well as children, and coaches as well as players."[1]

Managing today's workforce is complicated. Managers don't have as many ways to influence employees as they did many years ago, and most managers have learned that fear and intimidation are not motivational strategies; coaching employees to repeat good workplace behaviors is the way to go. Most organizations are operating with fewer employees being asked to do more, so it is more important than ever to create workplaces that are positive and reinforcing. Why is it so difficult for most managers to even think about rewards and recognition? It isn't that they aren't good people; it probably has more to do with the pressures they face to achieve sometimes-unrealistic financial targets. They just don't have time to consider what might be missing from their work environments that would greatly help them achieve their objectives: highly motivated employees!

No matter what's happening in the world of work, it's important to reward employees for good performance. According to Karen Renk, executive director at the Incentive Marketing Association and quoted in *Workforce*, "Leading companies have maintained their recognition programs, even during this economic downturn. This sends two important messages: One, you're letting employees know that their hard work is appreciated; and two, you're letting them know the company is stable and focused on reaching its goals."[2]

Rewarding employees is a great way to boost morale and motivate employees. Before you create an elaborate rewards and recognition program, we strongly advise you to find out what will work for your employees. Often, managers are convinced they know exactly what people want when it comes to rewards and recognition, but unless you ask people, how do you really know what will work for them? So, ask your employees what would work for them. You can do focus groups or just ask a representative group of people. Don't rely on your leadership team to tell you what they think; you want this program to work throughout the organization—and odds are, what the executives want won't be what your employees really need and/or desire.

The most cost-effective reward and the most valued for nearly everyone is a simple "thank you" for a specific job or for completing a project or for going above and beyond. It sounds like such a no-brainer, but you would be amazed at how few managers effectively use those two simple but powerful words.

It is increasingly apparent that one of the best ways to reward today's busy employees is to give them time off or the ability to work from home from time to time. Though flexibility isn't possible in all organizations or for all jobs, if your organization is able to occasionally be flexible, this will go a long way toward providing a real incentive to your employees.

When you plan your rewards and recognition programs, remember to match the reward to the person and to the achievement, and be sure that whatever you do will reinforce your organization's values. Also, consider how and when you provide recognition to employees. Hard as is it to believe, there are people who don't like to be praised in public; they would rather you quietly rewarded them for their accomplishments. Though most people thrive on public recognition, you should tread lightly before you do anything in a big public setting in order to determine what will be most effective for that person or group.

There are as many ways to reward employees as you can possibly imagine. Some organizations have had effective "employee of the month" programs for years, and they still work. These tend to be most effective in larger organizations, because in smaller firms you may quickly run out of people to acknowledge. Some organizations have a program in which selected employees meet with the CEO for lunch or coffee. These can be great idea generators or they can turn into "gripe sessions." If you go this route, consider the personality of your CEO or leader. Is this the type of person whom employees want to get to know, or would your staff be intimidated by the power the CEO holds? If you do these types of meetings, you may want to have the HR director there to facilitate the session and someone to jot down the ideas that are generated.

Many organizations still reward employees for length of service, and this can be a very effective way to acknowledge the contribution an individual makes. Length of service awards aren't nearly as important in a world in which people change jobs more frequently than in the past. Other organizations have safety awards to reward employees for going for long periods of time without an accident or safety violation. Although these awards are great, we want to encourage you to consider more personal types of rewards and recognition programs—ones that have significant impact on the recipient and on the organization.

Recognition as a Retention Tool

For some organizations, employee recognition can make all the difference in retaining staff. The Ritz-Carlton Hotel Company uses a system that defines, executes, and rewards. The company has demonstrated that employee recognition really does make a difference in retention. It has the lowest employee turnover rate of any hotel chain and feels that recognizing its employees is a major driver for its high retention rates.

High retention rates are good for the bottom line. "With engaged employees, I can drive our revenue per available room 20–30 percent higher than if I have employees who come in and just do their jobs," says Kathleen O. Smith, senior vice president of human resources at the company's headquarters in Chevy Chase, Maryland.[3] Giving employees the resources they need to do their jobs, recognizing a job well done, stating clear expectations, and showing interest and concern in them as individuals are all employee drivers. Recognition includes small, on-the-spot monetary awards given by supervisors when they catch an employee delivering extraordinary service as well as handwritten postcards given by and to staffers at any level when they see or receive first-class service.

Ritz-Carlton also does more formal recognition. Managers are asked to name a "Five Star" employee quarterly. They are recognized every day in their hotel and then, once a year, one of the "Five Star" winners receives a trip, with a guest, to any Ritz-Carlton hotel.

One organization we know does "surprise Tuesdays." Not every week, but once in a while and always on a Tuesday, the president of the firm gives something away. Sometimes it is a gift card to a local ice cream shop for everyone; other times it is a drawing for an American Express Gift Card for $100 or more. He has given away gas cards (especially popular when gas is at a high price). Another week it might be pizza for lunch for everyone. The best part of this is the surprise! People talk about it. It is part of the culture so that new employees hear about it during their first week from coworkers. The best part is no one ever quits on Monday—just in case!

If you are creating a program in which prizes are given, remember that people want choice, and they want items they can use in their personal life. You don't necessarily have to provide luxury items, but consider some of the programs that allow you to offer a choice to your employees—either online or in a catalog. That way, they get to pick something that will be rewarding to them or to their family. If the award means something to them, every time they use the item they've chosen, they will hopefully remember it came from your organization to acknowledge something they did above and beyond their normal job.

Keep in mind that having strong rewards and recognition programs won't matter if you don't have strong leadership and a positive work environment. Work on those areas of your organization first and then focus on rewards and recognition.

Tips for Designing an Effective Rewards/Recognition Program

- Carefully think through who is eligible. Consider at what level of the organization you cut off eligibility (for example, directors and above are not eligible).
- Promote the program using a wide range of media, including newsletters, emails, mail to employee homes, and so forth. (Involving families in rewards programs can be highly motivational to the employee who wants to win.)
- Ensure the program is fair and equitable.
- Publicize the criteria for any formal program.
- Have start and end times so that you can make the program lively.
- Publicly thank the award winners whether in an "all hands" meeting, in a newsletter, or on your website (or all three).
- If your organization works in teams, consider having a team award as well as individual awards.
- Peer recognition is valued, so consider having awards voted on by employees.
- Truly reward. Don't just have an employee of the month plaque that is passed around so that everyone gets it once!

How to Determine What Will Work at Your Organization

1. Gather a representative group of employees (ages, genders, races, levels in the organization) for a focus group. Be sure to have representatives of multiple generations to ensure all needs are met.
2. Use a trained facilitator to conduct the sessions.
3. Make sure that no promises are made regarding what can or cannot be included in the program.
4. Have your mission statement and values displayed around the room to remind the participants that any recommendation they make must match your organization's vision.
5. Once you have the data from the focus group(s), take the best suggestions that match to your values and will fit your budget.

No-Cost Rewards

- Verbal thank-you.
- Handwritten thank-you note.
- Letter of appreciation from the CEO or other senior leader for a job well done.
- Recognition at an "all-hands" meeting.
- Assignment to a highly visible team or task force.
- Recognition in newsletter.

Low-Cost Rewards

- Gift cards to local restaurants.
- Spot cash awards for excellent performance.
- Movie tickets.
- Company logo merchandise.
- Reserved parking place.
- Day off with pay.
- Lottery tickets.
- Lunch for the team.
- Round of golf with an organization leader.
- Lunch with the CEO or president.
- Flowers, balloons, or plant delivered to the office.

Discussion Questions

1. Why is recognition important to today's employee?
2. What is the best and most cost-effective way to reward someone?
3. What are some of the ways that recognition plays into employee retention?
4. What are some of the most important things to remember when putting rewards programs in place?
5. How often should we change our rewards and recognition programs?
6. What are some ways to publicly reward employees?

SECTION 3

TOTAL REWARDS

17

The Legal Landscape of Compensation

While President Franklin Roosevelt was in Bedford, Massachusetts, campaigning for reelection, a young girl tried to pass him an envelope. But a policeman threw her back into the crowd. Roosevelt told an aide, "Get the note from the girl." Her note read, "I wish you could do something to help us girls.... We have been working in a sewing factory...and up to a few months ago we were getting our minimum pay of $11 a week.... Today the 200 of us girls have been cut down to $4 and $5 and $6 a week." To a reporter's question, the president replied, "Something has to be done about the elimination of child labor and long hours and starvation wages."[1]

Federal, state, and local laws can significantly impact employee compensation. These laws govern overtime pay and protect employees from discrimination. It is important to appreciate the legal environment when designing and managing compensation. Discussed here are federal laws. Guidance should be sought for state-specific wage and hour laws and regulations.

The Fair Labor Standards Act (FLSA), 1938

The FLSA requires that employees be paid at least the federal minimum wage for all hours worked and overtime pay at time and one-half the regular rate of pay for all hours worked in excess of 40 hours in a workweek.

Minimum Wage

Covered nonexempt workers are entitled to a minimum wage of not less than $7.25 per hour, effective July 24, 2009. Many states also have minimum wage laws and where an employee is covered by both, he or she is entitled to the higher minimum wage.

> ➔   For more information regarding the federal minimum wage, visit *www.dol/gov/general/topic/wages/minimumwage*.

Overtime Pay

Unless an employee is exempt from the overtime provisions of the FLSA, he or she must receive overtime pay for hours worked in excess of 40 in a workweek. The rate of overtime pay cannot be less than time and one-half the regular rate of pay. There is no limit on the number of hours an employee 16 years of age or older may work in a workweek. Overtime is paid on hours actually worked and not time compensated. For example, if an employee receives eight hours of holiday pay for Monday and works an additional 36 hours from Tuesday through Friday, he or she is not entitled to overtime because no work was performed on Monday.

A workweek is a fixed and regularly recurring period of 168 hours—seven consecutive 24-hour periods. It does not have to coincide with the calendar week, but may begin on any day and at any hour of the day. Different workweeks may be established for different employees or groups of employees.

An employer cannot average hours over two or more weeks. Normally, overtime pay earned in a particular workweek must be paid on the regular pay day for the pay period in which the wages were earned. Public-sector employers may grant compensatory time off in lieu of overtime wages. Employers in the private sector must pay their employees overtime pay earned.

Exemptions

The FLSA provides exemptions from both minimum wage and overtime pay for employees employed as bona fide executive, administrative, professional, and outside sales employees and certain computer employees. In order for an exemption to apply, an employee's specific job duties and salary must meet all the requirements of the Department of Labor's regulations.

To qualify for an exemption, employees generally must:

- Satisfy all the requirements of salary-basis test discussed below.
- Be paid on a salary basis—that is, the employee must regularly receive a predetermined amount that cannot be reduced because of variation in the quantity or quality of work performed.
- Be a highly compensated employee. Under the current FLSA regulations, a highly compensated employee receives a total annual compensation of at least $100,000 (which includes at least $455 per week paid on a salary or fee basis, and can include commissions, nondiscretionary bonuses and other nondiscretionary compensation).

    → See The Salary-Basis Test and Thresholds (below).

- Satisfy the duties test for the particular exemption.

    → Appendix: FLSA Duties Test Checklist.

The Salary-Basis Test: to meet the requirements of the salary-basis test, an employee:

1. Must regularly receive a predetermined amount of compensation as required by the Department of Labor's regulations each pay period on a weekly or less frequent basis.
2. Cannot have his or her compensation reduced because of variations in the quality or quantity of the work performed.
3. Must be paid the full salary for any week in which the employee performs work.
4. Need not be paid for any workweek when no work is performed.

The Salary-Basis Test and Thresholds

The overtime rule of the FLSA was last updated in 2004. The salary threshold for the salary-basis test has been set at a weekly salary of not less than $455, or $23,660 per year. In 2016, a rule was proposed to raise the threshold to $913 weekly, or $47,476 per year, and these thresholds would automatically be updated every three years beginning in January 2020. In addition, the rule proposed to raise the salary threshold for highly compensated employees from $100,000 annually to $134,004, with the same provision for automatic updates every three years. It is important for organizations to regularly check the Department of Labor's website at *www.dol.gov/WHD* for the most current information regarding overtime and the salary threshold for the salary-basis test.

An employee is not paid on a salary basis if deductions are made from the employee's predetermined salary:

- For absences caused by the employer.
- Because of operating requirements of the business (e.g., there is no work to do, but the employee is ready, willing, and able).
- For absences for jury, witness or temporary military duty except for offset of fees received.

Deductions may be made for *full-day* absences without violating the salary-basis test for the following reasons:

- Sicknesses or disability under a bona fide plan or policy (sick leave policy, short or long-term disability plan),
- Personal reasons (vacation, personal business), and/or
- Suspensions for misconduct under written policy that applies to all employees.

The following deductions are also permitted without violating the salary-basis test:

- Pro-rated pay for partial initial/terminal weeks. (For example, an employee resigns and her last day is Wednesday. You need not pay her the full week.)
- Unpaid federal FMLA leave (partial- and full-day absences).
- Violations of major safety rules (partial- and full-day absences).

The following practices are permitted without violating the salary-basis test:

- Deducting from accrued leave accounts (full- or partial-day absence).
- Tracking hours worked.
- Requiring employees to work a specified schedule.
- Making bona fide, across-the-board changes in schedules.
- Salary plus.

As long as the employee is being paid the minimum weekly amount on a salary basis as required by the regulations, it is okay to pay additional compensation, such as commissions, bonuses, or additional compensation based on hours worked beyond the normal workweek. For additional hours worked, the employer can compute pay on an hourly, daily, or shift basis provided the employee is guaranteed the required minimum weekly amount.

SECTION 3

The Duties Test: The categories of employees under the duties test include:

- Executive.
- Administrative.
- Professional.
- Highly Compensated.
- Computer Employee.
- Outside Sales.

➤   Appendix: The FLSA Duties Checklist.

There are some things that employers can and should do to assure that they are in compliance with the overtime provisions of the FLSA, which include:

- Auditing all positions that are classified exempt to determine if they meet the salary requirements and duties test.
- Assuring that all employees they treat as "salaried nonexempt" are paid overtime rates when they work more than 40 hours a week, in addition to their fixed salaries for working up to 40 hours a week.
- Having a policy that requires employees to get approval before working overtime.
- Training employees whose positions are nonexempt on appropriate timekeeping and overtime policies and procedures. Even if an employee works overtime without permission, the employer must pay them for all hours worked. However, they may also discipline them for violating a policy that prohibits unauthorized work hours.

Child Labor Provisions

Child labor provisions ensure that when young people work, the work is safe and does not jeopardize their health, well-being, or educational opportunities. The child labor laws are designed to protect against workplace hazards impacting the employment of youth under the age of 18 years. They provide restrictions on the hours and condition of employment for children. These restrictions can vary depending on the type of industry.

Record-Keeping and Posting Requirements

Employers must display a poster containing the provisions of the FLSA. In addition, they must keep certain records for non-exempt employees, including payroll records, collective bargaining agreements, sales, and purchase records for at least three years. Wage computation records such as time cards, electronic time records, or piece work tickets should also be retained for three years.

These records must include:

1. Employee's full name and Social Security number.
2. Address, including zip code.
3. Birth date, if younger than 19.
4. Sex and occupation.
5. Time and day of week when employee's workweek begins.
6. Hours worked each day.
7. Total hours worked each workweek.
8. Basis on which employee's wages are paid (for example, "$9 per hour," "$440 a week," "piece work").
9. Regular hourly pay rate.
10. Total daily or weekly straight-time earnings.
11. Total overtime earnings for the workweek.

12. All additions to or deductions from the employee's wages.
13. Total wages paid each pay period.
14. Date of payment and the pay period covered by the payment.

➤ For additional information about the Fair Labor Standards Act, visit the Department of Labor's website at *www.dol.gov/whd/flsa*.

Portal-to-Portal Act, 1947

The Portal-to-Portal Act amended the Fair Labor Standards Act and defined general rules for hours worked. Hours worked ordinarily include all the time during which an employee is required to be on the employer's premises, on duty, or at a prescribed workplace. These rules are applicable in calculating hours worked for purposes of paying overtime. These include on-call/standby time, preparatory/concluding activities, waiting time, travel time, and training time.

- **On-call pay** is pay that employees receive when they are on call but not actually working.
- **On-call/standby time.** An employee who is required to remain on call on the employer's premises is working while "on call" and is eligible for overtime compensation.

    An employee whose activities are not restricted, but who is required to remain on call at home, or otherwise be available and have access to a phone or beeper so he or she can be reached, is not working (in most cases) while on call and would not be eligible for overtime compensation. However, if the employer placed additional constraints on the employee's freedom, the employer would be required to compensate this time.

- **Preparatory/concluding activities** that must be compensated include activities such as putting on or taking off safety gear or making deliveries for the employer on the employee's way to or from work. The key to whether or not the time is compensable is determining whether or not the activity is an indispensable part of the employee's job activity, or if it is solely for the benefit of the employer.

- **Waiting time.** Whether waiting time is hours worked under the Act depends upon the circumstances. If an employee is engaged to wait, it is work time and counts toward the 40-hour workweek. For example, a fireman who plays checkers while waiting for an alarm has been "engaged to wait" and is working during this period of inactivity. On the other hand, an administrative assistant who arrives at work 30 minutes before the start of her workday and reads a book during that period of time is not engaged to wait.

SECTION 3

The Case of Dedicated Debbie

Debbie often arrives at work 30 minutes early to avoid rush-hour traffic. When she arrives, she begins working, resulting in two and one-half hours of overtime every week. Even though the time was not authorized, her employer has to count those hours and pay her overtime. What should her employer do? Although they can't refuse to pay the overtime, they can put Debbie and other nonexempt employees on notice that any overtime must be authorized. If the employees fail to gain this authorization, they can be disciplined in accordance with the organization's policies.

- ◆ **Meals and breaks.** Rest periods of short duration, usually 20 minutes or less, are customarily counted and paid for as working time. Bona fide meal periods (typically 30 minutes or more) generally need not be compensated as work time. The employee must be completely relieved from duty for the purpose of eating regular meals and not be required to perform any duties while eating.
- ◆ **Travel time.** The kind of travel involved determines if the time spent traveling is compensable time. Commuting to and from work is generally not compensable time.
- ◆ **Training time.** Attendance at lectures, meetings, training programs, and similar activities need not be counted as working time only if all four of these criteria are met, namely: It is outside normal hours, it is voluntary, it is not job-related, and no other work is concurrently performed.

Employee Commuting Flexibility Act, 1996

The Employee Commuting Flexibility Act amended the Portal-to-Portal Act to allow employers and employees to agree to the use of employer-provided vehicles for commuting to and from work, at the beginning and end of the workday, without the commuting time being counted as hours worked. In order for this commuting time not to be considered hours worked, the use of the employer's vehicle must be within the normal commuting area for the employer's business or establishment, and the use of the vehicle must be subject to an agreement between the employer and the employee or employee's representative.

Guidelines for Travel Time

Guidelines for travel time include:

- ◆ Employees who travel in the course of a workday, such as from one work location to another, are entitled to compensation for their travel time. Travel to work-related meetings is compensable.
- ◆ Time spent traveling out of town on a single-day trip is compensable. However, time spent traveling to and from the airport or other transportation terminal in the morning and evening can be considered to be the equivalent of the home-to-work commute and is not compensable work time.
- ◆ An employee who travels away from home overnight is not working when he or she is a passenger on a plane, train, boat, bus, or automobile outside of regular work hours.
  - ▷ Any time that the employee spends traveling as a passenger on a weekend will be counted as time worked if the travel cuts across the hours the employee would normally work during the week. For example, an employee whose normal work schedule is 8:30 a.m. to 5:30 p.m. flies on a Sunday. The flight departs at 10:00 a.m. and arrives at 12:00 p.m. The time spent traveling (two hours) must be counted as time worked.
  - ▷ Any time that an employee spends working while a passenger must be counted and paid as work time.

Guidelines for Training Time

Training time is generally considered as hours worked. However, the time spent at a training event does not need to be compensated if the following four conditions are met:

1. Attendance is voluntary.
2. Attendance is outside of normal working hours.
3. The event is not directly job-related.
4. The employee performs no productive work during this period.

Many states laws regulate wages and hours worked. Some states, such as California, have daily overtime requirements. Employees are entitled to the maximum protection afforded under both federal and state law. Therefore, it is important that an employer be familiar with any state or local requirements.

Equal Pay Act, 1963

The Equal Pay Act was an amendment to the Fair Labor Standards Act. It prohibits sex-based compensation discrimination. Under the Act, employees must be performing equal work in jobs that require equal skill, effort, and responsibility, and that are performed under similar working conditions within one establishment. The exceptions to the act include pay that is based on:

*   Seniority.
*   Merit.
*   Quantity or quality of work.
*   Any factors other than sex.

Title VII of the Civil Rights Act of 1964 (Title VII), the Americans With Disabilities Act (ADA), and the Age Discrimination in Employment Act (ADEA)

> All of these laws, discussed in Chapter 3 (The Legal Landscape of Employee Rights), prohibit discrimination in all aspects of employment including pay, job assignments, benefits, and any other term or condition of employment.

The Lilly Ledbetter Fair Pay Act, discussed next, significantly changed the statute of limitations for filing a claim of discrimination.

In addition to prohibiting discrimination against older workers, the ADEA does allow companies to set mandatory retirement age for certain highly paid executives.

Lilly Ledbetter Fair Pay Act, 2009

This law amends Title VII, the ADA, and the ADEA by providing that the period of time for filing a charge of discrimination (either 180 or 300 days) begins when:

1. A discriminatory compensation decision or other practice is adopted.
2. An individual becomes subject to the decision or practice.

3.   An individual is affected by the application of a decision or practice, including each time wages, benefits, or compensation is paid.

Effectively, under the Lilly Ledbetter Fair Pay Act, the statute of limitations for filing a charge of discrimination starts each time an employee receives a paycheck based on a discriminatory decision. Each paycheck that delivers compensation that was based on a discriminatory decision is a wrong that is actionable under the equal employment opportunity statues, regardless of when the discrimination began.

Under the law, an unlawful employment practice occurs when "a person," is affected by a discriminatory compensation decision or practice. A person could include the spouse of a deceased worker claiming that pension benefits are reduced because of a discriminatory decision.

> ➔   The Equal Pay Act and the Lilly Ledbetter Fair Pay Act are enforced by the Equal Employment Opportunity Commission. For additional information, visit *www.eeoc.gov/laws/*.

Discussion Questions

1.   What steps have you taken to ensure that your organization is in compliance with the overtime provisions of the Fair Labor Standards Act, including auditing your positions, reviewing your policies and procedures about overtime, training managers about the law's requirements, and notifying your employees about their status?

2.   What steps does your organization take to assure that non-exempt employees are not working unauthorized overtime?

3.   What are some of the proactive steps that an organization can take to identify and eliminate pay inequities?

4.   There is often confusion about paying employees for travel time, training time, breaks, and so forth. What does your organization do to ensure that managers are briefed on these subjects?

18

Compensation: An Introduction

Five dollars a day is what Henry Ford paid to assembly line workers in 1914. It was more than double what his competitors were paying. Why did Ford take this revolutionary approach? He wanted to attract the best and the brightest—the best mechanics and workers for his plant.

Lead, lag, or meet the market—which compensation strategy should an organization follow? How and when should this be decided? Compensation, as part of the total rewards structure, is a key strategy for successful organizations. In order to meet its mission, it must attract and retain people who have the appropriate knowledge, skills, aptitudes, competencies, and attitudes to get the work done.

- A company leads the market when it decides to pay its employees more than the identified market rate.
- A company lags the market when it decides to pay its employees below the established market rate.
- A company matches the market when it pays the "going" rate.

The challenge for organizations is to develop a compensation philosophy and a pay system consistent with their objectives and that will reinforce the culture, the climate, and the behaviors needed for the organization to be effective and successful. The approach taken and the pay system implemented must fit the organization's strategy and management style. Further, compensation philosophy needs to be reviewed frequently to ensure that it still meets the business needs and continues to align with the vision and mission of the organization. As an organization moves through different stages of its organizational life style, its compensation philosophy needs to be revisited and may need to be adjusted.

Sample Compensation Philosophy Statement

Our compensation program is designed to assure competitive and fair pay practices which enable us to attract, motivate, reward, and retain the most qualified employees in order to provide service to our customers that exceeds their expectations. To accomplish this, we have established the following principles to guide our decision-making:

- We maintain a competitive salary structure consistent with our external market. We review positions against relevant market data and make necessary adjustments according to market conditions and organizational financial resources. New positions are established consistent with external market conditions and internal equity.

- We promote internal equity so that positions with similar scope, responsibilities, and market value are compensated at a similar level. To ensure internal equity, we consider a combination of performance, experience, level of contribution to the organization, and tenure.

- We remain fiscally responsible with regard to economic conditions and budget constraints in order to maintain the financial viability of our organization.

- We administer the compensation program in compliance with laws providing fair and equitable treatment for employees regardless of race, color, creed, religion, gender, national origin, age, marital status, disability, military status, sexual orientation, or any other protected characteristic.

Compensation has progressed since Henry Ford paid his workers five dollars a day. In addition to direct compensation or pay systems, employers today must consider indirect compensation or benefits as part of its total rewards system. A total rewards program includes base pay, pay differentials, bonuses and cash incentives, and stock-related rewards. These elements are discussed in this chapter. Other elements include employee benefits, performance feedback and recognition, opportunities for career growth, and workplace flexibility, which are discussed in other chapters.

A compensation system must be:

- Compatible with the organizational mission and strategy.
- Compatible with the culture.
- Appropriate for the workforce.
- Externally competitive.
- Internally equitable.

Developing a Pay System

The first step in determining how to pay employees is to develop a salary structure, which involves analyzing, evaluating, and pricing the jobs in the organization.

→　　See Chapter 19 (Developing a Salary Structure).

With this structure in place, pay systems can be developed. Pay systems, which focus on pay adjustments or increases, can be structured in a number of ways, and must fit the culture and align with industry standards.

- Pay for performance or merit pay systems tie pay increases to an employee's performance. Organizations that implement these systems often want to distinguish and reward performance excellence, and discourage a culture of entitlement. Seniority and years of experience are not factors that are considered. Increases are often tied to performance appraisal ratings. The challenge for employers is that they must be able to defend differences in salary increases and performance appraisal ratings to assure fairness and equity.

  Employers are turning to variable pay to reward employees for performance. Contributing to this trend are salary budgets, which in recent years remained relatively flat and low, and emerging trends in performance management, which are putting less emphasis on ratings or rankings. According to a survey conducted by WorldatWork in 2016, the percentage of companies using variable pay rose to 84 percent, and a combination of awards based on both organizational success and individual performance continues to be the most popular variable pay program.[1] Variable pay is a type of incentive pay, which is also discussed in this chapter.

- Single-rate or flat-rate systems generally pay one rate to all incumbents in a job, regardless of performance or seniority. These systems are often found in the public sector, for elected jobs, or in union hourly positions. The rate of pay is generally the market rate.

- In a time-based or step-based system, the rate is based on longevity, and pay increases occur on a predetermined schedule, such as an automatic step-rate, in which an employee who reaches a certain seniority level advances one step in the pay scale. In variations of this system, the size or the time of the increase may vary (the employee advances two steps rather than one) if the employee exhibits exceptional performance. Seniority is the basis for any pay adjustment.

- In a productivity-based system, pay is determined by the employee's output. Variations include a straight piece rate where there is a base pay rate plus additional compensation for output, or a differential piece rate, in which the employee is paid one piece rate up to the standard and a higher rate after the standard is exceeded. These are most common in assembly and manufacturing situations.

- Person-based systems pay people based on their value, rather than on the marketplace value of the job they hold. Examples include:
  - ▷ Skill-based pay, which is easy to apply in a production work group in manufacturing, where it is easy to identify tasks and needed skills. Employees earn pay increases at a rate commensurate with their ability to acquire new skills.[2]
  - ▷ Knowledge-based pay typically centers on career ladders, which identify expertise levels within the same occupation or discipline. For example, analysts at all levels of expertise perform work of the same basic type, but do so at varying levels of knowledge, skill, responsibility, and complexity of work. The vast majority of scientific, engineering, and professional occupations lend themselves to this approach. Their knowledge and expertise in their field grows over time and it becomes the metric for shaping their roles in their organizations.[3]

Other ways that base pay can be adjusted include:

- **Cost of Living Adjustments (COLAs)**, which are across-the-board wage and salary increases that bring pay in line with increases in the cost of living to maintain real purchasing power. They are based on the consumer price index (CPI).
- **Lump-sum increases**, which are one-time payments that typically do not affect or increase an employee's base pay.
- **Market-based or equity increases**, which occur when a market study (or salary survey) is conducted to determine if salaries are still competitive. The results may be individual employees receiving adjustments to their base salary and/or salary grades being adjusted.

Another consideration in developing pay systems includes pay differentials. Pay differentials are adjustments or additions to base salary. They can include:

- Overtime, as required by the FLSA.
- Geographical differentials, which are adjustments to pay rates based on location and are often used to attract workers to a certain location.
- Shift pay or shift premiums, which are paid to workers who work other than the day shift. They may be a percentage of base pay or be factored into the hourly rate.
- Emergency-shift pay, which occurs when employees receive extra pay when they are called back into work for an emergency, such as a power failure or when a computer system crashes.
- Premium pay, which is paid to employees in some industries when they work holidays or weekends, or in other extenuating circumstances.
- Hazard pay, which is additional pay for working in dangerous and/or extremely uncomfortable working conditions.
- On-call or call-back pay, which may be required under the Portal-to-Portal Act.

    ➔ See Chapter 17 (The Legal Landscape of Compensation) for more about the Portal-to-Portal Act.

    On-call pay is received when employees are on call but not actually working. Call-back pay is paid to employees who are called to work before or after their scheduled work day.

- Reporting pay, which is paid when an employee is called into work and there is no work available.
- Travel pay, which is paid to employees traveling to work assignments.

    ➔ This is also discussed in Chapter 17 (The Legal Landscape of Compensation).

The Annual Raise & General Electric[4]

Executives at General Electric (GE) are reviewing whether to continue the practice of making annual updates to compensation and rethinking how they define rewarding their employees. Recognizing that in the upper echelons of the U.S. labor market, a broader shift in total rewards is underway as organizations compete over younger workers for whom other perks, such as parental leave, paid time off, more flexibility, and work-life balance, may be as important as pay. Senior employees nearing retirement are also looking for more flexibility. Fueling this new look at total rewards is the reality that younger workers tend to change jobs more frequently and have shorter tenures with one organization. Waiting a year for an annual reward may be too long. The 124-year-old GE has long been a trend-setter with its management ideas taught at business schools. GE is now striving to be more nimble and flexible, much like the startup firms in the technology sector that are disrupting many established business practices. Employers should be aware that, though these changes are addressing the mostly skilled workers in the higher levels of the economic ladder, workers at the bottom end of the labor market have different needs. A one-size-fits-all approach could result in unintended consequences.

Incentive Pay

Incentive pay rewards employees for their individual and organizational results. Measures of success can include profits, customer satisfaction, or overall organizational performance.

Individual incentives are paid to employees who achieve goals and objectives that have been determined in advanced and achieved within a certain, defined time period. Individual incentive plans must be separate from base pay and can take the form of commissions, cash bonuses, recognition programs and awards, or piece rate awards, which allow workers who are more productive to earn more money.

As more companies are offering variable pay to reward employee performance, a combination of awards is often used—awards based on both organizational success and individual performance. Many employers are offering variable pay programs throughout their organizations, from hourly workers through the executive suite, in an effort to promote teamwork and cultivate a culture that everyone contributes to the overall success. These organizations view such programs as a way to attract and retain better talent at all levels.[5]

Group incentives are often implemented to increase productivity and foster teamwork while sharing success and financial rewards with employees. They do not take into account individual performance. One example is gainsharing programs, which involve employees and managers in improving productivity as well as sharing the benefits of success. When a profitability goal is met, each member receives the same cash reward.

In group performance plans, another type of group incentive, members are rewarded for meeting or exceeding performance standards. The performance criteria can be qualitative or quantitative and standards are often predetermined.

Finally, there are organization-wide incentive plans. Profit-sharing plans allow employees to share in a company's profits. They can be:

- Cash bonuses or payments in addition to normal base pay, which are considered direct pay and taxed accordingly; or
- Qualified plans under the Employee Retirement Income Security Act (ERISA) and the Internal Revenue Code, which distribute pre-tax dollars to eligible employees, are typically based on a percentage of the base salary.

> ↠ The ERISA is discussed in Chapter 20 (The Legal Landscape of Employee Benefits).

Performance-sharing plans are similar to group performance plans, in which the criteria are based on qualitative factors such as customer satisfaction and quality.

Finally, there are stock ownership plans that allow employees to receive or purchase company stock and share in its ownership. Employee Stock Ownership Plans (ESOP) are generally a defined contribution plan in which the employer makes contributions of cash or stock to a tax-deductible trust in the employees' names.

Establishing Cash Incentive Plans

Contributed by John D. White, President of JD White & Associates, Inc., McLean, Virginia

- This is a big undertaking. Don't underestimate it.
- Provide a rationale. Why is the company doing this? How will this help us to fulfill our mission?
- Make sure the senior team is 100 percent behind this. Set expectations at the outset and have discussion. They are going to be the champions.
- Have broad participation. Ideally, everyone in the company should be eligible.
- Establish percentage of pay targets, with executives receiving a larger percentage of pay.
- Establish company objectives each year.
- Have individual employee objectives link to company objectives.
- Avoid the entitlement mentality. Cash incentive payments will be tied directly to company success.
- Clear financial measurements must be in place so that all staff members realize what is required for payments to be triggered.
- However, in evaluating each staff member have broader measurements than just financial. Use this plan to reinforce the type of behaviors you want.
- Secure input from staff and managers during the plan design process.
- Be ready to tweak the plan as you go forward.
- You can't communicate enough.
- Extensive training (both management and employees) will be required.
- If you can't do all (or most) of these things, don't do the plan at all. A half-baked plan is worse than not having a plan at all.

Sales Compensation

Common methods for paying sales personnel include:[6]

- **Salary only (or straight salary)**, which provides a specific amount each pay period and covers all expenses incurred by the salesperson in the performance of assignments.
- **Sales commission (or straight commission)**, which is usually a percentage of net sales. If no sales are made, no money is received by the salesperson.
- **Salary plus commission/bonus**, which combines the two previously mentioned methods and provides a level of security in periods of economic downturns or depressed demand.
- **Salary plus bonus**, with the bonus based on individual or group performance and tied to some performance indicator.
- **Commission plus bonus**, with the bonus providing an additional incentive to accomplish a desired target.

Key Factors in Sales Compensation Plan Design[7]

A sales compensation plan should directly support the overall marketing and sales plan. The sales force has a direct and measurable impact on the overall revenue. Thus, a larger percentage of a salesperson's cash compensation is typically put at risk. There are three key factors in a salesperson's earnings:

- **Quota.** The top-level quota is divided up and assigned to the sales force in a process called allocation. Quotas are typically set so that approximately 70 percent of the sales force will meet or exceed their quota and about 30 percent will not.
- **Territory assignment.** There are many different ways to set up territories for the sales force, but a sound approach provides sufficient sales coverage for optimum sales with lowest cost. In a balanced configuration, each territory has a comparable number of new and existing customers and comparable potential revenue from each group. In a size configuration, large, medium, and small customers are grouped together with different teams of sales representatives handling each category. In an industry configuration, sales representatives specialize in understanding the needs of a specific industry. In a sales process configuration, customers are classified as either existing or potential, with sales reps specializing in addressing their needs.
- **Sales plans.** In designing individual sales plans, determine eligibility by considering the degree of customer contact and the degree of persuasion to buy services and/or products. Other questions to consider when determining eligibility:
  - ▷ Who is the primary contact during the selling process?
  - ▷ What is the principal activity/role of the position?
  - ▷ What type of sale?

Compensating Employees in a Global Environment

Organizations with employees in other countries face added challenges and complexities, including tax implications, in their compensation design and strategy. It is best to develop a global compensation and benefits strategy early and to seek professional advice from consulting or accounting firms with international specialists for expatriate and foreign national employment situations.

Common approaches to determining compensation packages for employees on international assignments include:

- **Straight negotiation**, where a package is mutually negotiated between the employer and employee.
- **Headquarters-based balance sheet**, in which the all expatriates working in the same position are paid the same based on standard of living in the headquarters' country regardless of their country of origin. Expatriate salaries are kept in line with staff at headquarters rather than their home-country peers or assignment-country peers.
- **Home-country-based balance sheet**, in which the expatriate receives a differential between his or her home-country costs and the costs of the country to which he or she is assigned (local or host country) to keep expatriate salaries in line with their home-country peers, not with those of their assignment-country colleagues.
- **Pure localization approach**, in which the expatriate receives the same compensation as local nationals working in the same position.
- **Higher-of-home-or-host country**, in which the expatriate is compensated at the higher cost of living, determined by comparing the standards of living of the home country and host country.
- **Lump-sum**, in which the expatriate receives a lump-sum payment rather than allowances or differentials.

Executive Compensation

Executive compensation varies by industry and organizational culture, but the majority of the plans have components of long-term and short-term incentives.

- **Short-term incentives** are generally cash bonuses, which represent a significant percentage of pay and are typically driven by annual objectives linked to company objectives.
- **Long-term incentives** typically include some sort of stock award, such as stock options, restricted stock, or others.

A common use of a deferred compensation plan occurs in the area of retirement planning. In many 401(k) plans, certain executives might not be able to defer their full desired amount under the plan because of non-discrimination testing issues. Companies faced with this issue often create a "401(k) excess plan" or a "401(k) wrap-around plan." These are non-qualified plans not subject to the same IRS regulations as those plans that aim to provide a benefit to all employees. This type of plan could allow the executive to defer an additional sum to the 401(k) plan over and above the amount allowed under the more restricted non-discrimination testing scenario.

Other components of executive compensation include:

* **Perquisites, or "perks,"** which are additional benefits that provide comfort and luxury to the work and/or personal environment. They may include generous pension plans, access to a company jet, club memberships, limousine services, annual tax/financial planning allowance to provide professional assistance in an area that is often time-consuming and a distraction to senior staff, or increased disability coverage because these programs have maximum dollar limits that cover less than the desired percentage of an executive's compensation.
* **Golden parachutes** that provide special payments in the event they lose their position, especially if there is a change of control because of a merger or acquisition. These are generally clauses written into their employment contracts.

Section 402 of the Sarbanes-Oxley Act, which applies to publicly held companies, bans personal loans to executives or members of the board of directors in for-profit companies. Executives include company presidents and vice presidents in charge of a principal business unit, division or function such as sales, administration or finance. It does not apply to loans taken from a 401(k) account, or loans for business purposes.[8]

> ⇥ The Sarbanes-Oxley Act is discussed further in Chapter 20 (The Legal Landscape of Employee Benefits).

Discussion Questions

1. Describe circumstances when a company would want to:
   ▷ Lag the market.
   ▷ Meet the market.
   ▷ Lead the market.
2. Describe the elements of your organization's total rewards program. What is the underlying philosophy of the program?
3. Describe any incentive plan that your organization has implemented. Have you considered other ways to reward your employees other than an annual raise?
4. If you were to design a pay system for sales employees in a large retail store, what would you consider and why? How would you set it up and why?

19

Developing a Salary Structure

BY MARY JANE SINCLAIR, SPHR

I worked at a company that conducted an employee opinion survey. One question asked if employees thought they were paid high, low, or average. The cumulative results correlated exactly with the salary survey results. In jobs where the salary surveys indicated that average salary was high relative to the market, the average employee responded that they were well paid. In jobs where the average salary was low relative to the market, employees responded that they were not paid well. My conclusion is that people have a pretty good sense of how well they are paid.

If you are about to develop and implement a salary structure, there are a few fundamental questions to be answered before you begin. In addition to compensation philosophy and strategy discussed in Chapter 18 (Compensation: An Introduction), consider:

- What is the size of your organization? Are you a small company with fewer than 500 employees? A large company with 10,000 employees?
- Where is the organization in its life cycle? Are you in a growth spurt with new products/services being introduced and new markets being penetrated? Do you have a startup organization with few staffers but growth planned?
- What work needs to be done to produce/provide the organization's goods or services?

These questions are also fundamental to workforce planning. Once these questions have been answered, it is necessary to address what employees are doing. This is accomplished by performing a job analysis—one of the most often overlooked, misunderstood, and poorly implemented processes.

Job Analysis

A job analysis identifies and describes what is happening in jobs in the organization. It helps to differentiate job requirements and performance requirements on the basis of job content, job specifications, and working conditions.

In conducting a job analysis, it is important to obtain information about:

- A job's context or its purpose, its work environment, and its place in the organization.
- A job's content or duties and responsibilities.
- The specifications and qualifications, which are often referred to as KSAs:
  - ▷ **K**nowledge, the information necessary for task performance.
  - ▷ **S**kills, the level of competency or proficiency.
  - ▷ **A**bilities, traits, or capabilities necessary.
- Behavior—how people in the job are expected to act in accomplishing the job.

To do this:

- Get direct employee and supervisor input.
- Collect data from multiple incumbents and supervisors.
- Use a technique that yields concise data, is easy to update, and limits bias.

Be wary of:

- Lack of management support.
- Insufficient training of those participating in the project.
- Incumbent distortion of data, either accidentally or on purpose.
- Insufficient time allowed for the project.

Conducted and implemented accurately, a job analysis will help organizations develop:

- **Job descriptions**—written descriptions that detail each job's requirements such as title and duties.

  ⇥   Job descriptions are discussed in Chapter 5 (Job Descriptions).

- **Job specifications**—written statements of the necessary qualifications for an incumbent to have a reasonable chance of performing a job. The focus will vary for trained and untrained workers.
  - ▷ **Trained**: Focus on length of service or previous performance.
  - ▷ **Untrained**: Focus on interests or ability to be trained.
- **Job competencies**—critical success factors that lead to enhanced performance. Competency models define sets of competencies required for success in a particular job. They identify core competencies that align directly with key business objectives.

Conducting a Job Analysis

These steps are essential in conducting a thorough and effective job analysis:

1. Identify the reason for doing the job analysis.
   - ▷ Determine desired outcome.
2. Select the method(s) to be used.
   - ▷ Decide what positions will be analyzed.

▷ Review available resources such as organization charts, job descriptions, work flow charts, and so forth.

▷ Determine sample size.

3. Choose the analysts.

▷ They may be external consultants or internal staff such as human resources or line personnel.

4. Train the analysts in the method(s) to be used.

5. Prepare for the analysis.

▷ Set up appropriate documentation.

▷ Establish time frames.

▷ Communicate the project and its purpose to the entire organization.

6. Collect data.

7. Review and verify.

▷ Involve supervisors to review what's been collected.

▷ Return to original source to verify data and ask any follow-up questions.

▷ Consolidate the results.

8. Develop job descriptions and job specifications.

Job analysis methods are described in the following chart.

Type	Methods	Comments
Observation	**Direct Observation** observes and records work. It observes things like input/output, tasks performed, work environment, tools and equipment, and who else is involved in completing the tasks. Cameras, video recorders, or personal observation are the most often used tools for this method. **Work Methods Analysis** is used by industrial engineers to determine standard rates of production, which are then used to set pay rates. This analysis includes two methods: time/motion study and micro-motion analysis.	Although these methods provide a realistic review, they must observe the complete work cycle to be effective. In some jobs the work cycle occurs at infrequent or irregular intervals. It is best suited for short-cycle jobs, such as production or processing. There are often issues that arise due to sample size, or workers changing what they normally do because of the observation. In addition, care must be taken to observe average workers under average conditions.
Interview	Involves questioning individuals about the work being performed, working conditions, success factors, and behaviors. Interviews are done with both the employee and the supervisor, and often involve group interviews with groups of employees who have the same job. Can be *unstructured* (no prepared questions) or *structured* (sequencing and questionnaires may be used).	Depending on conditions, the workplace is the best option for the interview site. Interviewers must be trained in conducting interviews and taking notes. Best suited for professional jobs.

SECTION 3

Questionnaire	*Closed-Ended Method* involves developing and distributing a well-designed questionnaire to collect a wide array of job data in a short period from both employees and managers. Two common methods are the Position Analysis Questionnaire (PAQ) and the Common Metric Questionnaire (CMQ). The PAQ consists of 195 job elements describing such human work behaviors as interpersonal activities, job context, mental processes, and work output. The CMQ has five sections of questions: Background, Physical and Mechanical Activities, Work Setting, Contacts With People, and Decision Making; and can also include a matrix to respond on frequency, criticality, and consequence of error. *Open-Ended Method* has no prepared inventories, but asks a series of questions about what is being done, when, how and by whom.	Questionnaires are best used when a large number of jobs must be analyzed and there are insufficient resources. They are less time-consuming and are usually replicable on a second administration. Problems can arise when the survey population finds that the language in prepared questionnaires does not match their jobs and often complain that the reading level is too difficult.
Work diary or log	Each of these methods involves asking the employee to record daily activities or tasks. Three of the most commonly used methods are: the *Diary Method*, which asks employees to write down what they do during the day; a *Job Analysis Checklist*, which has employees check items on a prepared list of tasks (these lists are either developed internally or purchased from an outside source); and *Task Inventories*, which have employees respond to tasks listed by interview.	Work diaries or logs should contain activities performed at infrequent or irregular intervals, such as weekly, monthly, or quarterly. They are useful when working with professions or on jobs requiring a high degree of technical or scientific knowledge. An oral record can be made using a digital recorder. Problems can arise when there is too much variance in writing skills, employees have difficulty remembering what they did earlier in the day, or when the tool being used does not include important parts of the job.
Combination	Combining the above methods may prove useful. For example, a questionnaire may be provided before a face-to-face interview is conducted, or an interview may follow an observation for clarification.	Each method has pluses and minuses and it is recommended that at least two methods be used.

→   Appendix: Job Analysis Interview Questions.

Job Evaluation

Once information has been collected in the job analysis, the job evaluation process begins. Job evaluation is a systematic approach to determine the relative level, complexity, importance, and value of each job. These factors may vary within the same industry, among industries, and within organizations. Even within a single organization, different skills will be valued differently in different areas. Job evaluation assesses both the job content and the value of the job.

Before embarking on job evaluation, consider the following:

- There must be clearly defined and identifiable jobs. If job descriptions exist, they should be reviewed and updated as necessary.
- All jobs in the organization must be evaluated using the method selected.
- Job evaluators need to have, or be able to attain, a thorough understanding of jobs within the organization. They should also be trained in the provisions of the Fair Labor Standards Act.
- Look at jobs, not at the people in them.
- Job evaluation is more art than science, but objective judgments can be made.
- Assessments must be made based on jobs being done in a competent and acceptable manner.
- The method selected must make it possible for jobs to be evaluated relative to other jobs in the organization.
- The results of the evaluation must be acceptable to all participants.
- The method selected will result in the organization's ability to examine duplication of tasks and reveal any gaps.

The following factors are typically included in most evaluation systems. This is not an all-inclusive list, and not all of these factors need be part of the system:

- Training, education, or qualifications.
- Complexity of work being done.
- Knowledge and skills needed.
- Interactions within and outside of the organization.
- Problem-solving.
- Independent judgment.
- Accountability and responsibility.
- Degree of supervision needed.
- Cross-training requirements.
- Decision-making authority.
- Supervision of others.
- Working conditions.
- Degree of difficulty filling the job.

There are several standard steps to be taken in job evaluation. Care should be taken not to skip or short-cut any of the steps if the results are to have credibility.

1. Introduce the concept of job evaluation to management and employees.
2. Obtain management approval as well as commitment to time and resources needed for the system to be successful.

3. Select and train a cross-functional job evaluation team.
4. Review and select the job evaluation method.
5. Gather information on all internal jobs. Use the most up-to-date job descriptions, any existing job process descriptions, and so forth.
6. Use the selected job evaluation method to compare and rank jobs in a hierarchy or in groups.
7. Link the ranked jobs to the compensation system or develop a new system.
8. Implement the job evaluation and compensation systems organization-wide.
9. Review the job evaluation system and the resulting compensation decisions periodically to ensure equitability and that the system remains current.

There are five common job evaluation systems:

- ♦ Ranking.
- ♦ Classification.
- ♦ Point Evaluation.
- ♦ Factor Comparison.
- ♦ Market Comparison.

Before making a selection, carefully review and research systems and examine their fit for the organization.

Type	Method	Pros and Cons
Non-Quantitative	*Ranking*—typically assigns more value to jobs that require managerial or technical competencies, those that supervise others, those with decision-making authority, and those that exercise independent judgment.	Advantages: Easiest, fastest, and least-expensive approach. Also easy to understand and communicate. Disadvantages: Subjective and often based on opinion. Often requires re-ranking whenever new jobs are created within the organization.
Non-Quantitative	*Classification*—uses job descriptions to develop a list of standards for each category of jobs. Matches all jobs to the standards for each category based on similarity of tasks, decision-making exercised, and contribution to the overall goals of the organization	Advantages: Simple once categories are established. New or modified jobs can be assigned within the existing system. Disadvantages: Subjective and jobs might fall into several categories. Similar titles might describe different jobs from different areas. Takes a great deal of care on the part of the evaluators.

Quantitative	*Point Evaluation*—the value of a particular job is expressed in monetary terms. First, identify compensable factors, then assign points that numerically represent the description and range of the job. Examples of compensable factors include skills required, level of decision-making, number of reporting employees, and working conditions.	Advantages: Often viewed as less biased than other methods because the evaluations do not assign total points until all of the compensable factors are identified and evaluated. Disadvantages: Subjective decisions are made about classification and associated points. Job evaluators have to be aware of their own biases and work to make sure they are not at work in the evaluation.
Quantitative	*Factor Comparison*—involves ranking jobs that have similar responsibilities and tasks according to the points assigned to compensable factors. Jobs are then analyzed in the outside labor market to establish a market rate. Jobs are compared to benchmark positions according to the market rate of each job's compensable factors to determine job salaries.	Advantages: Results in customized job-ranking. Disadvantages: Time-consuming and subjective process.
Quantitative	*Market Comparison*—job evaluators compare compensation for the organization's jobs to the market rate for similar jobs.	Advantage: Jobs are tied to the market and the rates can easily be modified as the market changes. Disadvantages: Requires careful selection of benchmark positions and accurate market-pricing surveys.

Compensable factors play a vital role in several of the job evaluation methods. It is critical that these factors be developed carefully.

- Identify the organization's internal values.
- Review the job content of the group of jobs.
- Identify five to 12 factors.
- Obtain buy-in for the chosen factors.
- Identify the highest and lowest levels/degrees of each factor.
- Identify a logical progression that reflects reasonable differences and creates intermediate levels.
- Develop a job-worth hierarchy consistent with the organization's perception of relative job worth.
- Establish the proper number of levels.

Quantitative evaluation methods use a scaling system to evaluate the value of one job as compared to another and assign a score. Quantitative evaluation methods include:

SECTION 3

- The **Factor Comparison Method** ranks jobs on compensable factors such as skill, responsibility, effort, working conditions, and supervision. It identifies factor weights and assigns dollar values to each factor. These dollar values are then added together for each individual position and the resulting total becomes the wage rate for the job.
- The **Point Factor Method** assigns a point value based on a compensable factor. Compensable factors reflect the dimensions along which a job is perceived to add value to the organization; these factors are used to determine which jobs are worth more than others. Each job receives a total point value and its relative worth can be determined. The Guide Chart-Profile or Hay Plan is a best-known method.

  Sample compensable factors are:
  1. Knowledge.
  2. Task Complexity.
  3. Independent Judgment.
  4. Customer Satisfaction.
  5. Error Impact.
  6. Degree of Confidentiality Required.
  7. Supervisory Responsibility.
  8. Mental/Visual Ability & Effort.
  9. Education.
  10. Physical Requirement.

The following is a sample Factor Summary Sheet using a senior computer programmer and showing the first five factors in the previous list.

Degree					
Factor	1	2	3	4	5
Knowledge	**90 points** Step-by-step instruction provided; no previous training	**180 points** Knowledge of basic, commonly used rule, procedure, or operations requiring previous training or experience	**270 points** Knowledge of extensive body of rules, etc., requiring extended training/experience to perform a variety of assignments	**360 points** Practical, wide-range knowledge of technical methods, principles, practices to perform assignments or carry out limited projects involving the use of specialized and complicated techniques	**450 points** Mastery of a professional or administrative field
Task Complexity	**85 points** Routine, repetitive duties, basic procedures	**160 points** Routine duties, limited deviations with defined choices	**250 points** Semi-routine duties requiring some discretion within prescribed limits	**330 points** Diversified or specialized non-routine work requiring discretion for determination of action	**425 points** Generally diversified, non-repetitive difficult work requiring independent action
Independent Judgment	**85 points** Closely supervised work is well covered by instructions; little initiative	**160 points** Work follows standard procedures with questionable cases referred to supervisor	**250 points** Work toward definite objectives using precedents; general supervision	**330 points** Limited supervision with course of action covered only generally in standard procedure	**425 points** Self-supervision with administrative direction only and absence of precedents
Customer Satisfaction	**75 points** Routine internal contacts limited to intermediate associates and supervisor	**150 points** Routine internal contacts to furnish/obtain information	**230 points** Frequent, routine internal/external contacts to furnish/obtain information	**300 points** Regular difficult contacts of significant importance	**390 points** Repeated, highly complex internal/external contacts of major importance
Error Impact	**75 points** Probable errors of minimal consequence	**140 points** Probable errors confined to small phase of departmental activity	**200 points** Probable errors possibly serious, but normally confined to department	**288 points** Probable errors having significant impact on phase of operations	**360 points** Probable errors having major impact on overall operations

SECTION 3

Completed Factor Summary Sheet for Senior Computer Programmer

Factor	Points
Knowledge	360
Task Complexity	252
Independent Judgment	336
Customer Satisfaction	234
Error Impact	288
Degree of Confidentiality Required	198
Supervisory Responsibility	96
Mental/Visual Ability & Effort	108
Education	90
Physical Requirement	20
TOTAL	1,982

Working With Pay or Salary Surveys

Once the value of each job has been established within the organization, it's time to look externally and gather information from salary surveys. Salary surveys should answer four critical questions:

1. What is the labor market for your jobs?
2. How will the data be used?
3. How frequently will you update the data?
4. How will you communicate the results?

Two considerations must be addressed: position match and data match.

Position Match

- Start with job families to match—low to high.
- Look for exempt and non-exempt positions to include.
- Match base pay to base pay.
- Match duties, not titles.
- Closely examine experience and education requirements.
- Look at scope of position in terms of company size, budget responsibility, industry, and so forth.

Data Match

- Use a simple average in evaluating the survey results, not the median.
- Use data with at least 10 participating organizations and 15 incumbents in the survey job.
- Use data that is as close as possible to your geographic labor area.
- Use three surveys at a minimum.

Once collected, review the data carefully. Consider how your job levels and families compare to the external data, internal equity, and financial impact of the results. For example, will salaries need to be increased?

Creating a Pay System

Depending on the pay philosophy the organization has selected, salary ranges or pay grades may be established. Salary ranges may be unique to each position or grouped into salary grades. If salary grades will be used, the right number of grades will have to be selected and developed.

- There is no magic formula for establishing the number of grades.
- They need to fit each organization's needs.
- They need to distinguish between different levels of jobs and provide room for salary growth.
- There should not be so many that the distinction between them is insignificant.

Many organizations have different grades for exempt and non-exempt positions. Others develop separate grades for executives. How broad these grades are is typically influenced by things like tenure and difficulty levels of the jobs within each category. Regardless of how the organization chooses to represent salary grades, the pay philosophy (lead, meet, or lag the market) will drive how midpoints (the middle of the range) will be set and the width and overlap of the grades. The organization should also consider its organization profile and the value of its overall rewards package.

The use of quartiles and percentiles shows how groups relate to each other and can be used to determine if an organization leads, lags, or matches the labor market. The following shows the range for one job grade as reported in a salary survey:

	First Quartile	**Second Quartile**	**Third Quartile**	**Fourth Quartile**
0%	25%	50%	75%	100%
$50,000	$60,000	$65,000	$70,000	$75,000
Entry		Midpoint		Maximum

A Startup Company's Approach

We have decided to lead the market in order to attract the top talent we need to continue our growth, but we don't have a broad total rewards package to offer. Thus, we will use a straight market pay strategy and target the 75th percentile of the market data. All of our jobs will have the 75th percentile from the market data as the midpoint. Because our salary grades will include many different positions, we will aggregate the 75th percentiles for all of the benchmark jobs that make up the salary grade.

Once midpoints are determined, the actual range for each grade must be established. There is no hard and fast number for range widths. Organizations should determine these widths after considering the impact these ranges will have in terms of employee motivation and longevity. Midpoints should be adjusted annually to ensure that the organization remains competitive.

Most organizations create wider ranges for higher-level jobs and narrower ones for entry-level positions. In typical pay structures:

- ◆ Executive grades have a range width between 50 and 60 percent.
- ◆ Professional grades between 40 and 50 percent.
- ◆ Hourly grades between 30 and 40 percent.

In addition, most organizations determine the difference they want to see between grade midpoints.

Developing a Salary Range

The organization wants a grade to have a 50-percent width and the midpoint is $50,000.
- ◆ The minimum is calculated by dividing the midpoint ($50,000) by 1 plus the width (50%) divided by 2 or (50%/2=25%).
- ◆ The maximum would be calculated by multiplying the minimum ($40,000) by 1.5.
- ◆ The difference between $60,000 and $40,000 is 1.5 or a 50% width.

Minimum	Midpoint	Maximum
=Midpoint/1+25% =$50,000/1.25	$50,000	=Minimum x 1.5 =$40,000 x 1.5
$40,000	$50,000	$60,000

→   Appendix: Sample Salary Structure.

Employees should understand that salary ranges are attached to jobs and are career ranges, and that minimums and maximums of salary grades should be taken seriously. When pay variations occur, they need to be addressed.

Pay variations include:
- ◆ **Green-circle rates**, which occur if employees' salaries are below the minimum. This may happen when trainees are hired and will be given raises as new skills are required. Once they are fully qualified, they should be at the midpoint of the range, because this is tied to market value.
- ◆ **Red-circle rates** are rates above the pay range maximum. Employees will generally only receive a raise if the maximum of the range goes up. This can happen when employees are moved into these pay grades as the result of transfers or recalls after a layoff.

If green circles happen as the result of implementing new grade structures, it is generally considered appropriate to adjust employees to the new salaries called for in the new grades. Red-circled employees are usually not reduced to the new maximum but rather are frozen at their current salary. One tool that is useful in these situations, as well as in measuring the effectiveness of a salary program, is a compa-ratio.

Compa-ratios index the relative competitiveness of internal pay rates based on range midpoints and are calculated by dividing the pay level of an employee by the midpoint of the range. Given a range of $6 to $10 an hour, a midpoint of $8, and a salary of $6 an hour, the compa-ratio is: $6 divided by $8 or 75%. A compa-ratio less than 1.0 means the employee is paid less than the midpoint. A compa-ratio greater than 1.0 means wages exceed the midpoint. These calculations can be used to assess employee, department, and company positions in salary ranges.

Minimum	Midpoint	Maximum
$6	$8	$10

Pay	Compa-Ratio = Pay/Midpoint
$6	$6/$8 = 75%
$10	$10/$8 = 125%

Two final topics to consider when developing a salary structure are broadbanding and salary compression.

Broadbanding

Broadbanding is the combination of a number of salary grades into new ones with a much wider spread between minimum and maximum. Whereas a typical salary range might have a width of 40 percent, a broadband range would have a width of 100 percent. This technique is very frequently used during reorganizations and results in fewer, wider ranges. It is an effective way to reduce the number of grades or classifications.

Its advantages include streamlining the organizational hierarchy, facilitating internal movement, and putting added trust in management. The disadvantages include the lack of a true midpoint and the inability to use compa-ratios. Broadbanding may also lead to inequities, a lack of cost controls and a severe reduction in opportunities for promotions.

Salary Compression

Salary compression occurs when the pay spread between newly hired or less-qualified employees is small in comparison to longer-term, more experienced employees due to rising starting salaries. This phenomenon generally occurs when organizations fail to raise pay range minimums and maximums over time, when there is a shortage of qualified candidates for particular jobs, and when hourly employees' overtime and base pay is higher than that of their supervisors.

Periodically monitoring market rates and the effectiveness of the organization's pay practices by studying compa-ratios will help prevent salary compression and should be a part of the organization's process improvement efforts. This is also important in monitoring pay equity in the organization.

Developing a salary structure is an often-overlooked activity that plays a key role in an organization's success when done with care and attention to the organization's goals. Many surveys have shown that people leave organizations when they feel they have not been paid fairly for what they do.

Time and resources spent developing a salary structure and communicating the process to all employees will result in fewer departures and higher motivation. Though not easily done, it is effort well spent.

Discussion Questions:

1. What information would be important for your organization to capture on a job analysis questionnaire?
2. Given the various methods for generating job analysis data and information (observation, questionnaire, diary/log, interview, or combination), which would be the most effective for your organization and why?
3. What compensable factors—those measurable qualities, features, requirements—are critical to jobs in your organization when conducting job evaluations?
4. How does your organization address pay rates below the minimum (green circle) and pay rates above the maximum (red circle)? How do you deal with employees who have topped out?
5. Considering geography and industry, what are some options for salary surveys for your organization?

About the Chapter Author

Mary Jane Sinclair, SPHR, is president of Sinclair Consulting in Wharton, New Jersey, and has more than 30 years of human resources experience with emphasis on compliance, compensation, management development, and training. She consults with a variety clients and industries including Fortune 500, privately held companies, government agencies, and non-profits.

20

The Legal Landscape of Employee Benefits

Prior to 1974, workers had no guarantee that they would receive the pensions promised by their employers. The movement for pension reform gained momentum in the early 1960s when the Studebaker Corporation, an automobile manufacturer, closed its plant and announced that the pension plan was so poorly funded it could not afford to provide all employees with their pension. Around the same time, President Kennedy created the President's Committee on Corporate Pensions. The issue came to a head in 1972 when NBC broadcast *Pensions: The Broken Promise*, an hour-long special that showed the consequences of poorly funded pension plans and onerous vesting requirements. On September 2, 1974, Labor Day, President Ford signed the Employee Retirement Income Security Act (ERISA) into law.[1]

Beyond the mandated benefits discussed in Chapter 21 (Employee Benefits), there are federal, state and local laws that affect employee benefits. It is important to have a basic understanding of them when designing a benefit program. Discussed here are federal laws. Guidance should be sought for state-specific laws and regulations.

Family and Medical Leave Act (FMLA) of 1993

FMLA is a mandated benefit that provides job protected leave to eligible employees. Employers with 50 or more employees (full-time or part-time) who work within 75 miles of a given workplace are required to provide this leave for certain qualifying events. An employee must have worked for the employer at least 12 months and 1,250 hours during the prior 12 months to be eligible. An employee generally must be returned to the same or an equivalent position unless he or she is unable to perform an essential function of the job because of the serious health condition.

Group health coverage must be maintained for an employee during his or her FMLA leave period on the same basis as such coverage was provided before the leave was taken. An employee's entitlement to benefits other than group health benefits during a period of FMLA leave (for example, holiday pay) is also required on the same basis as they are provided for other forms of leave.

Eligible employees may take up to 12 weeks during a compliance year specified by the employer because:

- Of the birth of a child or the placement of a child for adoption or foster care (leave for this reason must be taken within one year of the event).
- The employee is needed to care for a family member with a serious health condition.
- The employee's own serious health condition makes the employee unable to do his or her job.

Eligible employees may take up to 26 weeks during a single 12-month period for military caregiver leave on a per-covered service member, per-injury basis:

- Because of a "qualifying exigency" arising out of a covered family member's active duty or call to active duty in the Armed Forces in support of a contingency plan.
- To care for a covered family member who has incurred an injury or illness in the line of duty while on active duty in the Armed Forces, provided that such injury or illness may render the family member unfit to perform duties of the member's office, grade, rank, or rating.

→   Appendix: Key Definitions Under FMLA.

Employees cannot waive their rights under FMLA, nor can an employer require an employee to accept a light-duty assignment instead of FMLA leave. However, an employer can offer, and the employee can voluntarily accept, a light-duty assignment while recovering from a serious health condition.

Employers may require employees to substitute accrued paid leave for FMLA leave, provided the reason for the leave is consistent with the employer's leave plan.

Employers are required to provide written guidance to employees, which can be included in the employee handbook. Additional notice advising the employee of his or her rights and obligations at the time the employee takes leave should also be provided.

The employee has an obligation to provide the employer with notice of the need for FMLA leave. When the leave is foreseeable, the employee should give 30 days' notice. Although the notice only needs to be verbal, it is good practice to require an employee who requests leave to submit a written request.

It is the company's responsibility to designate leave as FMLA covered leave and to assure that the employee has been advised of all of his or her rights under the law. There may be times that the employee does not specifically request a leave. Nevertheless, there may be an underlying situation or issue that would lead the employer to suspect that a leave may be warranted. Situations involving chronic absenteeism could be symptoms of serious medical conditions. Leave may be delayed for an employee's failure to comply with the employer's notice policy. In certain circumstances, if the employee fails to comply, a company may count any absences during the delay (in notification) as non-FMLA absences and apply the employer's attendance policy to those absences.

If an employee is placed on FMLA leave, all contact with the employee and the company should take place through one designated source, such as the human resources department. This will assure that all communication is consistent with policy and the legal requirements.

Employers may, and it is a good practice to, require that a leave to care for the employee's own, or a family member's, serious medical condition be supported by a certification issued by the attending healthcare provider. There are additional certifications for Military Caregiver Leave.

→ The Family and Medical Leave Act is enforced by the Department of Labor's Wage & Hour Division. Additional information can be found at *www.dol.gov/whd/fmla/index.htm.*

Finally, many states have family and medical leave legislation with requirements that exceed those of the federal law. Employees are entitled to the maximum protection afforded under both federal and state law. Therefore, it is important that an employer be familiar with any state or local requirements.

Employee Retirement Income Security Act (ERISA), 1974

ERISA established uniform and minimum standards for employee benefit plans. It set increased reporting requirements, required that pension funds be separate from operating funds, set vesting schedules for retirement plan participants, required employers to provide summary plan descriptions of its plans to employees, and set minimum standards for fund management.

- **Employee participation**. ERISA set eligibility requirements for retirement plan participation. In general, employees must be 21 years old and have completed 12 months of service.
- **Fiduciary responsibility.** ERISA established the prudent person rule, which states that an ERISA plan fiduciary has legal and financial obligations not to take more risks when investing employee benefit program funds than a reasonably knowledgeable, prudent investor would under similar circumstances.
- **Vesting schedules.** ERISA defined minimum vesting schedules for retirement plans for funds contributed by the employer. Vesting is the point at which the employees own the contributions of the employer. Employees always own their personal contributions If employees are not immediately vested when they are eligible to participate in the plan, their vesting is delayed in one of the following ways:
  - ▷ **Cliff vesting**, in which participants become 100 percent vested after a specified period of time; or
  - ▷ **Graded vesting**, in which participants are partially vested each year for a specified number of years.

> The Economic Growth and Tax Relief Reconciliation Act (EGTRRA), 2001, amended ERISA by providing for three-year cliff vesting and six-year graded vesting (20 percent after two years and 20% per year thereafter). It also increased the permissible compensation limit ($200,000), allowed for higher limits on annual pensions ($160,000), permitted catch-up contributions for employees age 50 and older, and modified distribution and rollover rules.

- **Reporting requirements.** ERISA requires employers to:
  - ▷ Prepare and distribute Summary Plan Descriptions (SPDs) to plan participants. SPDs are written summaries about the plan's provisions, policies and rules, and the participants' rights and benefits. They must be written in language that can be easily understood.

    ▷ Prepare and distribute Summary Annual Reports (SARs) containing financial information about the plan.

    ▷ Prepare and file an annual report (Form 5500) with the IRS, and make it available for inspection by participants. Form 5500 is required for qualified retirement plans and for employers that have at least 100 employees participating in welfare plans. Employers with fewer than 100 plan participants are required to file Form 5500-SF. These forms must be electronically filed each year for the employee benefit plan to satisfy annual reporting requirements.

- The Pension Benefit Guaranty Corporation insures payment of certain pension plan benefits if a private-sector defined benefit pension plan does not have sufficient funds to pay the promised benefits.

The Department of Labor's Employee Benefits Security Administration (EBSA) has jurisdiction over ERISA reporting, disclosure, and fiduciary responsibility. The Internal Revenue Service (IRS) has jurisdiction over funding, eligibility, and other tax-related matters. In order to receive tax advantages for its benefit programs, employers must conform to the Internal Revenue Code.

> See *www.dol.gov/agencies/ebsa/employers-and-advisers/plan-admin-istration-and-compliance*, which contains guidance on health insurance, COBRA, retirement, and 401(k) plans; reporting and filing requirements; and employer's fiduciary responsibilities.

Retirement Equity Act, 1984

The Retirement Equity Act provides certain legal protections for spousal beneficiaries of qualified retirement plans. It requires written approval from a spouse if the participant did not want to provide survivor benefits and put restrictions on the conditions that could be placed on provider benefits. It also provides for Qualified Domestic Relations Orders (QDROs), which recognize the right of a spouse, former spouse, child, or dependent to receive a portion of an employee's pension benefits. QDROs are issued by state courts under domestic relations laws.

Health Insurance Portability and Accountability Act (HIPAA), 1996

HIPAA contains provisions for:

- Portability by providing for continuity of group health coverage. Health plans can apply only limited exclusions for preexisting medical conditions and must allow certain enrollments during the year.

- Nondiscrimination by prohibiting employers from conditioning or varying eligibility, continued eligibility, or premiums for health coverage based on an individual's health status.

- Guaranteed renewability, which generally requires insurers to renew group coverage sold to employers, except in specified situations. Insurers may not deny an employer continued access to coverage except in limited circumstances, such as non-payment of premiums or noncompliance with material plan provisions, including participation and contribution rules.

HIPAA's requirements for healthcare coverage portability, nondiscrimination, and renewability are part of three different federal laws: ERISA, the Internal Revenue Code, and the Public Health Service Act (PHSA). The Department of Labor, the Internal Revenue Service, and the Department of Health and Human Services are responsible for implementing these provisions and have issued final regulations implementing the HIPAA portability and nondiscrimination provisions. Legislation enacted since the regulations were issued, including the Genetic Information Nondiscrimination Act (see Chapter 3, The Legal Landscape of Employee Rights) and the Patent Protection and Affordable Health Care Act, has affected the HIPAA portability, nondiscrimination, and renewability obligations.

> ➤ HIPPA also has privacy standards, which are discussed in Chapter 29 (Risk Management).

> ➤ For additional information, see *www.hhs.gov/hipaa/index.html* and *www.dol.gov/EBSA.*

Older Worker's Benefit Protection Act (OWBPA), 1990

Older Worker's Benefit Protection Act amended the Age Discrimination in Employment Act (ADEA). It prohibits discrimination in employee benefits and requires employers to offer workers who are at least 40 years old benefits that are equal to, or that cost the employer as much as, the benefits offered to younger workers. It also sets minimum standards for an employee waiver of the right to sue for age discrimination, ensuring that the waiver is knowing and voluntary. Older workers must be given 21 days to consider the waiver or agreement and consult with an attorney. If a group of employees is being terminated, the workers must receive 45 days. These waivers are legal agreements that carry a number of binding provisions. For this reason, legal advice should be sought.

> ➤ The Age Discrimination in Employment Act is discussed in Chapter 3 (The Landscape of Employee Rights).

> ➤ The OWBPA is also discussed in Chapter 30 (Ending the Employment Relationship).

Uniformed Services Employment and Reemployment Rights Act (USERRA), 1994

The Uniformed Services Employment and Reemployment Rights Act was passed to ensure that discrimination does not take place against individuals who serve in the Armed Forces. It:

+ Prohibits discrimination on the basis of military obligation.
+ Requires military leave for up to five years (extended in some circumstances).
+ Requires oral or written notice of the need for leave.
+ Gives employees on military leave the same non-seniority-based benefits and rights generally provided to other employees with similar seniority, status, and pay on other types of leave.
+ Gives employees on military leave the same seniority-based benefits they would have received if they had not taken military leave.

- Requires that military leave not create a break in service for retirement plan purposes.
- Requires employers to give affected employees notice of rights and obligation under the law.
  - → The USERRA is enforced by the Department of Labor (DOL). For additional information, please visit their website at www.dol.gov/elaws/vets/userra/userra.asp.
  - → The DOL has developed a model poster, which can be found at www.dol.gov/vets/programs/userra/USERRA_Federal.pdf.

Many states may provide protections for employees beyond the requirements of USERRA. Therefore, it is important that an employer be familiar with any state or local laws.

Mental Health Parity Act, 1996

The Mental Health Parity Act requires the same dollar limits for mental health and medical benefits. It does not apply to substance abuse nor require a plan to offer mental health benefits.

Patient Protection and Affordable Care Act (PPACA or ACA), 2011

The Patient Protection and Affordable Care Act of 2011 is an integral part of healthcare reform. It has placed many new compliance obligations on employers that are complicated and technical. Employers should seek continuing advice from their benefits and legal consultants, especially since many provisions take effect on a phased basis.

Requirements and prohibitions affecting employers and plans include:

- Lifetime and annual dollar limits on "essential health benefits" are prohibited.
- There can be no retroactive revocation of coverage except for fraud/intentional misrepresentation of a material fact.
- Coverage for adult children up to age 26 is required.
- There can be no pre-existing condition exclusion for any participant.
- Coverage of certain preventive health services and immunizations without cost to covered individuals is required.
- Insured plans are now subject to nondiscrimination rules currently applicable to self-insured plans.
- Participants may choose any available primary care provider.
- Access to emergency services in and out of network without prior authorization must be provided.
- Internal and external claim appeal procedures and notification requirements of those procedures are required.
  - → For more information on healthcare reform, including a number of FAQs, please visit www.dol.gov/agencies/ebsa/laws-and-regulations/laws/affordable-care-act/for-employers-and-advisers, and www.hhs.gov/healthcare/about-the-law/read-the-law/index.html.

Tax Provisions of the ACA

The Affordable Care Act includes requirements for employers regarding heathcare coverage. The size and structure of your workforce determines your responsibility. For example, employers with fewer than 25 full-time equivalent employees may be eligible for a certain tax credit and those with fewer than 50 employees may be eligible to buy coverage through the Small Business Options Shop. Employers with 50 or more employees are required to file an annual information return, reporting whether and what health insurance they offered employees.

→ For more information on the tax provisions, please visit *www.irs.gov/ affordable-care-act/employers.*

Revenue Act of 1978

The Revenue Act of 1978 added two sections to the Tax Code that resulted in the favorable treatment of certain employee benefits discussed in Chapter 21 (Employee Benefits).

Tax Reform Act

The Tax Reform Act simplified many sections of the Tax Code and limited salary deferral contributions and compensation and restricted retirement savings for family-owned businesses.

The Omnibus Budget Reconciliation Act, 1986

The Omnibus Budget Reconciliation Act reduced compensation limits in qualified retirement programs.

Securities and Exchange Act, 1934

The Securities and Exchange Act affects company stock option and purchase plans. It requires the registration of all securities sold, and disclosure and restriction of "insider" trading.

Sarbanes-Oxley Act (SOX), 2002

The Sarbanes-Oxley Act applies to publicly-held companies. Section 306 of the Act requires plan administrators to notify plan participants of blackout periods for 401(k) or defined contribution plans. During a blackout period, a temporary suspension on stock trading, executive officers, and directors are prohibited from trading stock they acquired as a result of their employment, such as through a 401(k) savings plan or profit-sharing plan that offers stock. Advance notice of the blackout period must be provided to executives and the SEC. Contents should include reasons for the blackout, expected dates for the blackout, and a statement that participants and beneficiaries should evaluate their current investment decisions in light of their inability to change investments during the blackout.

A second SOX notification requirement in Section 306, geared at protecting workers, requires companies to notify employees at least 30 days prior to a blackout. Notice may be sent electronically.[2]

Discussion Questions

1. Employees do not always make a direct request such as "I need FMLA leave," yet the employer is responsible for providing an employee the job-protected leave if they have sufficient information that a leave is necessary. What steps can an employer take to assure that leaves are appropriately designated?

2. What are some of the ways that employers comply with their reporting requirements under ERISA?

3. What are the advantages and disadvantages of outsourcing the administration of FMLA, COBRA, and other benefit requirements?

21

Employee Benefits

In her history of the Cadbury family's chocolate business, Deborah Cadbury describes the innovative practices its founders implemented:

> Should anyone fall ill, a doctor was hired in 1902 for the staff. The medical department expanded over time to include four nurses and a dentist, who were available to all employees free of charge. Free vitamin supplements were provided for those lacking stamina, and a convalescent home...was built for staff in need of a rest. These amenities may seem quaintly paternalistic by modern standards, but at a time when employees could be subjected to unhealthy or even dangerous working environments, it is small wonder that workers were queuing up to join Bournville.[1]

Employee benefits are an integral part of a company's total rewards program. They play a large part in employee satisfaction, motivation, and retention. In its report "Building a Better Benefits Program Without Breaking The Budget: Five Practical Steps Every Small Business Should Consider," MetLife reports, "Of employees who say that they are satisfied with their benefits, 81 percent are also satisfied with their job. In comparison, of those who are dissatisfied with their benefits, only 23 percent are very satisfied with their jobs."[2]

Creative Benefits Strategy

By Gary B. Kushner, SPHR, CBP

President and CEO, Kushner & Company (*www.kushnerco.com*)

Creative benefit strategies today focus around the two most costly benefit programs: health and retirement benefits. Given not just the changes in the landmark 2010 Patient Protection and Affordable Care Act (PPACA), but also the dramatic shift in the number of dual-income family units, most organizations need to focus their attention not just on a continuous cycle of health-benefit-slashing by increasing deductibles, copays, coinsurance, and premium co-share, but also on the impact on recruiting and selection. By 2014, many employers may be able to leverage their competitive advantage by merely offering a cost-effective health benefit program tailored to their organization and employee needs. Further, by incorporating targeted prevention and wellness benefits, the wise employer can also not only save long-term healthcare costs within its plan, but can also see decreased levels of absenteeism and presenteeism, reduced ancillary benefit costs (workers' compensation and disability, for example), and even increased levels of talent engagement.

Within the retirement benefit arena, employers are rethinking some outdated designs that encouraged employees to leave the workplace at earlier ages. Given that today a worker planning on retiring at age 65 might in fact have as long a retirement life as she did a work life, both the financial and sociological implications are causing many to attempt to remain in the workplace. This too can provide a savvy employer with well-skilled older workers.

Thus, organizations should carefully consider what the benefit components of their Total Reward strategies are attempting to accomplish, and re-examine possibly outdated modes of thinking.

Mandatory Benefits

Social Security provides financial security to qualified workers when they retire or became disabled, or to their surviving dependents in the event of a worker's death. Workers earn credits to qualify for benefits, and full retirement benefits are indexed to the individual's age. Disability benefits are paid to workers who have not reached full retirement age once eligibility requirements are met.

Social Security tax, paid by both the employer and the employee, is calculated as a percentage of salary up to an annual maximum. The percentages and annual maximum can change each year.

Medicare provides hospital and medical benefits to people age 65 and older, or younger if they have certain medical conditions or disabilities. It is also paid by both the employer and the employee as a percentage of salary with no annual maximum.

Medicare has four parts:

1. Hospital insurance (Part A) for inpatient care in a hospital or skilled nursing facility.
2. Medical insurance (Part B) for doctors' and other medical services and supplies.
3. Medicare Advantage (Part C) allows people with Part A and Part B to receive all of their healthcare services through one provider organization.
4. Prescription drug coverage (Part D) for medications doctors prescribe for treatment.

If an individual continues to work after age 65 and receives healthcare benefits from his or her employer, the employer benefits are primary to Medicare.

➔ For additional information, see the Social Security Administration website at *www.ssa.gov* and the Center for Medicare and Medicaid Services website at *www.cms.gov*.

Unemployment insurance provides temporary financial assistance to eligible workers who lost their jobs through no fault of their own. Individual states are responsible for administering and distributing unemployment insurance funds within the guidelines established by federal standards. Funding is based on a tax paid by the employer, with an experience rating based upon the number of workers that have been terminated.

To be eligible for unemployment insurance, an employee must:
- Meet the state requirements for wages earned or time worked during an established period of time referred to as a "base period."
- Be determined under state law to be unemployed through no fault of your own.
- Be available and actively seeing work.
- Not refuse suitable employment.

Employers can manage their experience rating by having sound employment practices such as:
- Strategic hiring procedures for sourcing, recruiting, selecting, and hiring.
- Workforce plans to avoid one department hiring while another is laying off employees with similar skills and competencies.
- Policies and practices to manage the workforce and assure that performance and behavior issues are promptly and consistently addressed.
- Reviewing involuntary terminations.
- Documenting all employment decisions, especially terminations.
- Monitoring employee resignations to screen for constructive discharge.
- Promptly responding to inquiries about unemployment claims, presenting evidence at unemployment hearings, and challenging decisions to grant benefits that the employer believes are not deserved.

➔ For additional information, visit the website of your state employment office. A list of these offices can be found at *https://us.jobs/ state-workforce-agencies.asp*

Workers' compensation provides benefits to employees who incur a work-related injury or illness. The programs are enacted and administered by the individual states. There is no federal mandate that states provide a certain minimum level of benefits.

Workers' compensation is a no-fault insurance plan paid by the employer. The amount that employers pay is experience-rated based on the percentage of employees in various job categories, and the employer's previous claim activity. Employers with a high number of claims are likely to pay more.

Benefits under workers compensation include:
- Medical care and expenses.
- Rehabilitation expense.

- Income replacement during the period of disability when the employee is unable to work.
- Benefits to survivors in the event of an employee's death.

The amount of the benefit a worker receives is tied to fixed schedules or actuarial tables that consider the seriousness of the injury, whether it is permanent or temporary, or a full or partial disability.

Employers can control costs by:

- Implementing safety programs that include training, injury prevention, and ongoing education and reinforcement;
- Providing transitional or "light duty" jobs that will allow employers to return to work earlier; and
- Consulting with occupational or medical specialists particularly for reoccurring or industry-specific issues.

> For additional information on each state's workers' compensation program, visit *www.workerscompensation.com*.

> For more information about workplace safety and security, see Chapter 29 (Risk Management).

The **Family Medical Leave Act (FMLA)** provides job-protected leave to eligible employees. This law is discussed in detail in Chapter 20 (The Legal Landscape of Employee Benefits).

Health and Welfare Benefits

Healthcare insurance is the most critical of the health and welfare benefits, and one that continues to be debated.

Indemnity (fee-for-service) plans are the least cost-effective. Individuals are free to use any qualified healthcare provider and the fees are generated when the services are used. There are limits on the dollar amount of coverage over time and annual deductibles are common. Reasonable and customary limits can be set on fees.

Managed-care plans focus on providing necessary treatment in a cost-effective manner. They include:

- **Health maintenance organizations (HMOs)** restrict the choice of physician to those in the group. These are generally prepaid healthcare plans where the providers are paid on a per capita basis rather than for actual treatment provided. A gatekeeper is usually used, typically the primary care physician, to determine whether or not patients need to be seen by a specialist.
- **Preferred provider organizations (PPOs)** combine features from the indemnity and HMO plans. They use a network of providers for services, but do not require a gatekeeper. The PPO negotiates fees with the providers, and deductibles are common. Individuals may use providers outside the network, but they will pay a higher percentage of the costs.
- **Point-of-service (POS) plans** include a network of providers, but the plan will pay for services of an out-of-network provider when a network provider refers the employee

for care. However, if the employee sees an out-of-network provider without a referral, a coinsurance payment is required.

- **Exclusive provider organizations (EPOs)** are restrictive in that only providers in the network may be used. No payment is made for out-of-network providers.
- **Physician hospital organizations (PHOs)** consist of hospital and physician practices that merge to market their services and negotiate with employer organizations.

Methods of funding health insurance include:

- **Fully insured**, in which a third-party carrier is paid premiums by the employer to cover medical costs and all related charges.
- **Self-insured**, in which the employer is funding the costs, assuming some or all of the risk as well as the role of the insurance company.
- **Administrative-services-only**, in which the employer assumes the risk, but hires an insurance company to administer the claims.
- **Third-party administrator**, in which the employer assumes the risk, but hires another company (not an insurance company) for claims administration.

> ⇢ Employee Wellness is discussed in Chapter 29 (Risk Management).

Other Healthcare Options

Dental plans are offered with varying levels of coverage including preventative or restorative work such as fillings, or major restoration such as bridges and orthodontia.

- Vision care plans provide reduced costs for eye exams, contact lenses, and glasses.
- Prescription drug plans usually require a copayment and the use of generic drugs. Some plans specify the pharmacies where prearranged reduced costs are available.
- Alternative healthcare or nontraditional care, such as acupuncture or chiropractic, is now covered by some health plans.
- Health savings accounts (HSAs) combine a high-deductible health insurance plan with a tax-favored savings account. Money in the savings account is used to pay out-of-pocket medical expenses. It belongs to the employee and earns interest. Employees can make contributions on a pre-tax basis up to the annual contribution limit. The account balance is portable, meaning the employees can take it with them when they leave the organization. However, funds used for other-than-qualified medical expenses will be included in taxable income and subject to an additional 20-percent tax, which is waived if payment is made after age 65 or the individual becomes disabled or dies.
- Health reimbursement accounts (HRAs) are employer-provided accounts. The money can be used by the account holder or employee to pay for qualified medical expenses on a tax-free basis. Balances can be rolled over, subject to limitations, provided the employer continues to offer the program. Account balances do not earn interest.

> ⇢ Appendix: Guidelines for Choosing a Benefits Broker.

SECTION 3

Employee Assistance Programs

Employee assistance programs (EAPs) can help employees identify and resolve concerns related to health, marital, family, financial, substance abuse, legal, emotional, stress, workplace violence, or other personal issues that affect job performance. They also serve as a resource to management. They can be in-house programs or offered through an outside contractor.

Services that the EAP can offer include:

- Identification and referral, which assesses the nature of the problem and develops a plan of action, either a short-term problem resolution through the EAP provider or a referral to an appropriate healthcare professional or other community resource.
- Monitoring and follow-up services regarding progress.
- Crisis intervention to employees and eligible family members.
- Critical incident interventions, such as situations of workplace violence or when a staff member has been seriously injured or died.
- Training and consultation for managers regarding management referrals to the EAP for employees with job performance or behavioral/medical problems.
- Consultation regarding the design and implementation of policies and practices for EAP referral and use.
- Program promotion and education.

> → Additional information can be found on the website of the Employee Assistance Professionals Association at *www.eapassn.org*.

> → Employee Assistance Programs are also discussed in Chapter 29 (Risk Management).

Maximizing the Effectiveness of Your EAP

By Tom Murphy, MS, LMHC (FL), NCC, CEAP
President, Spenser & Associates, Inc. (*www. spenserandassociates.com*)

Over the last 20 years, EAPs have expanded their service delivery to incorporate certified practitioners of crisis intervention, and licensed mental health, social work, and counseling professionals to support employees and family members with a wide range of issues. A broad brush umbrella of services offered by EAPs may now include:

- Short-term assessment and counseling services.
- Consultation to assist managers and supervisors in their duties of maintaining a productive and cohesive workplace.
- On-site crisis intervention pertaining to an abnormal, dramatic event in the workplace.
- Referral databases that assist family members in the areas of health promotion.
- Services for dependent or elder family members.
- Information regarding their children going off to college.

EAPs have become a deeply valued added human resource partner, integral to the success of any organization and management team, and have proven to be a trusted consultant and coach to all in the American business marketplace.

SECTION 3

Other Core Benefits

Section 125 (Cafeteria) Plans were named for Section 125 of the Revenue Act of 1978.

- Premium-only plans allow employees to pay their premiums for healthcare, dental care, life insurance, and disability coverage with pretax dollars.
- Flexible spending accounts allow employees to set aside money on a pretax basis to pay for dependent care or unreimbursed medical expenses. Money not used will be forfeited.
- Full cafeteria plans allow employees to choose from a menu of eligible qualified benefits, paying with benefit credits. Unused credits can often be cashed out.

Group-term life insurance provides benefits to dependents in the form a lump-sum payment to beneficiaries. The benefit may be a flat amount or a multiple of the employee's salary. The employer usually pays the premium.

- Supplemental insurance may be available for an additional premium usually paid by the employee.
- Excess group-term life insurance, any life insurance in excess of $50,000, is viewed as imputed income by the IRS when the premiums are paid by the employer, and the employee pays taxes on it based on a table provided by the IRS.

Paid leave provides employees paid time off for various situations. Employers should look at industry and geographic practices in determining their leave policies.

- Holiday pay is typically provided for between six and 12 holidays each year.
- Vacation pay can typically be an earned or accrued benefit. There are legal and financial considerations for carrying vacation days forward and a cap on how many days can be carried over can be set.
- Paid-time-off banks combine many forms of paid leave into one bank allowing employees to use the time as they see fit to handle illnesses, personal needs, vacation, and other matters.
- Bereavement leave is provided to attend funeral and other services for close relatives.

Income replacement generally takes the form of:

- Sick leave, which is provided for employees to use when they are ill or needed to care for sick family members.
- Short-term disability coverage, which allows employees to receive a percentage of their wages (50–70 percent) generally after a waiting period and for up to six months. It is required by law in California, Hawaii, New Jersey, New York, Rhode Island, and Puerto Rico, and in the railroad industry.
- Long-term disability coverage, which provides continued coverage to disabled employees when short-term disability ends and can last from two years until age 65.

Employers may also offer:

- Transportation assistance.
- Tuition reimbursement.
- Prepaid legal insurance plans.
- Childcare and eldercare services.

Retirement Plans

Deferred compensation provides employees with income at a future time for work performed now. In order to provide tax-deferred income in the present, the plans must be qualified or meet certain characteristics under the Employee Retirement Income Security Act (ERISA). These plans are attractive because they help with recruitment and retention of employees, provide retirement income for workers, and provide tax deferrals for all plan participants.

Qualified plans under ERISA must:

- Be in writing and be communicated to employees.
- Be established for the exclusive benefit of employees/beneficiaries.
- Satisfy rules concerning eligibility, vesting, and funding.
- Not favor officers, shareholders, or highly compensated employees.

There are two types of qualified retirement plans: defined benefit plans and defined contribution plans.

Defined Benefit Plans

In traditional defined benefit plans, the employer generally funds the plan (makes all the contributions) and bears the risk. There may be provisions for employee contributions in addition to the employer's contribution. The benefit amount received is based on a pre-determined formula.

> → Defined benefit plans are insured by the Pension Benefit Guaranty Corporation, discussed in Chapter 20 (The Legal Landscape of Employee Benefits).

Types of defined benefit plans include:

- **Flat dollar formula**, which pays a set dollar amount for each year of service.
- **Career-average formula**, which bases the benefit on the average earnings during employment with the organization.
- **Final-pay formula**, which bases the benefit on the average earnings during a specified number of years, such as the last five years or the three highest-paid consecutive years.
- **Cash-balance plan**, which defines the benefit by using a hypothetical account which receives a pay credit based on a set rate, such as five percent of salary, and earned interest. The accounts are portable meaning employees may take it with them if they leave. At retirement, employees receive either a lifetime annuity or a lump sum.

Defined Contribution Plans

Defined contribution plans rely on contributions from the employees and employers into individual retirement accounts. Benefits are determined by fund performance.

Organizations may also offer nonqualified (or excessive) deferred plans to provide additional benefits to key executives. They do not receive favorable tax treatment under ERISA, nor are they protected by the PBGC. Employees can defer reporting income and the plans are not subject to the limits placed on qualified plans. Employer contributions are not deductible.

Types of defined contribution plans include:

- **Profit sharing**, in which employers make contributions from the company's profits.

- **Money purchase**, in which the employer makes a contribution based on a fixed percentage of eligible employees compensation, whether or not the company made a profit.
- **Employee Stock Ownership Plans (ESOPs)**, in which the employer makes contributions of cash or stock to a tax-deductible trust in the employees' names.
- **401(k) plans**, in which employees can make a tax-deferred contribution up to the limits established by the Economic Growth and Tax Relief Reconciliation Act (EGTRRA). Employers may make contributions as well, the limit of which is the same for profit sharing plans. 401(k) plans were established by the Revenue Act of 1978.

Other Tax-Deferred Retirement Plans

- **Individual Retirement Accounts (IRAs)**, to which yearly contributions can be made. They may or may not be taxable, depending on whether the employee is covered by a retirement plan.
- **Roth IRAs**, which provide tax-free income growth. Contributions are not tax-deferred.
- **Simplified employee pension** for self-employed individuals and very small businesses.
- **Savings Incentive Match Plan for Employees (SIMPLE)**, generally for small businesses. They can be 401(k) plans or IRAs.
- **403(b)** for tax exempt organizations.
- **457 plans** for employees of states and certain tax-exempt electrical cooperatives.

Communicating Benefits Information

Practically, benefits are not valuable unless employees know about and use them. Ongoing communication helps in making choices that meet individual needs.

There are a number of ways to communicate with employees about their benefits, including:

- In-person group meetings.
- Benefits fairs.
- One-on-one meetings.
- Emails, conference calls, and webinars.
- Company intranet or website with internally prepared benefit material.
- Online interactive tools.
- 1-800 number to "Benefits Advisor."
- Communications personalized to the individual employee.
- Personalized total compensation statements.

> → Required communications regarding benefits are discussed in Chapter 20 (The Legal Landscape of Employee Benefits).

Most suppliers of healthcare and financial services offer online tools to help educate employees about how to best use their benefits. In addition, emerging tools such as blogs, videos, social media, and mobile access can be incorporated into a communication program. However, don't forget paperwork, which can be more effective than emails. By sending communications to an employee's home, family members also get the message. Using brief printed communications to direct the recipients to an online resource can get vital information to employees and their families while still lowering printing and mailing costs.

Discussion Questions

1. What is your organization doing to address benefit costs, especially healthcare? Are these strategies working?
2. What strategies can an organization use to promote greater employee participation in retirement plans?

Creative Benefits Communications

Comcast started using Jellyvision Benefits Counselor, an interactive on-line tool that walks an employee through the process of selecting medical benefits, during its annual enrollment period in 2009. It has since expanded its use to allow new hires to use the tool and active employees to review information, and has added modules for life, dental, and vision insurance. The tool is outside the firewall, making it accessible to employees and their family members.[3] Trustnode Inc., a startup in San Francisco, develops decision support tools based on animated stories to educate employees on benefits.[4]

---

3. What can organizations do to promote wellness for their employees?
4. What is your organization doing to communicate with its employees about benefits? Is it effective?
5. What are the advantages to outsourcing benefits administration? What experiences can you share? What lessons have you learned?

SECTION 4

EMPLOYEE DEVELOPMENT

22

Assessing Employee Development Needs

Needs assessment is a process for identifying what knowledge, skills, and abilities are needed to move your organization forward. It is a method for pinpointing reasons for gaps in performance and/or a method for identifying new and future performance requirements. Too many organizations skip this critical step and jump right into creating development programs. Without the assessment step, costly and time consuming mistakes can occur when organizations make assumptions about what their employees need.

Making assumptions about training needs without doing a needs assessment can totally derail a comprehensive employee development plan. For example, let's say you've finally been given a budget to do some employee development. You've been asking for it for years and finally made the case that employee development is an engagement and retention tool. You're excited to get started, so you call someone you met the previous week at a networking event and ask them to come in and do some training for your employees. The class is scheduled and either no one shows up, or people come and the evaluations are terrible and you're devastated!

What went wrong? Well, in your excitement to get started, you skipped the needs assessment phase. This is where you uncover what your workforce needs to enhance their skills. So, take the time to do it and the chances of having a successful employee development plan go up!

In Chapter 2, we discussed the importance of doing a workforce plan. If you've taken that step, you probably discovered that some of your employees don't have all the skills or abilities needed to move your organization to the next level. You can use the information from the gap analysis to set the agenda for your employee development programs; if you haven't already done the gap analysis, here are some other ways to conduct a needs assessment so that you can design a training and development program that will have maximum impact on your organization. Just a reminder: As with any data-gathering, be careful to calibrate expectations. If employees think that just because they suggest something to you, it will happen, you will have a lot of unhappy employees to deal with. Let them know you are talking with a lot of people and gathering as much data as possible before training plans are finalized, and that you sincerely appreciate their suggestions—no matter how far out they may be—but you can't promise that everything they asked for will be part of the final plan.

Needs Assessment Methods

Performance appraisals. Analyze the development recommendations made by managers during the appraisal process to gather information about what training and development programs are needed at this time. Using this method presumes that the managers in your organization who completed the appraisals have been honest in what they have identified as development needs. If your managers have been trained in how to evaluate development needs, using information collected in performance meetings can be one of your best ways of determining what training and/or development is needed at this time in your organization's lifecycle. If you find your managers themselves need training on how to determine what an employee needs to improve, you may have just discovered one of the first training sessions you need to have in your management training curriculum.

Employee or managerial interviews. For example, if your organization has a call center and you want to know what development needs exist, interview a percentage of the employees in the call center. Interviews are one of the easiest ways to collect the information you require. Sometimes, even a brief discussion with employees will point you in the right direction, and then you might want to have a more in-depth discussion with their supervisor or manager to confirm your assumptions. If you need to get more information, consider a formal interview process, conducting either in-person or phone interviews. Develop your questions in advance and summarize your interviews immediately after the event so that you don't miss anything. Look for trends as you gather data. For example, if you hear from several employees that they'd really like to improve their business writing skills and you confirm that with their managers, you can be sure that the employees and the organization will benefit from a program on business writing.

Focus groups. This is another effective way to gather data. Bring together a group of people who share similar expertise, and ask their opinions and ideas about a specific topic. The size of the group should be no less than five or six people, and no more than 12. Focus group facilitation requires preparation and a trained facilitator. Facilitators need to remain objective and nonjudgmental, and be able to encourage everyone to participate. In addition to the facilitator, have a note-taker so that the facilitator can focus his or her attention on asking the questions.

Surveys and questionnaires. Developing good surveys is not easy, but a well-crafted questionnaire can provide valuable data for you in order to determine your training and development requirements. Before you put a survey together, consider these questions:

- Will you be asking closed questions where responses can be easily tabulated or open-ended questions where participants record their own thoughts?
- How will the data be analyzed?
- Can you use an online survey provider, such as Survey Monkey?

Developing questions for interviews, focus groups, or surveys is critical to the needs assessment process. You want to ensure that your questions are easily understood and not misinterpreted, which might result in inaccurate data. Carefully review your questions and the order in which you ask them, and be sure not to ask questions that require two answers (for example, "Why do you do send the ABC summary on Tuesday and what is it used for?"). We strongly recommend that, if you are putting your own survey together, you do a test before sending it to the target audience.

Observation. Watching people actually doing work or listening in on phone calls can be an effective way to gather data, but be sure that the employees are notified ahead of time as to what you are doing and why. Otherwise, you may do more harm than good by creating anxiety and unrest.

Once you've completed the needs assessment, the next step is to come up methods to develop the skills and abilities of your employees.

    ➔   See Chapter 23 (Best Approaches to Developing Employees) for employee development options.

Tips for Preparing and Implementing Surveys and Questionnaires [1]

1. Familiarize yourself with the background situation. Speak with appropriate sources to determine and clarify jargon or technical terms.
2. Define the goal.
3. Determine whether questions from previously developed surveys can be used in their entirety or in part.
4. Determine whether any commercial surveys or questionnaires can be customized.
5. Determine whether confidentiality will be maintained.
6. Determine how results will be analyzed.
7. Consult with an in-house technical specialist if an electronic survey will be used or if computerized analysis will be performed. Determine if outsourcing will be necessary.
8. Decide whether color schemes should be used.
9. Decide how the results will be presented.
10. Ensure that each question has a purpose.
11. Determine which type of question (closed or open-ended) will elicit the best response. Maintain simplicity if the survey will be sent to a large number of people.
12. Arrange questions in a logical sequence from general to specific.
13. Ensure that each question asks for only one piece of information.
14. Avoid leading and biased questions.
15. Avoid negatively phrased questions.
16. Avoid personal or identifying questions.
17. Ask questions that the respondents are qualified to answer.
18. Avoid jargon, abbreviations, or colloquialisms.
19. Use gender-neutral terms.
20. Write questions that are clear and concise.
21. Position difficult or sensitive questions at the end.
22. Number questions.
23. Provide space for comments.
24. Limit the use of commas.
25. Use boldface or italic type and underline, when appropriate.
26. Use plenty of white space.
27. Number pages.
28. Write instructions on how to answer questions.

SECTION 4

29. Explain complicated or confusing terms.
30. Write a cover letter.

    a. State the purpose of the survey.
    b. Provide a history of the previous research or findings, if appropriate.
    c. Show the benefit to the user.
    d. Explain why the respondent was selected.
    e. State when and how the form should be returned.
    f. Thank the respondent for completing the survey.

31. Pilot test the questionnaire or instrument after it has been developed.
32. Make appropriate modifications based on the results of the pilot test.
33. Conduct a second pilot, if necessary.
34. Make final modifications.
35. If a paper survey, use quality paper.

Discussion Questions

1. How can you use data from performance appraisals to determine employee development needs?
2. How can you use employee interviews to determine employee development needs?
3. How can you use focus groups to determine employee development needs?
4. How can you use surveys to determine employee development needs?
5. How can you use observation to determine employee development needs?
6. Name three to four things to keep in mind when preparing a survey or questionnaire.

SECTION 4

23

Best Approaches to Developing Employees

Warren Bennis, organizational consultant and author said, "You need people who can walk their companies into the future rather than back them into the future."[1] This highlights the need for making a real effort to be constantly providing opportunities for employees to learn and grow. Otherwise, organizations won't be positioned for growth and will not produce the value required to succeed in today's increasingly competitive marketplace—whether it is to add value for shareholders or for members.

Not only is employee development critical for organizational growth, it is even more crucial for attracting, engaging, and retaining the talent your organization has or wants to hire!

If you did a needs assessment as outlined in Chapter 22 of this book, you know what new skills and abilities your current and/or future employees need to develop their talents and abilities, it is time to put a plan into place to address what is needed. Before you consider the next step, consider that, whatever you decide to do, it is critical that any training, development, or organizational development process or initiative have support from the top of the organization. Any program that doesn't have top management understanding and commitment will be severely limited in the basic change it can effect. In fact, every level of the organization should be committed to employee development, and HR plays a key role in this by providing expertise and resources, and sponsoring and supporting all training events. That being said, it is also critical that employees know they are responsible for their own development. Certainly, the organization can help them by providing opportunities to learn and grow, but they must constantly be striving to improve their own skill set.

All employee development programs must be linked to your organization's strategic plan and your workforce plan so that the end result of any employee development is to move the organization closer to its stated goals and objectives. Any training program should be integrated with a comprehensive development program to reinforce the organizational culture. The responsibilities for an effective employee development program are shared by the organization's top level of management, HR, the organizational development (OD) function (if applicable), the employee's manager, and the employee, with the greatest responsibility on the employee to take advantage of what is available within the context of his or her job.

Employees need to recognize that it is essential for them to continue to learn so that they will be effective in their current jobs and able to move into other positions as their skills increase. Career development supports continuous learning. Remember: Do not ever make any promises in this process. For example, never say, "If you take this class, you will be promoted." All discussions should be around skill-set improvement—not how to get a promotion!

Sometimes there is confusion about some of the terms used. For example, what is training and what is OD? Training usually refers to instruction provided for a current position and has a relatively narrow focus, whereas organization development usually is broader in scope and may or may not be focused on the employee's current position; however, it may be necessary for organizational success.

And what is organizational development? OD focuses on the overall improvement of an organization—its policies, procedures, structure, and culture. OD has a large component of change management to it: How and why does the organization need to change to move forward, and what will be the impact of those changes on the employees and the culture? These are the types of issues tackled by OD experts.

Once you've collected information (by completing a needs assessment, from the performance appraisal process, individual development plans (IDPs), or other sources) about what your employee development needs are, what options do you have to provide development opportunities for your employees? The possibilities include:

- Training.
- Coaching.

    → See Chapter 24 (Coaching as an Employee Development Strategy).

- Mentoring.
- On-the-job training.
- Job rotation.

Training

If you decide training is the way to go, be sure you develop objectives that tie to the strategic goals of your organization. It is important to note that training doesn't miraculously lead to results. Managers play a critical role in making sure investments in learning and development pay off.

It used to be so simple. If you wanted to train employees, you put together an instructor-led class, and many training and development experts feel that the classroom is still the best way to deliver training. When we gather people into a classroom to learn together, to collaborate on new ideas, to problem-solve, or to help each other—the classroom becomes a place to practice what it takes to succeed at work. But now, there are so many other ways to deliver training:

- **In-house programs conducted in a classroom setting.** This type of training can be costly and labor-intensive. The program has to be developed. The participants need to be scheduled. You need a space and equipment, and it is harder and harder to get managers to allow their employees to take time from the busy workday to attend training programs. On the plus side, this type of training has some real benefits, as employees learn not only from the instructor but from each other, and they get the opportunity to meet and interact with coworkers from other departments. Also, any in-house training program is by definition, specific to your organization; therefore, case studies and examples can be taken right from the workplace with no fear of confidentiality issues. If you decide in-house training is the way to go to provide development opportunities for your employees, the next decision is whether to use your own staff to deliver the programs or to bring in outside resources.

Instructor-led training has greatly diminished as employers realize that employees want more control over their own development. They want to learn on their own and when they want to learn—not when you want to schedule a class.

◆ **Public workshops/seminars** (you send a person or group) are readily available and can be cost-effective. Keep in mind the content will be generic and your employees will lose the specificity of in-house training. On the plus side, professional trainers will present the material and the content is typically well prepared. Another benefit is your employees will be able to expand their professional network with other participants.

◆ **Online training**, or **e-learning**, is a popular and effective way to provide training experiences for your employees depending on your workforce. In today's world, few people aren't computer-literate, but don't go down this path without considering whether this is totally true of your employees. You can develop your own training programs, video them, and put them on your intranet for employees to watch when they have time. You can buy programs from reputable vendors to put on your intranet or to be housed on the vendor's server and accessed with a password assigned by your company. There are many platforms available for creating and hosting live meetings, webinars, and distance learning. This way they participate along with others around the country or world, and have an opportunity to ask questions and get answers online. Technology advances appear almost daily in the training and development world. You just have to decide what will work best for your employees and your budget. Just like you would for any solution, do your research, ask your network for recommendations, and try out what's available before signing any contracts.

Consider making any training program you offer available on any mobile device. This is extremely important for today's worker who wants to access development opportunities when and how he or she wants. Providing training in a way that is easy to access should increase participation and help your organization attract, engage, and retain your talent.

◆ **Massive Open Online Courses (MOOCs)** are online courses for an unlimited number of people and provide open access to the courses on the web. Many MOOCs are produced by major colleges and universities; others are conducted by nonprofits, including the American Council on Education and the Bill and Melinda Gates Foundation, and still others by major providers such as Coursera. Some are free to the participant whereas others are fee-based. The value of MOOCs is that the learner has access to world-class information that might not be otherwise available.

◆ Universities and colleges offer **development programs** that can either be brought in-house to your organization or you can send your employees to a public offering. These programs tend to be more effective for management-level staff. One of the benefits of sending your employees to these programs is the networking opportunities they present. If your organization has an educational assistance program where employees can take classes or training at local universities or colleges, you will want to develop a policy that outlines what classes are accepted and what the payment limit is. You also will need to determine whether you want to tie the payment to a grade received in the class and whether you will reimburse employees for degree programs. You also should have an approval process whereby the employee gets the class approved prior to taking it, and many organizations have clauses that require repaying the tuition if the employee leaves the organization within a certain time.

➙   Appendix: Sample Tuition Reimbursement Request Form.

◆ Some organizations have started their own training facilities, commonly called a **corporate university**, to provide training and development opportunities to their own employees. This is not an easy process, and it takes resources to pull it off, but it can be rewarding. What differentiates a corporate university from a traditional training program? Training departments tend to deliver training in a fragmented, decentralized way, and often it is in reaction to something (needs identified on performance reviews, for example). Training departments offer open enrollment courses with people participating as needed.

Corporate universities pull together all learning in a managed way by seeing employee education as a business initiative. Corporate universities have clear goals and strategic plans, and are typically proactive with activities linked to business goals.

➙   For additional information on starting a corporate university, see
            www.corpu.com.

The Motley Fool has a corporate university. According to Tom Gardner, CEO, "The highest priority is to develop people."[2] He founded the company and teaches in the university. He says that their training costs have not gone up and that all their senior executives teach something. Motley Fool started the university as an investment in their employees after an employee survey showed that employees felt the company didn't give them opportunities for growth.

Motley Fool shared some tips for organizations that might be considering using the corporate university model[3]:

▷ Focus on high-potential employees.
▷ Give them real-world problems.
▷ Use your own employees to teach classes.
▷ Must have top management support.
▷ Think of it not as training but as lifelong learning.

According to James Bailey, Ave Tucker Professorial Fellow of Leadership and director of executive development programs in the department of management of the George Washington University, as reported in the *Washington Business Journal,* "It's [corporate universities] is not that new of a phenomenon…back in the 1950s, IBM was among the first organizations to put a university concept in place."[4] He said that putting a corporate university together "is a struggle between doing something in-house versus outsourcing. The problem with doing it internally is, if it isn't a core competency [of your firm], you're not going to do it well."[5]

SECTION 4

Developing an In-House Training Program

If you decide to go the route of developing your own training programs, here are some tips:

- Start with something you can handle. Don't expect to have a full-blown university style program in year one.
- Find subject matter experts in your organization who will be willing to train others on what they do best.
- Provide everyone who will be a presenter with a course in presentation skills.
- Make training mandatory.
- Find a champion in the organization that will help sell the program.
- Bring in a leader to kick off each program to set the tone that training is important here.
- Exchange presenters with organizations in your network. That way, your employees get to hear from someone from the outside without you investing a lot of money.
- Consider putting a certificate program together whereby if an employee takes a certain number of your in-house programs, they receive a framed certificate of achievement.

Adult Learners

As adult learners advance through the cycles of life, learning becomes self-initiated, self-directed, and self-motivated. One way to encourage employees to learn and grow is to use something called individual development plans that detail the employee's specific intentions around learning and outcomes. They also lay out the support to be provided by the manager and the organization.

Other training methods that work well with adults include role-plays and case studies. It is important to know your employees well enough to determine what to include in the training process to maximize their ability to learn and grow. In the past, employees depended on their employer to provide necessary training in the form of subject matter knowledge, using predefined, fixed methods of training. In today's workplace, employees learn and grow through their experiences, and it is the employees' responsibility to seek out learning experiences to add to their skill set.

SECTION 4

Mentoring

"My mentor gave me confidence in my first teaching job for a class of special needs students. He provided technical assistance through lesson plans and management techniques, emotional support by validating what I already knew and he acknowledged my fears and anxieties without letting me wallow in them. He used humor to diffuse tension. All that and more in just one week—I don't know what I would have done without him."

—from a first-year teacher in Prince William County Schools, Virginia

Mentoring is a no- or low-cost development process that can pay huge dividends for the individual and the organization. Mentoring can be an asset in the hiring process; it helps the prospective employee see that the organization will invest in his or her future development, and it can be a retention tool as well, because it can help a new hire quickly assimilate into the organization. The mentoring process creates cross-organizational connections and builds channels of communication—often between people who might not have worked together other than through a mentoring relationship.

When designing a mentor program, take these things into consideration:

- Goals—must link to the organization's strategic goals or a specific development goal.
- Leadership support—must have resources to support the program.
- Customization to organizational strategy and culture.
- Have clear definitions and criteria for success.
- Include guidelines, structure, and chain of command.
- Provide training for mentors—provide resources for them to use when mentoring.
- Include an evaluation process—how to know whether goals are met.

Mentoring programs can be formal or informal; each has its value. Informal mentoring happens all the time without a lot of effort on the part of the leadership and can last for as long as needed. Social networking tools, such as LinkedIn, can facilitate informal mentoring relationships outside the organization. Formal programs usually involve a highly developed selection process where mentors apply, are evaluated, and then are carefully matched with people who want or require a mentor.

Some of the most powerful mentor relationships occur when an employee is mentored by someone outside his or her current department. For example, an HR manager may decide to seek a mentor in the finance department to expand his or her knowledge of that function and explore the linkages between HR and finance.

A broad definition of a mentor is anyone who has knowledge or experience the other person doesn't have. Mentors don't have to be high up in the organization, so don't overlook anyone in your organization as a potential mentor. For example, ask a Millennial to mentor Baby Boomers in maximizing use of technology. Mentors can provide information or knowledge that isn't found in any book or other resource. If you use mentoring, be sure to do mentor training and, if possible, have coaches for mentors so that they have someone to go to for information they need to help their mentee.

10 Potential Gains for the Organization (That Provides Mentoring)[6]

1. The existence of a broad-based mentoring program strengthens the organization's image as being a caring, sharing, and helping community of employees.
2. Mentoring offers a completive edge in recruiting efforts, particularly in times and areas of labor shortages.
3. Mentors can facilitate, strengthen, and often shorten the new employee's induction and orientation process.
4. Mentoring supplements traditional and special employee training by helping trainees quickly apply their learning and develop mastery of a subject.
5. Research strongly indicates that a quality mentoring program significantly improves employee retention rates.
6. A community of mentors in an organization creates a more open, cooperative, and receptive environment for fresh ideas, and for the quick and easy exchange of important information.
7. A mentor's help often improves a new employee's personal productivity, internal motivation, and sense of responsibility for results.
8. Mentoring can be used to build a more inclusive, equitable, and democratic work environment.
9. Well-trained mentors learn to avoid many of the common negative and unproductive personal reasoning practices and behaviors such as "group think," rationalizing questionable proposals, or unfairly discounting the legitimate needs of other individuals or groups.
10. A productive mentoring network in an organization improves the entity's quickness of response, adaptability to change, and the broad sharing of new and emerging opportunities.

SECTION 4

On-the-Job Training (OJT)

OJT is how many people learn new skills or take their abilities to a new level. However, there is some risk in putting people into jobs for which they aren't fully trained. Before you take this route, consider the impact on others in the organization, as well as the amount of time a manager or lead person in the organization will need to devote to providing oversight to the employee being trained. OJT should be combined with other forms of development, including training, mentoring, and coaching, to allow the person to learn as quickly as possible.

Job Rotation

When you've identified a skill or development need, consider where else in the organization the person could improve that particular skill. Is there a manager who is particularly good at this and could the employee be assigned there for a period of time to gain valuable experience? Job rotation requires collaboration and cooperation among departments, but can be highly effective and is certainly cost-effective.

Management Role in Employee Development

Lack of managerial involvement is the most common reason that employee development initiatives fail to produce improved performance. Training can't work miracles, and rarely alone does it improve performance. Managers need to follow up after training to ensure that learning is reinforced. Developing people is one of the greatest joys of managing others. It is a wonderful experience to help move a good employee to another level of performance. Being known as a manager who develops people will greatly enhance your reputation and will encourage others to want to work in your department.

Managers can provide direction and create learning opportunities, but remember that it is still up to the employee to learn and grow. Managers also help to set goals and can assist employees in recognizing areas in which their skills are lacking. Managers can provide valuable insight into opportunities for growth and development, can serve as mentors, and can offer employees cross-training experiences to build skill sets.

Some managers hesitate to provide growth opportunities for talented staffers because they fear they will lose them to another position or department. It must be noted that this is a strategy that almost always backfires. A talented employee who is not offered development opportunities will find ways to get them—even at the risk of leaving your company—so it is always smarter to actively participate in the development of your team.

Evaluating Employee Development

"The true impact of a training program will be best predicted by the work environment participants return to after the event. More specifically, this refers to the type of leader they work with and report to after their respective training."[7] Before you start any development initiative, consider how you will measure results. Every training class should include an evaluation to measure what the participants learned and to help you evaluate the effectiveness of particular trainers. At a minimum, do a yearly summary of training effectiveness prior to planning your next year's development schedule. Don't get caught up in a numbers game of how many people attended classes; you want to know what the impact was on the people who participated. You can also follow up any development opportunity with a quick, online survey asking a few questions to gather data about what the participants learned. You can use on-line surveys such as Survey Monkey in a very cost-effective way to gather this data.

→   Appendix: Sample Training Evaluation Form.

Bottom line: The real measure of employee development effectiveness is the success and growth of the organization!

Training and development cost money and time. In today's fast-paced business climate, sometimes time is even more difficult to come by than money, as managers don't want to allow their employees to take time away from their assigned tasks to attend training, or meet with a mentor, or whatever. Organizations constantly ask themselves how much training is worthwhile. Before you embark on a needs assessment, we highly recommend you investigate what resources you will have so that expectations aren't set too high. Some organizations set their training budget as a percentage of their overall budget (for example, allocating 1 percent of revenue to employee development), whereas other organizations set their budget based on what they think that particular year's budget will allow. It is sad to see that training and development budgets are usually one of the first line items to be cut when budgets are tight—especially because Millennials and I-Gen are looking for more and more development to increase their skill sets. This is a trend organizations can't afford to ignore if they want to attract and retain younger workers to balance out the aging workforce.

It is possible to train and develop with minimal cost impact to the organization by using resources you already have on hand. For example, consider videotaping a lecture by your CEO on leadership and using that at a "lunch and learn," where employees bring their lunch and spend their lunch hour watching the DVD. A member of the HR or training department could facilitate the session, take questions back to the CEO, and distribute the responses via email. This is a no-cost way to get information out to employees.

Consider using subject matter experts from your organization to share their knowledge with others in your firm. Asking a subject matter expert (SME) can provide a real morale boost for that person and also help his/her own professional development. Also consider "borrowing" SMEs you admire from companies in your area. We are not suggesting you call your competitors to ask for their marketing manager to come to talk to your sales department, but what about asking someone from a successful company in your town in a totally different field from your firm? You could reciprocate by sending one of your superstars to speak at their company someday. This is a highly effective way to expose your employees to new ideas with minimal cost impact—and also may increase your firm's standing in the community.

Discussion Questions

1. Discuss the difference between training and development.
2. What are some low- or no-cost ways to develop employees?
3. Why is it important to have top management support for training and development?
4. What are some cost-effective training methods?
5. When might job rotation be an effective training tool?
6. Name three to four ways mentoring can impact an organization.

24

Coaching as an
Employee Development Strategy

BY JENNIFER WHITCOMB

In the past, organizations engaged executive coaches to help fix undesirable behavior. Today, coaching is seen in a more positive light and is more about creating an opportunity to develop and enhance the performance of high potentials. In some organizations coaching is so highly valued and perceived as a perk that executives feel they are missing out if they are not given the chance to work with an executive coach.

The International Coach Federation (ICF) defines coaching as partnering with clients in a thought-provoking and creative process that inspires them to maximize their personal and professional potential.

Coaching can be considered a just-in-time, immediate activity to enhance leadership skills. The coaching process is flexible and can take place face-to-face, over the phone, or via Skype. Coaching is tailored to the individual's needs and goals with identified success factors. Coaching is more than a meaningful conversation; it's about working toward the desired results with the client. Coaching is ideally adapted to the client's learning style preferences. The client learns "how to learn"; this is what Chris Argyris from Harvard Business School refers to as "double loop learning."[1] The client not only learns about the challenge he or she is facing, but also learns about his or her underlying assessments, values, and beliefs that he or she holds around the challenge—thereby deepening the learning and potentially replicating the results.

The metaphor for coaching can be described as "polishing the diamond"—someone who has excellent skills in some areas, yet needs support to achieve goals in other areas. For example, a leader can demonstrate exemplary business development skills yet need support to better manage internal relationships or navigate the political landscape.

The Role of HR in Coaching

Ideally, coaching is part of a larger leadership development initiative and is tied to the organization's overall goals and leadership competency model. Human resources often takes the lead in the process from identifying the high potentials and, when needed, assigning a coach. It is sometimes best to avoid coaching requests that are designed to "fix it." Another activity or intervention might be better suited to solve the situation, unless the person is a senior leader in a critical role.

It might be helpful to create an intake and/or agreement form for coaching. Human resources can be involved in the process of creating the internal coaching agreement, which can include the parameters of the coaching relationship. This form can include coaching goals and measures of success, number of coaching hours, length of coaching engagement, and cancellation policy.

Human resources will often have a cadre of coaches from which a client can select. Two to three coaches may be contacted to see if they are available to take on an assignment, be informed about the potential client, and agree to be interviewed.

The coaching relationship between coach and client is considered highly confidential. Once the human resources professional has engaged the coach, then he or she should avoid talking with coach about the content of the coaching conversations. To find out how the client is doing, talk directly with the client periodically, or his or her manager. You may need to talk with the coach independently if the client misses appointments or there is a change in the contract.

Typically, the coach will set up a three-way conversation with the client and client's manager at the beginning, mid-point, and end of the engagement. At the beginning, it is to determine if the client and coach are in alignment with the goals of the manager, and to ask the manager to support and provide feedback on the coaching goals.

Reasons for Using an Executive or Leadership Coach

- When a high potential leader is identified and an assessment determines that coaching is a good fit.
- When the organization wants to support the development of an executive and this is in support of leadership and organizational goals.
- To provide support to successfully transition a leader to a new organization or role.
- To sharpen the skills of leaders who have been identified as a high-potential and future leader.
- To support top producers.
- After a person has been promoted, to help him or her acclimate successfully to the new position.
- When a leader wants to increase his or her effectiveness with his/her team and stakeholders.
- When a leader needs to improve his/her communication strategy to effectively reach his or her audience.
- When a leader wants to capitalize on his or her strengths.
- When a leader gets derailed by a slippage in work performance.
- When a leader needs to improve communication style or work relationships or manage the political environment.
- As a confidant to senior leaders to help him/her make better decisions with challenging issues.
- To resolve tension between leaders. (A coach can mediate and help create partnership.)
- To support a larger leadership development initiative.

Is the Client Coachable?

Ideally, the person to be coached shows interest and welcomes the opportunity to be coached. He or she should see coaching as a positive development experience, and be open to growth and learning.

The manager is also an integral part of the process by providing the time needed for the coaching engagement and providing feedback to the client on how he or she is achieving his or her goals.

Choosing a Coach

Experience. Find out how long the coach has been working in the field and the level of client that he or she has coached to. What other relevant experience does he or she have? Does he or she have experience in your industry? Or, has the coach been in a leadership role himself or herself?

Results. Ask for examples of the results that the coach has achieved when working with clients. What outcomes have resulted from his or her work, and how have the client achieved their goals?

Coach training. What kind of coach training does the coach have? Ideally, the coach has attended a training program from an accredited school with at least 100 hours of coach training. How long was the training program and when did the coach graduate from the program? What other development has he or she done since completing the initial coach training?

Philosophy and approach. What is the coach's philosophy to coaching? What is his or her coaching process? A solid coach process includes some form of assessment (either confidential interviews of peers and manager, or formal assessment), providing feedback, development of goals, and designing activities and practices to support the achievement of the goals. These goals may be documented on an individual development plan that sometimes is submitted to human resources.

Qualification/certification. What qualifications does he or she have as a coach? Credentials from the International Coach Federation range from an Associate Certified Coach (ACC) with minimum of 100 coaching hours, to a Professional Certified Coach (PCC) with 500 hours of coaching and a Master Certified Coach (MCC) with 2,500 hours of coaching. Coaches also can be certified from the coaching school they attended.

A Typical Engagement

Most coaching engagements are between three and six months. If the engagement is less than three months, then it may be unlikely that the results will be achieved. It can often take up to six months for behavior change to occur. Coaches often meet on average with clients twice a month for an hour to an hour and a half, either face-to-face or over the phone. These arrangements can all be tailored to what's best for the client.

The process often looks like this:

Initial meeting. Once the coach has been selected, an initial meeting can take place with the client. In this meeting the client and coach discuss how they will work together, the coaching philosophy and process, goals and desired results, and logistics.

Assessment. The coach can be provided with assessment results from Myers-Briggs Type Indicator, 360 assessment results, or any other recent assessments. The coach also may choose to do confidential interviews of various stakeholders, including the manager, direct reports, and peers. Gathering feedback on the client provides the coach with others' perspective on the person, and helps with the development of the coaching goals.

SECTION 4

Feedback. Once the information has been collected from interviews and/or assessment, the coach presents the feedback, highlighting a few themes that became apparent. During this discussion, the client and coach select which areas to work on.

Goal development. Goals are developed from feedback results and from conversations with the client and manager. These goals can be formed into an individual development plan or goal worksheet. The measures of success with the desired results are included.

The coach and client begin regular meetings, working toward the goals. The client chooses the agenda for the meeting, and the client and coach determine a successful outcome for the meeting. The coach works with the client asking questions, providing observations, facilitating activities, and developing new practices in support of the goals and outcomes. The coach rarely provides advice, as often the coaching process sees the client as being resourceful, creative, and whole. The coach guides the client, versus directing the client.

Some Tips to Consider When Engaging a Coach

Before	Determine the success factors and goals for the coaching engagement by asking the potential client and his or her manager. What results are expected from the completion of the coaching engagement?
	Provide several coaches for the leader to choose from and provide their biographies. Encourage the leader to interview coaches to determine a good fit for him/her.
	Develop a pool of coaches to select from. Each coach should hold a coaching credential from the International Coach Federation (ACC—Associated Credentialed Coach, PCC—Professional Certified Coach, MCC—Master Certified Coach). Interview these coaches yourself to determine their fit to the organization, organizational level experience, and industry level experience.
	Determine the coachability of the leader. How willing is this person to learn or make changes? How open is he or she to the process?
	Describe coaching as an investment and a positive opportunity for growth. Also explain that this is a confidential relationship between the coach and client. As an HR professional you might check in with the client periodically to see how it's going, if the client feels that he or she is getting the results he or she needs, etc.
	Refer to the organization's core competencies.
	Emphasize the value of the executive and that coaching is to help support him or her.
	Provide different coaches when there is a potential conflict of interest such as reporting relationship. For example, retain a separate coach for the direct report and the manager.
	Avoid promising results from completing the coaching engagement such as promotion or another assignment.
	Create an intake form with the request for coaching and length of the engagement.
During	Check in with coaching client to see how it's going after the engagement has started, midway, and at the end.
	Check in with the manager to get a sense of how the client is progressing.
After	Check back with the client to determine if he or she has achieved the results desired and to receive feedback about the coach.
	If the coach has not touched base with you at the end, you may want to close out the business side of the coaching relationship.

Coaching can be a valuable resource and benefit to the individual client and the organization. If the client is open to the process and the organization positively supports this form of leadership development, it can generate sustainable results.

Discussion Questions

1. How is coaching used effectively in today's organizations? How does this compare to how coaching was used in the past?
2. What role (s) does HR play in the coaching process?
3. Name three or four reasons for engaging a coach.
4. How can you determine if a client is "coachable"?
5. What should you look for when selecting a coach?
6. Describe a typical coaching engagement. How does it start? What are some of the steps taken in the coaching process?

About the Chapter Author

Jennifer Whitcomb is a Master Certified Coach (MCC) and Principal of the Trillium Group, a San Diego–based firm that provides executive coaching, leadership development, and mentor coaching. She is a faculty member of the Georgetown University's Leadership Coaching Program.

25

Performance Management

Michelangelo is often quoted as having said that inside every block of stone is a beautiful statue. One need only remove the excess material to reveal the work of art. Applying the concept to education (or performance management), it would be pointless to make comparisons among children (or employees). Rather, the energy would be on chipping away at the stone to remove whatever was in the way of mastery. Give everyone an A—a possibility to live into and not an expectation to live up to.[1]

The purpose of any performance management system should be to ensure that individual employees and the organization are producing their best: their best work, their best products or services. Managing performance for each individual employee is a process that starts with having a clear and documented description of the job's roles and responsibilities. On the first day of employment, managers should set the framework for success, explaining job duties, expectations, and job-related behaviors. Employees should receive a copy of the job description. Goals and objectives should be discussed. Finally, employees should be briefed on company culture so they can gain an understanding of what success looks like in the new organization.

Acclimating New Employees

Pixar Animation Studios spends a good amount of time when new employees begin working there. Pixar stresses that new employees are not expected to demonstrate their worth right away; they were picked because Pixar knows they are great. Pixar wants its employees to be part of its community and company. The company stresses that employees' initial time should be spent observing and absorbing everything around them—to take time to know how the company works. This gives them a chance to see others receive feedback and realize that work only gets better because of it.[2]

Performance management requires continual attention to each employee, monitoring and evaluating his or her performance against the job's requirements and standards for success. This includes noting and acknowledging all incidents throughout the year, both positive and negative, and addressing situations that need adjustment or improvement when they occur. This ongoing approach assures that performance management is a process, not an event.

Performance management is under scrutiny and performance appraisals, which have traditionally been an integral part of performance management systems, are being carefully studied and reconsidered. Some organizations are abandoning them in favor of more flexible approaches. Understanding the traditional approach helps explain the emerging trends and future direction of performance management

Appraisals and Traditional Approach

There are varying methods of performance appraisals. Many of these methods have existed for a long time and were developed during the industrial era. Whichever method an organization may use, it should ensure that it aligns with its mission, values, and strategic objectives. These methods include:

- **Category Rating Methods** include different types. The most common and frequently used is a *graphic scale*, which rates the employee for each performance factor and for overall performance. Two other types of category ratings are the *checklist* with words or statements best describing the employee's performance that can be weighted for quantifiable results, and *forced choice* with statements that best/least describes the employee's characteristics and performance.

- **Comparative Methods** compare employee performance against others. Whereas these may be useful for some types of decisions, such as when organizations are faced with reductions in force, companies are abandoning these methods. There are three types of comparative methods: *ranking*, which lists employees in a work group from highest to lowest without considering the degree of difference between each; *paired comparisons*, which pairs and compares each employee with every other peer, one at a time, using the same scale for performance; and *force distribution*, in which a manager must place a certain percentage of employees into each of several categories based on overall performance without considering the degree of differences.

- **Narrative Methods** are particularly time consuming for use on an ongoing basis. There are two types of narratives. The first is *essays*, which reviews personal, job, or organization characteristics relative to the employee's behavior and contributions. The second is *critical incident*, which describes behavior that makes a difference in the success or failure of a work situation. Incidents must be recorded as soon as possible after events. Documenting such incidents has value for any organization regardless of the method of performance appraisal in use.

- **Special Methods** include *behaviorally anchored rating scales*, which are numerical scales anchored by specific narrative examples of behavior that rate an employee's performance of a specific task and *management by objectives*, which allows employees and managers to set objectives for the coming year.

A performance appraisal instrument or form has been an established part of the overall performance management process. Indeed, there are many sample performance appraisals forms to which organizations can refer when developing their own instrument. Review several examples and gather ideas, but be wary of defaulting to just one of these samples. If you wish to use such an instrument, design one that is right for your organization.

Typically, a performance appraisal form will list a number of performance factors. These factors have to make sense for your organization otherwise they have no relevance. If you are measuring something, make sure it reflects the needs of your organization. The number of factors used should be reasonable for the organization's size and culture, somewhere between five and 10. The factors should also be defined.

> ➜ Appendix: Sample Performance Factors.

The aspect of performance appraisals most recently being debated is the rating system; for example, the graphic scale type of category rating method described above. If this approach is taken, an organization should ensure that the factors it has chosen are quantifiable. For instance, factors related to quality, output, or safety are objective and can be quantified. A factor such as strategic or independent thinking is subjective and may say more about the rater than it says about the employee being evaluated. If a rating scale is used, the organization must decide which rating style best suits its needs and how it will define each of the ratings. For example:

Rating Style	Advantages	Disadvantages
Three Ratings: Exceeds Expectations, Meets Expectations, Below Expectations	Simple, consistent, pass/fail	Too black and white, no judgment, no variation
Four Ratings: Exceeds Expectations, Meets Expectations, Below Expectations, Does Not Meet	No middle, forces decision, rewards the positive	Reduces judgment, skew to higher level, no average
Five Ratings: Outstanding, Exceeds Expectations, Meets Expectations, Below Expectations, Unacceptable	Bell curve, familiar, separates the exceptional	"C" grade for someone who meets expectations, manager vs. employee perspective

> ➜ Appendix: Sample Performance Ratings and Definitions.

> ➜ Appendix: Sample Performance Evaluation.

Beware of Rating Errors

Ratings are not fail-safe. A research study of what ratings actually measure revealed that 62 percent of the variance in the ratings could be accounted for by individual raters' peculiarities of perception. Actual performance accounted for only 21 percent of the variance.[3] Managers need to guard against these common rating errors, which distort objectivity either favorably or unfavorably. They include:

SECTION 4

Error	Description
Halo/Horn Effect	One outstanding quality/negative dimension becomes the basis of the whole evaluation.
Critical Incident	A single episode, whether positive or negative, is given undue emphasis.
Contrast	Employees are compared to one other individual rather than against an established standard. The good performer might suffer if compared against a stellar performer.
Similar-to-Me	One employee who is similar to the manager is evaluated more favorable than others with different attitudes and backgrounds.
First Impression/Recency	An employee is evaluated based on performance early in the year/immediately preceding the performance appraisal rather than performance throughout the year.
Past Anchoring	The manager rates performance based on prior years' performance evaluations instead of taking a fresh look.
Central Tendency	The manager rates all employees as average failing to distinguish among performance levels.

Although most of these errors are subconscious, managers should be aware of them and recognize those to which they may be susceptible so that objectivity is not impaired.

Emerging Trends

Why has this disillusionment with the traditional approach to performance appraisals evolved? The existing methods and approach are rigid and embody the following:

- Idiosyncratic rater effect.
- Form-focused, not people-focused.
- Judgmental, not supportive or developmental.
- Time-consuming.
- Rating-focused, not future-focused.
- Fuel anxiety, not engagement.
- Less meaningful in today's fast-paced, service-oriented institutions.
- Forced to coincide with conceptual pay models as opposed to true performance.[4]

The way we work and the nature of the work performed in today's organizations have changed. Organizations are becoming less hierarchical in their management structure. There is more of a focus on teams, which means that feedback and input about performance—individual performance and team performance—may be sought and given from more than one person and not just an employee's manager who has formal managerial authority. In addition, organizations are finding that the traditional process of an annual performance review is time-consuming and expensive.

Accenture is joining a small but prominent list of major corporations that have had enough with the forced rankings, the time-consuming paperwork, and the frustration engendered among managers and employees alike. Six percent of Fortune 500 companies have gotten rid of rankings, according to management research firm CEB.[5]

Do these criticisms mean that all organizations should abandon the traditional approach? That is something each must decide for itself. Some are totally embracing a new approach whereas others are making incremental changes. What an organization should consider is its industry and the nature of the work its employees perform. There are many types of jobs that may still align with the traditional approach, such as jobs in manufacturing or some jobs in call centers—jobs in which the work may be of a repetitive nature with little room for creativity and in which the tasks being performed are highly quantifiable.

An example of a new method can be found in the sweeping changes the consulting firm Deloitte made to its performance management system in 2015. It moved to an approach that was nimbler, real-time, and more individualized for the employee. Deloitte was adopting a focus that would fuel future performance rather than assessing what occurred in the past. The objectives of this new system are to recognize performance, to see performance clearly, and to fuel individual performance.[6]

To achieve the second objective, team leaders are asked to answer—on a periodic basis, not just once a year—four future-focused questions regarding what they would do with each team member, rather than what they think of the person. Two questions use a five-point scale from "strongly agree" to "strongly disagree" to measure:

1. Overall performance and unique value to the organization: *Given what I know of this person's performance, and if it were my money, I would award this person the highest possible compensation increase and bonus.*
2. Ability to work well with others: *Given what I know of this person's performance, I would always want him or her on my team.*

The remaining questions use yes-or-no responses to identify:

3. Problems that might harm the customer or team: *This person is at risk for low performance.*
4. Potential: *This person is ready for promotion today.*[7]

To support the last objective of Deloitte's system—fueling performance—frequent conversations or check-ins between employees and team leaders are an integral part of the process.

Common Elements

Whether an organization wants to embrace the traditional or seek a new approach, there are a number of elements to consider—namely, developing objectives, assessing performance, providing feedback, documentation and data, and fueling future performance.

Developing Objectives

Objectives establish direction for the future and help to identify expected results. To be effective, they must align with team, departmental, and organizational objectives. Objectives should be flexible, taking into consideration changes in business conditions or plans. Changes in the business environment occur at a faster pace than they did in the past. Organizations today are reviewing and revising goals on a quarterly basis to ensure that employees stay focused on what matters most throughout the year.

Well-written objectives:

- Use action verbs, clearly stating what will be done and the expected results.
- Have results that are quantifiable, observable, or verifiable.
- Include activities and results that are within the employee's control.
- Assure that targets are realistic yet challenging.
- Support business goals.
- Involve assignments that contribute to job responsibilities or address a developmental need.
- Use time lines or milestones by which to assess progress.

Finally, well-written objectives are SMART, meaning they are:
S—Specific.
M—Measurable.
A—Attainable.
R—Relevant.
T—Trackable.

➤   Appendix: Setting Performance Objectives.

Performance Assessment

Performance assessment is an analytic or evaluative process that determines how an employee is doing in the particular role or job he or she performs for an organization. Results will vary depending on the nature of the job. For example, sales employees may be evaluated on reaching a certain volume or dollar amount, a customer service representative may be evaluated on reaching a certain level of customer satisfaction, or a technical advisor may be evaluated for developing and implementing a new system successfully.

- Evaluate the employee against his or her job—that is, the specific requirements of position. Determine to what extent the employee met the position's requirements using measurable, job-related criteria.
- Evaluate the employee against his or her accomplishments.
- Evaluate the employee against objectives and expectations.

If there are gaps between what is expected and what the employee achieved, those gaps should be identified, documented, and discussed. A plan to address those gaps should be developed, and that plan should identify any actions for improvement, including developmental needs. Of course, the employee's performance may have gone beyond what was expected. In either case, that is where fueling future performance plays a role in performance management.

In the traditional approach, performance assessment is usually associated with giving ratings to performance factors. With the emerging approach, performance assessment can be more of a reflection of the organization's values. Just because a performance factor is not quantifiable, does not mean that is not important. Rather than giving a rating or score to a factor (or value), the performance assessment is an opportunity to explain how an employee exemplifies a certain factor or lives the organization's values. For example: *"Creative thinking is an important part of your job as a designer, and you demonstrated your abilities in creativity with the new product line you developed. Through the prototype, you showed innovation and the ability to produce the products in a cost-effective manner."*

If there are behavioral expectations associated with a job, it is important that those expectations are clearly written and communicated for the particular role. If performance ratings are being used, standards that match those ratings should also be clearly defined. This will facilitate an objective evaluation that minimizes any bias and provide meaningful information to the employee. For example:

Behavior	Behavioral Expectation		
Communication	Entry-Level Employee: Effective written communication skills: basic writing skills and proof reading ability		
	Performance Standards		
	Below Expectations	Meets Expectations	Exceeds Expectations
	Even with guidance, fails to prepare straightforward communications in a timely and accurate manner; work products require moderate to extensive revisions.	With guidance prepares straightforward communications in a timely and accurate manner; work products require minimal corrections and revisions.	Independently prepares communications in a timely, clear and accurate manner; work products require few, if any, corrections and revisions.

Performance Feedback and Conversations

Performance appraisals answer an important, fundamental question for employees: "How am I doing?" People want feedback, some more frequently than others, because feedback provides:[8]

- Reassurances that they are contributing and doing the right things.
- Awareness of the impact of performance on desired results, such as customer satisfaction.
- A measure of the adequacy of performance (quality, quantity, speed, etc.).
- Recognition of the importance of and value of their performance to the organization.

During the feedback stage, the manager is asking and answering the following questions:
- What?
  - ▷ What is the behavior that is not working?
  - ▷ What is working?
  - ▷ What is the expectation that is not being met?
  - ▷ What is the expectation that is being met?
- So what?
  - ▷ What is the impact?
  - ▷ Why is it a problem? Why is it great?

- Now what?
  - ▷ What can the individual do differently to achieve the desired results?
  - ▷ If not, what is the consequence?

Feedback should be ongoing. Frequent feedback lets employees know they are making a contribution and that their contributions are valued. That's what motivates and retains people. Providing feedback about day-to-day accomplishments, rather than waiting until exceptional or ineffective performance is observed or, worse, once a year, is very powerful. To be effective, feedback must be a two-way communication process:

- The manager's responsibilities include providing feedback in a constructive, candid, and timely manner.
- The employees' responsibilities include seeking feedback to ensure they understand how they are performing and reacting well to feedback they receive.

Having effective, ongoing performance conversations between managers and employees is probably the single-most-important determinant of whether or not a performance management system will achieve its maximum benefits.[9]

> Organizations that have abandoned categorical rating type feedback are finding that the performance management discussion is negative. Without a rating to focus on in the conversation, managers may find it harder to deliver a clear message.[10] This is unfortunate. The purpose of feedback and a performance discussion was never to justify a grade or a number; rather it was to provide qualitative feedback.

Managers, team leaders, even peers have to be comfortable with giving qualitative feedback. Yet these conversations don't come naturally for many individuals. The following are guidelines that may help:

- Create a positive, communicative atmosphere.
- Be sure to allow ample time for the meeting, and don't allow interruptions to occur.
- Engage in dialogue. Listen to the employee's perspective.
- Provide specifics and avoid vague, general statements. For example: *"You failed to deliver the product specifications on time which demonstrates poor preparation and resulted in budget over-runs."*

  ↱   Chapter 26 (Critical Conversations) has additional guidance.

Since its founding in the 1860s, Kimberly-Clark, a leading global company has consistently been recognized as a great place to work with strong values and commitment to its employees. As it grew globally, leadership identified gaps related to performance management. To address these gaps, the company implemented a performance management system to support their global employee base. The system not only allows for feedback to be provided from manager to employee but also for feedback to be shared between team mates. The system was deployed in 18 languages and was customized according to the workflow in each country.

As a user of the system himself, Kimberly-Clark's CEO Tom Falk stated, "For us to win, we must set clear objectives for performance and leadership required to create a stronger, faster Kimberly-Clark. Our Performance Management process is a critical part of this goal."[11]

Documentation and Data

A strong rationalization for the traditional performance appraisal instrument has been that it provides documentation for future management decisions, such as an out-of-cycle raise, a promotion, or a termination. Yet, many a human resources professional, when faced with a request by a manager to terminate an employee because of performance, is perplexed after reviewing the last annual performance appraisal, which had nothing but positive comments and ratings. Clearly, it was not fail-safe.

Documentation of employee performance and conversations with the employee about the performance, whether positive or negative, should be created and maintained. As organizations are moving to more frequent assessments and check-in discussions with employees, there's no reason a one-page assessment that addresses the employee's contributions cannot be prepared. Also emerging with the redesign of performance management systems is the use of new technology to capture and analyze performance-related information.

General Electric (GE) has introduced a phone app called PD@GE that employees use to assess both subordinates and superiors in order to facilitate more frequent feedback.[12] The consulting firm Accenture is also building a proprietary app that will more easily chart ongoing performance discussions. With the human resources function becoming more data- and analytics-driven, the ability to leverage technology to capture this information can both help identify trouble areas in which concerns show up repeatedly and target developmental programs. Capturing information real-time in one digital app has the potential for greater legal defensibility around employment decisions.[13] Of course, managers and employees alike will need to be trained on the appropriate use of such apps to assure they are not being misused and are effective. Information placed in such apps should be used to facilitate, not replace face-to-face conversations.

Fueling Future Performance

When managers assess employees' performance, they determine if an employee is experiencing any gaps or if an employee is exceeding performance expectations. Whatever the manager concludes, the next questions he or she should ask are *"What about the future? How does the organization help the employee grow in his/her current role or prepare for a future role?"*

SECTION 4

If there are gaps in performance, an employee is often placed on a performance improvement plan. These are positive plans that can and should be implemented at any time. They focus on specific gaps or opportunities and address what can be done to correct them.

Performance improvement plans have between three to five tasks that need to be achieved. Each should include:

- A task definition that describes specifically what needs to be completed.
- An action plan that describes how the task will be completed and how the results will be measured.
- An expected date when the task needs to be completed.

> After reviewing a proposed performance improvement plan with human resources, the manager asks, *"What do we do if the employee does everything on the plan?"* Taken aback, the HR manager responds, *"That's the objective. A performance improvement plan is just that: a path to improvement, not a path to termination."*

When an employee falters, it is easy to focus on what he or she does wrong. However, there may be other factors contributing to the problem, such as:

- **Training.** Is an experienced employee, who moves quickly and summarizes critical information, training a new employee? Is the new employee too intimidated to ask questions? Is the trainer training while being expected to meet deadlines? In other words, the training took place, but the learning did not.
- **Colleagues and constituents.** Are others not holding up their part of the bargain, missing meetings, or forgetting to do things?
- **Customers.** Customers do not come in neat tidy packages. Are they part of the problem?
- **Life.** Are there other factors, such as illnesses, families, automobiles, or dogs and cats, affecting the employee's ability to focus on the task at hand?

None of these variables eliminate the responsibility of the employee to meet performance expectations. They do, however, affect how a manager approaches performance issues and must be considered before an employee is held solely accountable. In addition to the above issues, a manager should also be asking:[14]

- *Were my work assignments clear?*
- *Was I available when I needed to be available?*
- *Were my deadlines reasonably based on the employee's workload?*
- *What did the employee need from me to do this assignment successfully?*
- *Did the employee have the resources necessary to complete the assignment?*
- *Were there extenuating circumstances that are not readily apparent that affected the employee's ability to meet the performance expectation?*
- *What are the specific facts of this performance issue?*

- *Did I establish a workable process for keeping track of the employee's progress on this assignment? Did I support the process by being available and supportive when the employee needed my help or input?*
- *How have I addressed similar performance issues with other employees in the past?*
- *Am I approaching this situation with a goal of creating an opportunity for this employee to be successful in the future?*

→ Appendix: Plan for Performance Improvement.

Fueling future performance, not merely improving performance, is a powerful objective that all organizations should embrace. It goes to the core of performance management. Recognize strengths and leverage employee talent. Grow the individual along with the organization. Continuous learning and improvement is necessary for any organization's success. Don't take for granted that good performers need no encouragement for continued growth. Put energy into inspiring everyone.

→ Chapter 23 (Best Approaches to Developing Employees).

Launching an Appraisal Process

When you design and implement a performance appraisal, consider:

- Is the appraisal process aligned with other HR systems? Are the performance factors, behaviors, and competencies the same as those used for recruitment, staffing, and development?
- Have key individuals been involved in the design? Will they be involved in the implementation process?
- Have you conducted a pilot test in order to evaluate the process and make improvements? Have you identified any flaws or omissions and made corrections? Are you certain that the managers and employees in the pilot understand and support the process?
- Have you communicated what you are doing so managers and employees understand it?
- Have you trained employees and managers on their roles and responsibilities?

A good communication plan is key to engaging employees and managers. Publicizing frequently asked questions and answers (FAQs) is an additional way to engage the staff and reduce anxiety. Training employees and managers ensures that they are motivated to use the system and will use it effectively. Topics can include roles and responsibilities, setting objectives, giving and seeking feedback, and how to use the appraisal instrument or automated system. Classroom training is a desirable format because it can train both groups on how to provide and receive feedback effectively and give them an opportunity to practice.

Generational Considerations

As younger generations enter the workplace, they bring with them different expectations. These differences impact the way they view the world, and the way they need and want to be managed. For managers to effectively manage performance, they need to be aware of some of the fundamental differences of these generations.

SECTION 4

People are different and individuals are unique, but common experiences shape a generation's thinking. We form most of our views during the first 10 to 15 years of life based on what was happening in society and the outside world during that time.

Baby Boomers are still a force in the workplace. Smart organizations will continue to engage this generation even as they prepare for retirement because they possess a great deal of optimism, institutional knowledge, and intellectual capital. Generation X-ers are adaptable, self-reliant, pragmatic, and creative. They love technology, have confidence in dealing with authority, and are willing to embrace diversity. They seek balance and flexibility in their lives. They want to see results and may sidestep rules in order to achieve them. They learn quickly and want development, continuous learning, coaching, challenging work, and innovation.

Millennials have high expectations and self-esteem, and are confident, goal oriented, and inclusive, as they were raised with diversity. They are tech-savvy and can multitask.

This generation needs a transactional approach in dealing with employers. Their ease with technology makes them would-be experts on everything and a good target for just-in-time strategic approaches to thinking, learning, and communicating.

Instant Gratification

Stephen P. Seaward, director of career development for Saint Joseph College in West Hartford, Conecticut, observes:

> The majority of Millennials never experienced life without a microwave, computer, ATM card, or television remote control.... Many had their first cell phones in their early teens with parents footing the bill. This instantaneous gratification...may have fostered unrealistic expectations with respect to goal-setting and planning. That, in conjunction with extreme parental influence, can prohibit creative problem-solving and decision-making.[15]

Legal Considerations

→   Chapter 3 (The Legal Landscape of Employee Rights).

→   Appendix, Guidelines for Documenting Workplace Issues

In preparing a performance appraisal, a manager is creating documentation regarding the employee. Poorly prepared appraisals could be used as evidence to show inconsistent treatment of employees. However, good documentation can support a decision for taking an adverse action against an employee, such as reassignment, demotion, or termination.

To assure that performance appraisals are legally defensible, they must be reasonable, generally understood, accepted as objective and fair, and focused on job-related activities and behaviors. They should not mention characteristics and traits that may relate to race, sex, age, or any other legal protections. Finally, they need to be reliable or consistent. If the same employee were rated by several different managers for the same review period, the results of the appraisal would be fairly consistent if the instrument and the process were reliable. Organizations should consider having a formal appeals process if an employee feels that his or her evaluation was not fair or lacked objectivity.

Discussion Questions

1. What are some of the major strategic choices organizations should make in implementing a performance appraisal?
2. What steps can a company take to assure its performance management system reflects its mission and values?
3. What are some of the values that cannot be quantified (for example, you exhibit the behaviors or you don't)? How can those values be evaluated?
4. How is your organization responding to the emerging trends involving performance management?
5. If an organization abolished performance appraisals, what should it do instead?

26

Critical Conversations

Although the folks at Starbucks sell coffee, other beverages, and food, they are really the most recent embodiment of a centuries-old tradition of coffeehouses that probably began in the Middle East, in cities like Bagdad and Tehran. These coffeehouses not only offer refreshment but also serve as hangouts for conversation, reading, writing, playing games, and now web-surfing. So though Starbucks' business focuses on refreshments, the environment it has created and reproduced in thousands of coffeehouses around the globe was really about creating a comfortable place for conversation—in essence for maintaining a centuries-old tradition.[1]

Critical conversations take place when a manager and/or an HR professional have to:

- Conduct an interview with a perspective employee.
- Discuss performance.
- Provide feedback.
- Discipline an employee.
- Refer an employee to an EAP.
- Resolve conflict or negotiate.
- Praise an employee for a job done well.
- Investigate an issue.
- Implement a management action, whether positive or negative (for example, tell an employee he or she is getting a raise or is getting reassigned to a position with less responsibility).

In this age of smart phones and iPads, we email and send text messages as a way of communicating. We tweet, short and to the point, in just 140 characters. All of these are one-way communications. They are not a substitute for conversations.

A conversation is a two-way dialogue where information is given and received. Conversations matter because they[2]:

- Help us to remain relevant.
- Enable us to connect with others in compelling ways.

219

- Enable us to find out what's going on with our employees, our peers and stakeholders.

Word About Email

Use email when:

- Your audience must get the message.
- Your audience is at a distance.
- A record is required.
- Multiple people must receive the message.
- A quick but not instant response is needed.
- Time is needed to compose the message.

Avoid email when:

- An immediate response is needed.
  ▷ Not everyone checks email regularly.
  ▷ Not everyone has constant access to email.
  ▷ Some individuals procrastinate.
- The message may be misunderstood.
- Dialogue is needed.
- The information is sensitive (bad news, confidential, proprietary information).
- You are agitated (flaming).

The goal of an effective conversation is to have a positive outcome. New ideas will be encouraged, everyone will be open to different approaches, and there will be opportunities for everyone to discuss differences and explain differing points of view. Having a critical conversation at work requires some preparation. A way to prepare for the next and all future conversations is to understand the anatomy of a conversation.

Get Good Information

Good information is relevant to the issue at hand—the subject of the conversations. Learning to ask open-ended questions in a manner that encourages ease and makes others comfortable is a key to meeting this purpose. For example:

- *Tell me more.*
- *Help me better understand.*
- *Can you say a little more about how you see things?*
- *Tell me why this is important.*

Be curious and probe. Ask who, what, when, where, and why questions, and clarify terminology and acronyms. It is also important to ask for concrete or relevant information. For example:

- *What leads you to say that?*
- *Can you give me an example?*
- *How would that work?*

It is equally important for the conversation and thought process to flow. Too many questions and interjections could disrupt this flow. Though you need to control the time and the discussion, don't control the direction of the discussion. Talking too much may be a barrier that contributes to the erosion of communication.

Push other people to be specific, using the following probes[3]:

- *Please fill me in on the details.*
- *Can you give me a specific example of what happened?*
- *Do you have a particular situation in mind?*
- *What exactly do you want me to do?*

We all see the world differently because we all have different information, are influenced by past experiences, and reach different conclusions based on our own information and experiences. Ask yourself, *"What information do they have that I don't have that leads them to that conclusion?"* Keep in mind that there are barriers to communication that include culture, gender, age, education, skill, experience, knowledge, style perceptions, and attitudes.

➔ Appendix: Checklist for Gathering the Facts.

Encourage Dialogue

It is important to listen and to encourage reactions and suggestions. Allow the other party to provide input and suggestions. Allow the other person to state his or her point of view without arguing or becoming defensive. Be prepared to adjust your viewpoints, if necessary. As you work to create a two-way exchange of information, stay flexible about who asks the questions and who states concerns or provides information first.

You can encourage dialogue by:

- Being at ease. It will put the others at ease.
- Getting the other person's perspective. Asking others to contribute and provide opinions is a compliment.
- Showing sensitivity. Listen for statements that may lead to new or additional information.
- Checking for understanding by repeating, paraphrasing, and taking time to reflect before stating your immediate reaction. Don't assume that everybody sees things the same as you.
- Using listening skills. Be patient.

Recognize that silence allows time to reflect and think about the information you've already received and to frame additional questions. Don't interpret it as a negative. Hear silence as it's intended.[4]

Be an Active Listener

Active listening means making a deliberate effort to understand what the other person's message is from his or her viewpoint, paying attention to all verbal and non-verbal signals, clarify meaning when you don't understand, and rephrasing and showing your desire to understand what is being said.

- Listen to learn. Be interested and show it.
- Seek understanding. Listen to words and clarify understanding.
- Turn off your listening filters. Don't allow yourself to think of anything except what the speaker is saying.

SECTION 4

- Be patient. Avoid interrupting the person during his or her explanation.
- Withhold judgment until you have all the facts.
- Focus on content as well as delivery.
- Pay attention to non-verbal signals.
- Recognize that listening is not waiting for your turn to talk. The absence of talking is not the same as listening. Pausing during your discussion may prompt the person to volunteer additional relevant information.
- Resist the urge to formulate a response until after the speaker is finished.
- Listen with compassion. Be aware of your tone of voice and body language.
- Listen for feelings as well as facts.
- Listen for what is not said, and use the opportunity to probe for more information.
- Listen for what you don't want to hear as well as what you do want to hear.
- Listen long enough to understand what the other person is telling you.

Give Good Information

When you give information, you want it to be relevant, precise, and accurate. You want to assure that the other person receives the message you intend to convey. Beware of providing too much information at one time. It could be overwhelming.

Be specific and provide details. For example, determine what facts and information the employee needs to do his/her job, such as policies and procedures, things that are new, and priorities. Ask yourself, *"What information do I have that the other person needs?"*

Lack of specificity causes problems. Tasks go uncompleted and questions fail to get answered because people are not mind readers. For example:

Nonspecific: You don't seem to care about your work performance.
Specific: You have missed four deadlines this month.[5]

Be honest and positive rather than negative. We hear and remember positive words better than negative words, and the listener is more likely to remember what you said if you use positive language. For example, say, *"I can have this ready for you on Friday"* rather than *"I can't have this ready until Friday."*[6]

Be accurate and check your facts. For example, don't tell an employee who is being laid off that his or her final paycheck will be a direct deposit when in fact it will be mailed.

When you are giving praise, come to the point quickly. Talk about specific actions that deserve recognition and appreciation, and explain how it made a difference. Describe the results you are recognizing and why they deserve appreciation. Match the recognition with the person. Not everyone wants the same kind of praise. Some respond well to public recognition, others to private.

When you are assigning tasks or new responsibilities, clearly communicate a description of the specific task and why it is important. Discuss job scope, performance expectations, and accountabilities. Describe the support you will be providing to the employee.

If you are giving constructive feedback, be timely and clear about your concerns. Talk about specifics—what you saw and heard—and avoid speculating about motivation and opinions. Be sensitive to the employee's feelings.

- Begin by providing positive feedback, and point out specific accomplishments and contributions.

- Emphasize problem-solving and concentrate on future actions and improvements.
- Explain the employee's behavior and the consequences of that behavior to the individual and the organization.
- Stress the requirements of the job.
- Allow the employee the opportunity to discuss his/her reactions.

Reframe the situation by choosing to see it in a new light, focusing on positive aspects. Putting a situation in the best possible context will allow everyone to move toward constructive action.

Maintaining Control of the Conversation

Maintaining control of a conversation allows you to:
- Have balance.
- Maintain the confidence and self esteem of all parties involved.
- Build constructive relationships and integrity.

Maintaining control means there are no distractions or interruptions, and allows for level-headed responses to others' emotions. It allows the parties to move away from past problems. Maintaining control allows you to deal with difficult people, situations, or issues.

When dealing with difficulty, recognize and remove the barriers to communications that include culture, gender, age, education, skill, experience, knowledge, style perceptions, and attitudes. Work to control emotional behavior—yours or the other parties.

Maintain control of emotions and attitudes by staying focused and objective, and modeling constructive behavior. Use a "soft" approach. Soften your voice, smile, posture, tone, eye contact, and body language to send a message of openness. Breathe deeply and don't become defensive.

Conversations About Performance

As more organizations look at emerging and smart practices for managing performance, there is agreement that more discussions need to be held. Organizations such as Deloitte are encouraging regular check-ins and, to ensure their frequency, empowering team members who are eager for guidance to initiate them.[7] Feedback discussions should have always been an important component of performance management and organizations are finally realizing it. One way to assist managers, team leaders, and team members is to develop questions to guide these important two-way discussions. Consider variations on the following:
- What's working and should be continued?
- What can you (I) do more of/less of to be effective?
- What will you be (should I be) doing over the rest of the month (quarter) to address the above?
- What can I do to assist you with this? (Here's what I need some help with and why.[8])

In Chapter 25, another approach was presented: asking *what, so what,* and *now what*?
- **What?** This helps to provoke a discussion around accomplishments, project status, or lessons learned. Both parties can explore what went right or what when wrong.
- **So what?** This brings clarity into the discussion, explaining why the accomplishments and lessons learned are important. It can help identify problems or measure potential.
- **Now what?** This provides an opportunity to explore deficiencies and corrective actions, and, equally important, an opening to explore growth potential and future opportunities.

Both approaches can facilitate a dialogue and ensure:
1. The atmosphere is positive and communicative.
2. The emphasis is on problem-solving and future actions rather than dwelling on the past.
3. The employee is involved in finding a solution.

Whatever the nature of the discussion, there should be mutual agreement at the end. If the employee is meeting or exceeding expectations, it's an opportunity to agree on a development strategy so the employee can advance within the organization. If the employee is experiencing gaps, explore reasons for these gaps as discussed in Chapter 25 and agree on a plan for closing the gaps. Either way, the individuals involved need to keep these discussions focused on facts.

Conducting Investigations

An employee makes a complaint and an investigation must take place. Why investigate?
- To obtain more facts.
- To resolve issues.
- To encourage a positive employee relations culture and enhance employee morale.
- To comply with legal and regulatory requirements such as EEOC guidance on sexual harassment complaints or the Sarbanes Oxley requirements.
- To avoid litigation.

An investigation is defined as a detailed inquiry or systematic examination—a search and examination of facts that are used to reach a conclusion. Simply stated, when facts are in dispute, investigate.

Investigations take skill and practice. The investigator must act without bias. Before beginning an investigation, managers and HR professionals should always check with internal resources, especially legal counsel. In some instances, it might be beneficial to engage an outside, impartial party to conduct the investigation. Keep in mind that interviewing witnesses to a situation is just one part of the investigation. Your organization may have specific procedures and practices regarding investigations, and they should be followed.

> ➔   Appendix: Checklist for Effective Investigation Interviews.

Discussion Questions

1. A manager has to sit down with an employee whose performance has been deteriorating and who has been exhibiting erratic behavior, and make a referral to the Employee Assistance Program. How should this manager prepare and what specific information should he or she provide to the employee?
2. Two employees on your team are always at odds with each other. One works hard at controlling his or her sometimes-explosive personality; the other appears calm and aloof, but frequently brings up facts that are outside the scope of the issue at hand, often in an accusatory manner. As you watch yet another tense situation about to explode, what advice would you give both of your teammates about controlling their emotions and the conversation?
3. What questions could you suggest for your organization to guide performance discussions?

SECTION 5

EMPLOYEE RELATIONS

27

Employee and Labor Relations

Two prime ministers are sitting in a room discussing affairs of state when a man bursts in, shouting and banging his fist on the desk. The resident prime minister admonishes him: "Peter, kindly remember Rule Number 6," whereupon Peter is instantly restored to complete calm, apologizes, and withdraws. After the scene is repeated, the visiting prime minister asks his host if he would share the secret of Rule Number 6. The host replies: "Very simple. Don't take yourself seriously." "And what are the other rules?" asks the visitor. "There aren't any," replies the host.[1]

The cornerstone of employee relations is not about rules. It is about an organizational culture that treats people fairly, professionally, and respectfully. A positive and respectful culture balances the needs of the organization and the employees. It drives recruitment, retention, morale, and productivity. It builds an atmosphere of trust.

The characteristics of a positive culture include:

- Opportunities for growth and advancement.
- Promotional opportunities.
- Rewards and recognition.
- Feedback and communication.
- Problem-solving and counseling.
- Fair and consistent treatment of employees.
- A safe and secure work environment.

Positive Culture and Policies

Through its employment and human resources policies and practices, organizations can set a framework for treating people with respect and fairness. Policies:

- Reflect the culture and values of the company.
- Set and communicate management expectations.
- Assure consistency in the way all people are treated.
  - ▷ How would you treat another employee in a similar situation?

- Recognize uniqueness and provide flexibility.
  - ▷ Would you treat an employee who has been with the company 12 weeks the same as someone who has been there 12 years?

In developing human resources policies, organizations should keep in mind that:
- Policies are management guidelines and not necessarily mandates.
- Policies are standards developed to assure a consistent approach to people management issues.
- A consistent approach should not ignore judgment and the particulars of each situation.
- Policies should be flexible and allow for management decisions to meet each unique situation.
- For policies to be effective, they must be communicated to managers and employees alike.
- For managers to make effective decisions, they have to be trained to understand the intent of the policies and how to apply the policies. It is important that managers receive guidance on assessing situations and applying policies in a fair and consistent manner.
- Policies are unique to each organization. Do research and understand what other organizations in your industry and geographic area are doing. Consider your organization's size. Resist the urge to cut and paste policies, even from trusted sources.
- Individual policies do not stand alone, but work together with others. For example, a violation of a drug abuse policy would be subject to disciplinary action under a conduct policy.

Policies also represent the organization's response to the external environment and can offer a degree of legal protection in areas such as harassment or discrimination. However, recognize that practices and precedents outside the boundaries of established written policies, or practices in lieu of written policies, can erode any legal protections and become de facto policies. In challenges to employment decisions, employers are often asked about the historical treatment of individuals in similar situations.

Employee Handbooks

Organizations often use employee handbooks as a way to communicate policies to employees and managers. They can also be used to communicate information about benefits. In addition to policies and benefits, handbooks may contain introductory information about the organization, an employee acknowledgment form, and information about other work rules.

Best practices regarding employee handbooks include:
- Tailoring it to your needs and don't adopt a "form" handbook, which often includes information that is not relevant to your organization.
- Avoiding including too much detail on procedures. It is best to consider a separate manual for managers.
- Providing an at-will disclaimer and make sure that there are no other statements that contradict it.

- Advising employees that the employer can modify or change policies, and will provide notification when it does.
- Reviewing it for inconsistency.
- Gaining advice, legal and technical, to assure that the policies and practices are sound and enforceable.
- Having employees sign for the handbook acknowledging that they have read it.

Update your policies and handbooks as conditions change, and have your employees sign acknowledgments of the changes. If you distribute the employee handbook electronically or via an intranet, you should obtain a written acknowledgment of any critical changes, such as the introduction of a dispute resolution or social media policy.

Employee Handbook Acknowledgment Form

I acknowledge that I have received, read, and understand the policies described in the XYZ Employee Handbook. I understand that these policies are intended as a guide to human resources practices and procedures. I understand that the company has the right to modify the handbook and any of the policies and practices described herein at any time. It is understood that future changes in policies and procedures will supersede or eliminate those found in this book, and that employees will be notified of such changes through normal communication channels. When notified of such changes, I understand that I am responsible for reading such changes, which will generally be posted on the Company Intranet before being published in print version, if applicable.

This handbook is not contractual and should not be relied upon as a contract. The employment relationship is based on the mutual consent of each party and can be terminated by either the employee or XYZ at any time. I understand that no manager or representative of XYZ, other than the Chief Executive, has any authority to enter into any agreement for employment for any specified period of time.

Please sign, date, and return to Human Resources.

➥ Appendix: Employee Handbook Table of Contents.

Employee Communications

Regular, open communication with employees is essential for demonstrating respect and fostering trust. Routine communication provides updates about the organization's strategy and policies, and how it is measuring up against its goals and plans. It is important to be honest and open about both positive and negative issues.

Employers should have a formal communication plan, which should incorporate a number of vehicles:

- Open-door policies foster a free interchange between employees and management, and provide a flexible and informal approach for communication.

SECTION 5

- Department staff meetings, all-hands staff meetings/town-hall meetings, and brown-bag lunches are excellent opportunities for in-person communication.
- Newsletters can be traditional paper editions or distributed electronically.
- Leverage technology through the use of email, blogs, Intranet, webcasts, and podcasts. This is a robust way to keep younger workers engaged.
- Story-telling can convey information in an engaging manner and stimulate conversation.
- Employee surveys can provide excellent information to an organization, provided it is committed to acting on the feedback it receives. If employee comments and feedback are ignored, it sends a negative message.

> See Chapter 14 (Employee Engagement).

A Sampling of Sound People-Management Policies

There are certain policies that an organization should consider implementing. The following provides guidelines on how those policies should be crafted.

Employment at Will

You can establish this policy with a simple statement that the organization maintains an "at will" relationship with its employees. At any time, with or without notice, employees are free to join or leave and the organization is free to establish or terminate the employment relationship.

Be certain that you do not make statements in an employee handbook or other policies that would violate this policy, such as having a probationary period for new employees or placing conditions on voluntary terminations.

EEO Policy

The policy should, at a minimum, prohibit discrimination based on all of the protections in federal nondiscrimination laws, as well as any additional protections under state or local law.

> See Chapter 3 (The Legal Landscape of Employee Rights).

It should:
- Apply to all employees and applicants.
- Ensure that all management and employment practices are administered without unlawful discrimination on any protected basis, as described Chapter 3.
- Define the covered practices, such as recruitment, selection, job assignment, transfer, promotion, demotion, layoff, discipline, termination, training, education, tuition, social and recreational programs, compensation, and benefits.
- Require all employment decisions be based on qualifications, such as skill, knowledge, and/or ability to perform the position being filled, and be clearly related to job effectiveness.
- Assign direct responsibility for this policy to supervisors and managers.
- Provide management staff with appropriate training and briefings on equal employment opportunity policies and procedures to assist in their implementation.

Though federal and state discrimination laws protect specific and varied characteristics, and although the EEOC and the Courts issue guidance and interpretations of these laws, employers should strive to be inclusive in their workplace practices. Implement positive practices and do not tolerate behavior that targets any employee because of a specific characteristic—for example, size, manner of dress, sexual orientation, or gender identity, to name a few.

Performance Management Policy

The policy should:
- Provide a process for managers to communicate job expectations and to formally evaluate performance against those expectations.
- Describe clear expectations that must be related to job performance—skills, behaviors, and tasks important for job success—and should be:
  ▷ Specific, measurable, and observable.
  ▷ Within the employee's control.
  ▷ Achievable with time and resources.
- Encourage informal evaluation and communication on a continual basis.
- Develop a culture of continued improvement.
- Require communication of performance expectations.
- Provide a process for performance improvement to correct performance below expectations.
- Provide a process for continued performance success for all employees.

  → See Chapter 25 (Performance Management).

Employee Conduct Policy

The policy should:
- Establish and define standards of conduct that are not acceptable, while stressing that the list is not all-inclusive and that there can be other infractions.
- Provide assistance to employees to change inappropriate behavior.
- Provide management a means to address issues.
- Provide management responses if behavior does not change.
- Provide a flexible approach (progressive or corrective discipline) process to address conduct.
- Provide a communication mechanism for employees and managers.

A corrective discipline process can include the following steps:
- Open dialogue/verbal counseling.
- Written counseling/letter of caution.
- Final written notice.
- Suspension.
- Termination.

A fair and defensible corrective discipline process allows management flexibility in determining whether all steps should be used in dealing with a specific problem and in deciding when immediate or severe action must be taken. Don't be too specific in your process and tie management's hands. Disciplinary action can and should start at any stage, depending on the severity of the behavior. Don't factor judgment out of the process.

Written disciplinary notices should include the date, the employee's name, the nature of the action being taken (for example, letter of caution), specific behaviors observed and the dates they occurred, and a statement that if the employee fails to correct his or her behavior, further disciplinary action may be taken, up to and including termination.

→   Appendix: Sample Categories of Unacceptable Conduct.

→   Appendix: Sample Disciplinary Notice.

Performance, Conduct, or Both

Employee performance is defined as the use of skills, knowledge, and tools to complete a task or assignment. There is a performance problem when an employee is unable to effectively accomplish his or her work. Performance improvement (PIP) is corrective action for addressing performance problems. Performance is different from conduct, which is behavior exhibited in the workplace.

There is a conduct problem when an employee exhibits behavior that is inappropriate in a business environment. Conduct problems are addressed with a corrective disciplinary action. Performance and conduct problems can occur simultaneously, and both sets of actions can be taken.

Drug Abuse Policy

The policy should prohibit employees from possessing, using, manufacturing, purchasing, dispensing, or selling illegal drugs on the premises, as well as consequences for violation. The policy should also provide for referrals to an Employee Assistance Program for drug, alcohol, and related mental health problems affecting job performance.

Harassment Policy

The harassment policy must be communicated to all employees, and it is advisable to do this in writing. It should cover:

- All forms of harassment, not just sexual harassment.
- All employment decisions (see "EEO Policy") or actions.
- Behavior that occurs wherever the company is conducting business (for example, work locations, a client site, a training facility, during travel on company business, during a company-sponsored event).

The policy should provide:

- A definition of harassment with clear explanations of prohibited conduct.
- A definition of the responsibilities of all employees, the responsibilities of management employees, and the responsibilities of human resources.

- Assurance against retaliation.
- A clear complaint process.
- Assurance of confidentiality to the extent possible.
- A clear investigation process.
- Assurance of corrective action when harassment has occurred.

Workplace Bullying Policy

Closely aligned to the harassment policy, a policy on workplace bullying should include:
- A definition of workplace bullying.
- A description of who is covered.
- Examples of behaviors that will not be tolerated and consequences of not adhering to the policy.
- A clear complaint and investigation processes.

Electronic Media Policy

Technology today comes in many forms and it keeps evolving. A policy on electronic media should define media broadly, including, devices such as laptops, tablets, cell phones and smartphones, cameras, recording devices, and any other emerging tools to access information.

The policy should address and set expectations for the responsible use of technology, including the systems that support the technology used in the workplace. This would include, but not be limited to, email, Internet access, and the use of any of the organization's networks. It should stress that:
- Any equipment and systems provided by the organization that support the media are the property of the organization and dedicated for business purposes.
- The organization has the right to monitor, retrieve, and read any information sent or received using the equipment and systems.
- The employees should not have any expectation of privacy while using the organization's equipment or networks, and that the organization has the right to review any electronic communications on its systems.
- Violation of the policy could result in disciplinary action.

Define what is considered an unacceptable use of technology, such as:
- Sending or receiving offensive or disruptive messages that could be violations of the harassment or non-discrimination policies.
- Using technology for soliciting, collecting, or selling for any non-business purpose.
- Sending, receiving, or disclosing confidential or proprietary information, copyrighted materials, or trade secrets without authorization, including downloading data or programs for personal or commercial use.

Finally, provide guidance on protecting the integrity and security of the systems and the information transmitted. Have provisions for password protection, downloading unauthorized software, intentionally introducing viruses, and alerting the appropriate management representatives about viruses and other security breaches or related issues.

SECTION 5

Technology is widely used today and organizations should not overreach in what they try to achieve with their policies. Set reasonable expectations, such as responsible personal use, but be open with your expectations so that employees and managers are clear about the rules. Seek appropriate legal and technical guidance, because the issues are constantly changing.

→   Appendix: Guidelines for Documenting Workplace Issues.

Social Media Policy

Social media is brave new world for employers, especially as the demographics of the workforce change. Younger employees are savvier with technology and the use of public, social platforms such as Twitter, Facebook, and LinkedIn, to name just a few. These platforms are changing constantly and it is impossible for employers to address all the things that employees can and can't do on them. Reasonable guidelines can be communicated in a policy, and should include a broad definition of social media and explain the employer's position on its responsible use as it pertains to the organization. In developing a social media policy, consider the following:

- No organization can be in the business of policing everything their employees do during and after working hours. An over-restrictive policy would be difficult to enforce.
- How far do you want to reach? Two concerns for employers are how employees are spending their time at work, and how employees are portraying your company online when they are not at work. The policy must address both types of online use.
- Do you want to permit social networking at work, at all? If you prohibit it, how will you monitor it? Allowing limited personal social networking during business hours assures employees that you are treating them respectfully and professionally. However, your policy must cover circumstances when employees abuse the privilege through excessive use or inappropriate postings.
- Do you want employees to identify with your business when networking online? Employees should be made aware that if they post as an employee of your organization, they will be responsible for any negative portrayals. Positive postings, however, can have powerful networking and marketing results. Conversely, if an employee posts something negative and his or her profile indicates the employer's name, it could have negative consequences for the employer, even if no reference is made to the organization.
- How do you define "appropriate business behavior"? Everything posted online is public, and employees have no privacy rights. Anything in cyberspace can be used as grounds to discipline an employee, no matter whether the employee wrote it from work or outside of work. There should be consequences for any information that negatively reflects on your business. Social networking policies should work in tandem with your conduct, confidentiality, harassment, non-discrimination, and electronic media policies.

Other issues to consider are:
- Who within the organization can be Facebook "friends"?
  - ▷ No restrictions.
  - ▷ Supervisors cannot friend direct reports, but employees can friend their supervisor.

    ▷   Supervisors and their reports cannot be friends.

    ▷   Only peers can be Facebook friends.

    ▷   Employees are prohibited from being Facebook friends with any coworker, regardless of position.

    The option you choose has more to do with your corporate culture, but there can be legal implications such as harassment liability. You should address this in your social media policy.

- Can a manager provide a recommendation for an employee on LinkedIn? Consider that if a manager provides a good recommendation for an employee, and the employee is later terminated for cause, the recommendation could be used as evidence if there is a subsequent lawsuit. Managers need to be aware that anything that they write about an employee in any public forum, whether positive or negative, could be used against the employer.

    →   **See Chapter 8 (Recruiting From Outside the Organization), which also discusses considerations for a social media policy.**

Workplace Violence Policy

The policy should:

- Provide a statement that violence (or threats of violence, including bullying) will not be tolerated. This could be included in a conduct policy.
- Define the prohibited conduct and give examples of violent conduct. The policy should strictly prohibit threats of violence, intimidation, physical altercations, and vandalism.
- Provide for disciplinary procedures for employees who engage in violence, up to and including termination. This should tie to the conduct policies. Employers should not hesitate to terminate employees in appropriate cases. Discipline may include mandatory counseling. Organizations may also want to reserve the right to remove the employee from the workplace until a fitness for duty certification can be obtained from a healthcare provider.
- Encourage reporting and implement investigation procedures. Employees should be encouraged to raise concerns about violent coworkers, and organizations should establish an effective method for investigating and resolving such complaints. Early intervention can be beneficial to all parties. Through an effective communication program, encourage employees to come forward when the first indications of violence are observed.

Leave Policy or Policies

Policies regarding leaves of absence must include mandatory leave for issues such as FMLA and military leave, and leave for jury and witness duty. Other types of leave that employers may want to provide include bereavement leave, emergency leave that can cover issues such as inclement weather or other unforeseen circumstances, education leaves, or sabbaticals. The policies should specify the conditions under which the leaves are paid and provisions for continued benefits as may be required by law.

Layoff and Termination Policies

Layoff policies should establish:

- The circumstances under which an employee can be laid off—generally a reduction in force.
- Any severance, notice, or pay in lieu of notice practices.
- Selection criteria for layoff.
- Provisions to conduct an adverse-impact analysis under attorney-client privilege.

In making selections of individuals for layoff, employers should consider:

- The organization's needs including those positions necessary to perform the work, what the workforce looks like today, and what you will need in the future—those knowledge, skills, abilities (KSAs) required to perform the work.
- Employees' KSAs, performance, reliability, and service.

Termination policies should provide for management review and awareness by establishing:

- An internal review and approval process, including notifications to senior managers for involuntary terminations; and
- An exit interview process for voluntary terminations to assist with future retention.

Labor Relations

I went to the miners' camp in Holly Grove where all through the winter...men and women and little children had shuddered in canvas tents that America might be a better country to live in. I listened to their stories. I talked with Mrs. Sevilla whose unborn child had been kicked dead by a gunman while her husband was out looking for work. I talked with widows, whose husbands had been shot by the gunman; with children whose frightened faces talked more effectively than their baby tongues.

"I think the strike is lost, Mother," said an old miner whose son had been killed.

"Lost! Not until your souls are lost!" said I.

—Mary Harris Jones in 1914[2]

The history of the American Labor Union is an important part of American History. It is also an important part of human resources history. Before organizations had HR professionals to ensure that employees were treated with fairness and respect, it was the unions that fought for workers' rights. Mother Jones was drawn to the miners, although it was child labor that aroused her most spectacular activities.

Today, organizations with an effective employee relations program and a culture of respect are likely to remain union-free. Throughout this book we have discussed these characteristics, and chapters are dedicated to rewards and recognition, workplace flexibility, performance management, effective conversations and feedback, coaching and counseling, compensation, benefits, and safe and secure work environments. Creating such a culture is the first proactive step. Maintaining the culture is the ongoing challenge.

Evidence of Union Activity

Early detection of and rapid response to union activity has long been key to union avoidance. Counsel should be sought at the first signs of union activity, direct or indirect, even if they seem isolated. Why is this so important?

- A bundle of isolated, minor occurrences may amount to evidence of a serious union campaign. Considering all such reports, HR and legal can assess the extent of a union campaign.
- If 30 percent of eligible employees in an appropriate bargaining unit sign union authorization cards, the company may be on its way to a unionized workforce. The next step is a secret ballot election.

Activities that may indicate early union organizing include:

- An employee handing out a union flier in the parking lot or wearing a pro-union T-shirt.
- Unusual off-site gatherings of employees—at barbecues, bowling alleys, and bars.
- Employees who have not had previous relationships suddenly become very involved with each other.
- Phone, photocopier, or fax machine use for personal business increases.
- Complaints or grievances increase in number (may be used as a union rallying point).

If union activity is suspected, supervisors should immediately report the activity to HR and/or senior management, and expert advice should be sought from legal counsel or consultants specializing in labor relations.

Activities that unions have traditionally used for organizing campaigns include:

- Telephone solicitation.
- Off-site meetings.
- Distribution of leaflets.
- Indirect influence.
- Picketing.
- Salting (placing union organizers as employees into companies).

More recently, technology has allowed unions to launch Internet and email campaigns. Social media is a powerful tool for member outreach and organizing, especially as unions shift their focus to younger workers. Although unions may be setting up Facebook pages to attract younger workers, companies can assure that their non-solicitation rules limit access to any company systems. Stress that company systems are owned by the company, are for company business, and may not be used for solicitation of any type.

Lynn Outwater, managing partner of Jackson Lewis LLP, in Pittsburgh, Pennsylvania, counsels[3]:
- Make sure supervisors treat workers equitably.
- Look behind disciplinary termination actions to make sure they're proper.
- Educate supervisors about what they can or cannot say legally about unions seeking to organize.
- Communicate your organization's employee-relations philosophy setting forth the employer's position on unions.
- Have lawful solicitation and distribution rules.
- Have lawful bulletin-board posting and email rules.

A common acronym that helps to remember behaviors that could result in an unfair labor practice is TIPS. Managers and supervisors should avoid:
- **Threats:** threatening any adverse action such as significant changes in benefits, de-motions or firing because employees are engaging in a protected activity.
- **Interrogation:** asking employees about union activities.
- **Promise:** suggesting or promising employment benefits, such as promotions or sal-ary increases, if the employee will refrain from union activities.
- **Spy:** spying on union-related activities during work time and non-work time, whether on or off company premises.

⇢   See also Chapter 3 (The Legal Landscape of Employee Rights).

Supervisors must understand that if a union representative contacts them directly, they should not look at any:
- List of employees that a union representative attempts to give them.
- Cards or letters with names on them.
- Papers that employees attempt to hand them.

⇢   Appendix: Guidelines to Address Union Activity.

Discussion Questions

1. Describe how an organization can create a culture of respect. What effect does the external environment, such as the economy, have on its efforts? What has your orga-nization done to foster a fair and respectful climate?
2. Discuss the ways that organizations communicate with their employees. What has your organization done that has been innovative and effective?
3. Employee handbooks can be distributed in hard or soft copy, or posted on an intranet. Discuss how your organization distributes its handbook and obtains employee ac-knowledgments. How does your organization handle updates and revisions? What steps do you take when a new policy is introduced?
4. What are the benefits of providing a separate policy and procedures manual for managers?
5. In today's environment, do you think that unions have outlived their usefulness? Why or why not? Discuss if there are circumstances or industries in which unions could still have an impact.

28

Moving From Conflict to Collaboration

In 1993, when she was Secretary of State, Madeleine Albright was a member of President Clinton's national security team. She and General Colin Powell, the chairman of the Joint Chiefs of Staff, did not agree on whether the United States and NATO should intervene to stop ethnic cleansing in Bosnia. In retrospect, Albright conceded that the general was right to be cautious, right to ask questions, and right to consider alternatives.[1]

A workplace conflict is a condition between or among workers whose jobs are interdependent, who are angry or frustrated, who perceive the other(s) as being at fault, and who act in ways that cause a business problem. Constant changes in today's workplace can fuel workplace conflict. These include changes in demographics and dimensions of diversity, and changes in organizational structure. Less hierarchical structures and a focus on teams require a more collaborative environment but provide a greater opportunity for differences. Over dependence on technology also contributes to the potential for conflict. The subtleties that accompany face-to-face communication, such as body language or facial expressions, are lost when using technology to communicate.

Chapter 26 discussed the need for developing skill in having critical conversations. Two alternatives to having effective conversations in crucial situations are to avoid them and suffer the consequences, or face them and handle them poorly.[2] Conflict is often avoided because of a lack confidence in the ability to defuse the situation and to provide the right solution. Will we get results or will we make a bad situation worse? Are the underlying issues understood by all the parties? Conflict at work can be perceived as negative, and there is a fear of being labeled a trouble maker for bringing an issue forward.

Conflict is not always negative. Conflict is often growth that is trying to happen. Distinguishing the differences between negative and positive conflict is the first step in moving to collaboration.

Conflict is negative when:
- Differences are not addressed.
- Expectations are not managed.
- Assumptions rather than facts are central to the disagreement.
- The individuals involved or affected don't want to be part of the solution.

In a good or positive conflict[3]:

- The value of conflict and differences are honored and respected.
- Issues are open and not masked.
- Ideas not personalities are central.
- Emotions are managed and points of view expressed in a skillful and respectful manner.

In a good conflict, relationships and the resolution process are valued. Just like positive critical conversations, collaboration at work requires some preparation in order to have positive outcomes. The resolution process involves three steps: Acknowledge it, assess it, and address it.

Acknowledge It

Acknowledging the conflict begins with dispelling the myth that conflict always has to be negative, and recognizing the characteristics and the advantages of a "good" conflict.

The parties involved must agree that there is a problem and identify the source of the tension. Creating an effective atmosphere is important to acknowledging the problem. For example, approach the other person and say, "We've been having difficulties lately when we talk about ____."

The sources of tension in a conflict can include:

- Relationships.
  - ▷ Fear of eroding good working relationships.
  - ▷ Fear of involving others.
  - ▷ Possessiveness of other parties, such as clients, employees, or teammates.
- Data—inaccurate or no information.
- Interest—competition between perceived or actual needs or conflicting interests.
- Structural/organizational issues (for example, limited resources or poor role definition).

Why do relationships matter? Flatter organizations and wider spans of control have dispersed power in organizations, giving lower-level managers and employees greater autonomy to take action and make decisions. With power dispersed, people need to negotiate solutions to problems with others over whom they may have little or no formal authority.[4]

Assess It

Assessing the conflict involves determining the facts and the individuals involved, including the differences in personal styles.

Avoid assumptions and get the facts by:

- Keeping the discussion focused on the information needed.
  - ▷ What are the important issues that must be identified?
- Maintaining control of the discussion.
- Varying the types of questions used.
  - ▷ Ask questions to uncover other's interests, needs, values, and assumptions.
  - ▷ Ask, *"Why is that important?"*
  - ▷ Get the other person's perceptions of the issues.
  - ▷ Ask, *"Would you clarify the point that you made about?"* or *"Regarding ____, what's important to you?"*

Getting the facts means getting and giving good information.

- Get to the root of the issue.
- Be specific and get the details.
- Be curious; probe.
  - ▷ Ask open-ended, who, what, when, where, why questions.
  - ▷ Clarify terminology.
- Avoid speculation.
  - ▷ Adjust your assumptions based on what you've learned.
- Encourage dialogue and create a two-way exchange of information.
- Beware of:
  - ▷ Finger-pointing and placing blame.
  - ▷ Identifying victims and villains.
  - ▷ Trivial issues and helpless stories.
  - ▷ Not identifying the underlying or root issue.

Not identifying the underlying or root issue. A critical success factor in moving to collaboration is to understand that individuals differ in their approach to conflict. Know your own style and learn to recognize the style of others. You can consciously choose to use a different style when appropriate and should practice using different styles. Recognize that all styles can work at one time or another depending on the situation.

Exploring Your Style

- *The hardest conflicts for me to deal with are _____.*
- *The thing I most fear in conflict is _____.*
- *I don't confront conflict because _____.*
- *When someone confronts me in conflict, I _____.*
- *My greatest strength in handling conflict is _____.*
- *When we have conflict on the team, we should _____.*
- *Conflict could help our team/organization if _____.*

→   Appendix: Managing Conflict Through Open Communication.

There are five recognized modes for dealing with conflict that describe an individual's behavior along two basic dimensions: (1) assertiveness, the extent to which the person attempts to satisfy his own concerns, and (2) cooperativeness, the extent to which the person attempts to satisfy the other person's concerns.

1. **Competing** attacks and likes to argue and debate. This type is competitive, assertive, and uncooperative, and can be threatening and intimidating, causing others to give in to avoid the argument. The competing type takes the stance of "win or lose," often pursuing his or her own concerns at the other person's expense. Competing means "standing up for your rights," defending a position which you believe is correct, or simply trying to win.

2. **Accommodating** is unassertive and cooperative—the complete opposite of competing. When accommodating, the individual neglects his or her own concerns because of high levels of concern about others. This type needs to please and be liked by others. Accommodating might take the form of yielding to another's point of view, or giving in during disagreements even when the individual believes his or her ideas are better.

3. **Avoiding** is unassertive and uncooperative; the person neither pursues his own concerns nor those of the other individual. This type will not commit and is unsure where he or she stands on issues. Often the individual conceals his or her interests. Avoiding might take the form of diplomatically sidestepping an issue, postponing an issue until a better time, or simply withdrawing from a threatening situation.

4. **Compromising** is moderate in both assertiveness and cooperativeness. The objective is to find some expedient, mutually acceptable solution that partially satisfies both parties. It falls between competing and accommodating. Compromising gives up more than competing but less than accommodating. This style is comfortable talking things through with others, but is intimidated by direct confrontation and will look to gain consensus or seek a quick middle-ground solution.

5. **Collaborating** is both assertive and cooperative—the complete opposite of avoiding. Collaborating takes a win-win stance and involves an attempt to work with others to find some solution that fully satisfies his or her concerns. This style approaches conflict with skill and balance, understands the value of positive conflict, and often acts as a mediator. The collaborator will explore the issues in much greater depth than the compromiser and work to find a creative solution. This style recognizes the importance of focusing on interests and creating options in order to arrive at that creative solution.

Each of us is capable of using all five conflict-handling modes. None of us can be characterized as having a single style of dealing with conflict. But certain people use some modes better than others and, therefore, tend to rely on those modes more heavily than others—whether because of temperament or practice.[5]

Address It

In their book *Getting to Yes*, Roger Fisher and William Ury present a four-step process for addressing and resolving conflict[6]:

1. Separate the people from the problem.
2. Focus on interests, not positions.
3. Create options.
4. Insist on using objective criteria.

A common mistake made in conflict resolution is to place too much emphasis on the individuals involved in the situation. This can be linked to a fear of not wanting to damage a relationship. If the real issue is not identified, collaboration cannot be achieved. In separating the people from the problem:

*   Focus on the problem, not the people involved.
*   Identify the real versus the perceived problem.
*   Explain the problem as you see it.
    *   ▷ Discuss the situation as you see it and ask for reactions.

- ▷ Find common issues and shared goals. *"We agree on the importance of _____. Shall we look into it further?"*
- ♦ Maintain constructive relationships.
- ♦ Give and get feedback. Don't assume that others see things the same way you do.
- ♦ Proactively work to uncover problems by asking questions. *"Is everything happening as you expected?"*

Tips on Managing Relationship Value[7]

- ♦ Create trust by demonstrating that your words and actions are in harmony.
- ♦ Communicate interests, capabilities, and concerns.
- ♦ Never sweep mistakes under the rug. Acknowledge and address them quickly.
- ♦ Ask for feedback, and never assume that the other party sees things the same as you.
- ♦ Work to uncover problems. The other party will respect you for it.

- ♦ Put your opinions aside and show interest. *"I'd like to hear more about the situation from your perspective."*

What if people are the problem? People problems often require more attention than substantive ones. In these cases it becomes necessary to[8]:

- ♦ Untangle substantive issues from relationship and process issues. Substantive issues include terms, conditions, prices, dates, numbers, and liabilities. Relationship issues include the balance of emotion and reason; ease of communication; degree of trust and reliability; attitude of acceptance or rejection; relative emphasis on persuasion; and degree of mutual understanding.
- ♦ Build a working relationship independent of agreement or disagreement. Agree to disagree.
- ♦ Negotiate the relationship and the people problems on their merits. Raise concerns without judging motivations.
- ♦ Distinguish how they treat you from how you treat them. Avoid responding in kind, which may only result in reinforcing the undesirable behavior.
- ♦ Most importantly, don't personalize the conflict. Focus on the issues. When dealing with difficult attitudes, ask yourself:
  - ▷ Why do I care about the issue?
  - ▷ Why does the other person care?
  - ▷ Is the problem the type of issue that can fuel a creative spark?
  - ▷ What are the consequences of not resolving the issue amicably—to me, to the other person, and to the organization, including its stakeholders?

Focus on Interests, Not Positions

Interests are rooted in needs, concerns, desires, and fears often shared by both parties. A position is a way to get what you want. An interest is what you need to accomplish.[9]

Consider the following situation. Bob and Jan are part of a team that provides customized products to their clients. Bob, in customer service, feels that the customer relationship is most important. Jan, in technical service, feels that product, excellence is most important. They frequently clash, as she accuses him of merely charming the client without understanding what it takes to produce a quality product and he retorts with comments about her poor interpersonal skills scaring away the customers. Now Bob has to call Jan and discuss some changes to a client's requirements. The client has asked for a technical representative to be at the meeting. Their mutual interests are the customer's needs and company reputation. Their approach to accomplishing the customer's needs vary.

Consider the following statement made to Dawn by her boss: "If you don't land a new account by the end of the month, I'm going to have to let you go."[10] Dawn's boss is obviously not pleased, but what is the true interest? Does he really want to fire Dawn, or is that the *position* he is taking to get her to increase sales? What does he *need to accomplish*?

Reveal your interests. Remember that in a good conflict, issues are not masked, but are in the open. Explain why your interests benefit the organization and others. Explain why it is important, not just what is important. Collaborate with the other party or parties to understand the underlying issue and avoid arguing over positions. Ask yourself, *"Do I have a good argument?"*

Create Options

Creating options moves parties off their positions. It provides an opportunity to explore collective versus individual points of view and creates synergy. Brainstorm to create options for problem-solving and positive outcomes. Be curious and express genuine interest. A good brainstorming session will offer several points of view rather than opposing points of view.

Don't use the brainstorming process to evaluate the ideas presented. Separate the process of generating ideas from the process of evaluating them. Every option should be on the table. Value the dialogue rather than the debate.

As you are creating options, ask yourself, *"What assumptions am I making, that I'm not aware I'm making, that gives me what I see?"*

And when you have an answer, ask yourself, *"What options are now possible, that I haven't yet considered, that would provide other choices?"*

Use Objective Criteria

Use of objective criteria allows for efficiency and fairness. Time will not be spent talking about positions, but rather possible standards and solutions. Objective criteria are independent of each side's will, are practical, and are legitimate. Fair standards may be based upon things such as market value, precedent, professional standards, scientific judgment, or equal treatment.[11] Safety or quality standards are examples of fair and independent standards. Objective criteria can include precedent, efficiency, and costs.

Objective criteria should appeal and relate to shared interests and shared standards. Shared interests can be common interests of the larger community, such as the organization or the industry in which the organization operates, as well as the mutual interests of the individuals involved. Objective criteria can be based on shared standards or values, such as equality, fairness, integrity, or quality.[12]

Research criteria that might best apply. Be prepared to show why those criteria are relevant. Look at external standards, as well as internal equity. In evaluating criteria ask, *"Are the standards and criteria considered fair and reasonable?"*[13]

Relevancy is important. It keeps the parties focused on the issues and prevents the conflict from being derailed. Always ask this question: *"Is it relevant to the issue?"*

Discussion Questions

1. Jake has the office next to Beth and she has a difficult time working with him. He constantly interrupts her when she's on the phone, talks too loudly, and asks nosy, personal questions. It seems as if he distracts her all day long. What would you do if you were Beth? What would you if Beth came to you and asked you to resolve the situation?

2. What are examples of relevant criteria you could use in the following situations?
    ▷ Giving an employee who has reached the top of a salary range a raise.
    ▷ Giving an employee an increase over and above the approved budget.
    ▷ Negotiating salary and relocation with new hires.
    ▷ Negotiating a severance package with an employee who is being terminated.

3. Organizations can do a number of things to address and manage conflict. These include training options for managers and employees, policies that address certain behaviors, and programs that offer guidance and assistance. What are the things your organization is doing or could be doing?

4. Conflict is not necessarily negative; in fact, it may result in positive outcomes. Give some examples of how conflict can be a positive force in your organization. What can you do to optimize it when it is a positive force?

29

Risk Management

On March 25, 1911, approximately 146 people, many in their teens, died or jumped to their deaths in the Triangle Shirtwaist Company fire. The fire engines at the scene did not have ladders that reached to the ninth floor where the blaze was raging. The fire escape, which did not reach to the street and was not built to accommodate more than a few people at a time, collapsed. The stairwell that led to the roof was burning. The one that led down to the street was padlocked from the outside so that the workers would be prevented from eluding inspection or making off with leftover scraps of cloth. Triangle's owners rebuffed the union's demand for sprinklers and unlocked stairwells. They were later tried for manslaughter, but acquitted in the absence of any laws that set workplace safety standards.[1] One hundred years later, we not only have workplace safety standards, but we have safety included in organizations' values.

Concerns about employee health and safety have evolved into risk management systems that also include concerns about individual and organizational security and privacy.

The DuPont Commitment: Goal of Zero Injuries, Illnesses, and Incidents[2]

We believe that all injuries and occupational illnesses, as well as safety and environmental incidents, are preventable, and our goal for all of them is zero. We will promote off-the-job safety for our employees. We will assess the environmental impact of each facility we propose to construct or acquire and will design, build, operate and maintain all our facilities and transportation equipment so they are safe, secure and acceptable to local communities and protect the environment. We will be prepared for emergencies and will provide leadership to assist our local communities to improve their emergency preparedness.

The Legal Landscape of Safety and Health
Occupational Safety and Health Act, 1970

Congress enacted the Occupational Safety and Health Act to ensure safe and healthful working conditions for working men and women by setting and enforcing standards, and by providing training, outreach, education, and assistance. The Act is enforced by the Occupational Safety and Health Administration (OSHA) within the Department of Labor.

The Act's General Duty clause requires employers to provide jobs and a workplace free from recognized hazards that are causing or are likely to cause death or serious physical harm. Both employers and employees are required to comply with OSHA standards, rules, and regulations.

Employees have a right to:

- Demand safety and health on the job.
- Request inspections.
- Have an authorized employee representative accompany an inspection.
- File a complaint.
- Be informed of workplace hazards.
- Receive training.

Employers must keep employees informed by:
- Displaying the OSHA poster.

> → See www.osha.gov/publications/poster.html.

- Providing copies of rules and regulations.
- Posting OSHA citations.
- Notifying employees exposed to hazardous agents at levels exceeding OSHA standards and informing them of corrective actions.
- Maintaining accurate records.
- Permitting authorized employee representation during an OSHA inspection.

Employers must keep employees safe by:
- Correcting violations.
- Allowing employees to refuse abnormally dangerous work.
- Providing personal protective equipment.
- Providing medical surveillance.
- Providing training.
- Enforcing safety rules and regulations.

OSHA has defined additional general industry standards that include, but are not limited to:
- **Emergency Exit Procedures** require an emergency action plan for continuous and unobstructed means of exit from any point in a building and requires maintenance of emergency systems.
- **Occupational Noise Exposure** established permissible noise levels and measurement procedures, and requires hearing conservation programs and audiometric testing for employees in environments with noise above permissible levels.
- **Machine Guarding** requires point of operation guards on certain machinery.

SECTION 5

- **Hazard Communication** requires that information about the hazards of chemicals in the workplace is disseminated. Chemical manufacturers and importers must evaluate the hazards, prepare labels, and make material safety data sheets (MSDSs) available to employees to convey their hazards. Employees must be trained to handle the chemicals properly.
- **Control of Hazardous Energy—Lockout/Tagout** requires affixing devices to machines and equipment to prevent unexpected start up or release of stored energy during maintenance.
- **Bloodborne Pathogens** requires employers to take steps to prevent exposure to pathogenic microorganisms in human blood that can cause disease. This includes written exposure control plans informing employees of preventive steps, post-exposure evaluation and follow-up, record-keeping, and incident evaluation procedures. The Needlestick Safety and Protection Act (passed in 2000) revised this standard to require employers to minimize workers' exposure to blood through needlesticks.
- **Confined Space Entry** requires permits for employees to enter spaces that may be filled with a hazardous atmosphere that is immediately dangerous to life and health.
- **Personal Protective Equipment** requires protection to be used if employees come in contact with hazardous materials.
- **Process Safety Management** requires processes to prevent or minimize the effect of catastrophic releases of toxic, reactive, flammable, or explosive chemicals.

OSHA Inspections

OSHA has the authority to inspect workplaces. It priorities the need for inspection in the following order:

- Imminent danger, a reasonable certainty that death or serious harm from an existing hazard will occur before the danger can be eliminated through normal enforcement procedures.
- Catastrophes and fatal accidents that resulted in a death or hospitalization of three or more employees as reported to OSHA within eight hours of the event to determine whether existing standards were violated.
- Complaints from employees of unsafe or unhealthful conditions and referrals from any source about a workplace hazard.
- Programmed inspections targeting high-hazard industries, workplaces, occupations with high injury/illness rates, and severe violators.
- Follow-ups on previously issued citations to ensure corrective action has been taken.

The following approach is used for conducting safety inspections:

- Opening conference, which discusses the purpose and scope of the inspection and the OSHA standards likely to be applied.
- Physical inspection of work areas for compliance with OSHA standards. If a complaint was filed, the specific area named in the complaint is inspected. Compliance with postings and recordkeeping requirements can also be reviewed.
- Closing conference, in which observations and corrective actions, along with possible violations, are discussed.

SECTION 5

OSHA at 40[3]

In the almost five decades since the Occupational Safety and Health (OSH) Act was signed into law and the Occupational Safety and Health Administration (OSHA) was charged with enforcing it, workplaces across the nation have realized a dramatic decrease in work-related deaths and injuries. Since 1971, workplace fatalities have been reduced approximately 65 percent, from near 14,000 to 4,836 in 2015—in a workforce that has doubled in size.

Enforcement of OSHA Standards

OSHA's success results from its strong enforcement of its standards. It has established fines and penalties that it can assess against organizations that violate the required standards. The categories of OSHA violations and penalties are:

- **Willful.** An intentional violation that the employer knowingly commits. Penalty up to $70,000 for each willful violation.
- **Serious.** A violation in which there is a substantial probability that death or serious physical harm could result. Penalty up to $7,000 depending on the gravity of the violation.
- **Other-Than-Serious.** A violation that has a direct and immediate effect on job safety and health, but probably would not cause death or serious physical harm. Penalty up to $7,000 for each violation.
- **Repeat.** A violation where OSHA previously issued a citation for a substantially similar violation. Penalties up to $70,000 for each such violation within the previous three years.
- **Failure-to-Abate.** Failure to correct a prior violation. Penalty of up to $7,000 for each day past the abatement date.
- *DeMinimus.* A violation with no direct or immediate effect on safety or health. No penalty.

OSHA Injury and Illness Reporting and Record-Keeping

Employers with more than 10 employees must report employee occupational injury and illness data. An occupational injury results from a work-related accident or exposure involving a single incident. An occupational illness is a medical condition or disorder caused by exposure to environmental factors associated with employment.

Employers are required to record work-related illnesses and injuries if they result in:

- Death.
- Days away from work.
- Restricted work or transfer to another job.
- Loss of consciousness.
- Diagnosis by a licensed healthcare professional.
- Medical treatment beyond first aid.

SECTION 5

OSHA Form 300 is a log of work-related injuries and illnesses that records specific details about what happened and how it happened.

OSHA Form 301, Injury and Illness Incident Report, includes more data about how the injury or illness occurred. It must be prepared within seven days for each recordable injury or illness and kept on file for five years.

OSHA Form 300A, Summary of Work-Related Injuries and Illnesses, shows the total injuries and illnesses by categories. Employers must post the log in a visible location in the workplace from February through April each year.

Starting in 2017, many employers will be required to electronically submit injury and illness data to OSHA. Establishments with 250 or more employees in industries covered by the record-keeping regulation will have to electronically submit injury and illness information from OSHA Forms 300, 300A, and 301 while establishments with 20–249 employees in certain high-risk industries will have to electronically submit only the information from OSHA Form 300A. This electronic reporting requirement will be phased in over two years.

> ⇥ For additional information on OSHA recordkeeping, visit *www.osha. gov/recordkeeping/index.html* and *www.osha.gov/recordkeeping/final-rule/index.html*.

All employers covered by the Occupational Safety and Health Act of 1970 must report to OSHA any workplace incident resulting in a fatality or the in-patient hospitalization of three or more employees within eight hours.

> ⇥ For additional information on OSHA, visit *www.osha.gov* and *www. dol.gov/compliance/guide/osha.htm*.

Workplace Safety and Health

Workplace safety is the absence from hazard, risk, or injury on the job, whereas workplace health focuses on environmental health hazards and infectious diseases that can affect the workplace. In addition, employers also incorporate employee wellness and fitness programs and employee assistance programs into their overall risk management in order to improve employee well-being, motivation, and productivity.

Safety Management Programs

Common characteristics of safety management programs include:
- Management commitment to safety and employee involvement.
- Ongoing worksite analysis to identify potential safety and health hazards, and prevent accidents.
- Hazard prevention and control programs.
- Corrective action.
- Ongoing safety and health programs.
- Systems to report and investigate accidents.

Safety committees comprised of employees and management representatives can encourage safety awareness, motivate peers, and identify and correct hazards. Employees doing the job know best about safe practices. Working with management, they must be involved in developing safe operating procedures.

SECTION 5

➤   Information on safety and accident prevention may be found at the
      National Institute for Occupational Safety's website: *www.cdc.gov/niosh*.

➤   Appendix: Safety Checklist.

Health Hazards

Environmental health hazards can be physical (heat, noise, ventilation, smoking), chemical (dust, fumes, gases, toxic materials, carcinogens, smoke), or biological (bacteria, fungi, insects, sanitary conditions).

Ergonomics addresses the way a physical environment is designed for the safety and efficiency of people. Poor design can cause musculoskeletal disorders including repetitive stress injuries, such as carpel tunnel syndrome, computer vision syndrome, or lower back pain. Ergonomics programs include:

- Work-site analysis.
- Job redesign.
- Surveys/monitoring/feedback.
- Training.
- On-site exercise programs.

➤   Additional information can be found at *www.osha.gov/dts/osta/os-hasoft/index.html#etool*.

Biological health hazards include infectious diseases such as the Hepatitis B and Hepatitis C viruses and HIV/AIDS, which are blood-borne pathogens, and tuberculosis, which is an airborne contagious disease caused by bacterial infection spread through casual workplace contact. Also included are future pandemics, communicable diseases new to the population that spread easily, infect humans, and cause serious illness, such as the Severe Acute Respiratory Syndrome (SARS). Employees with infectious diseases who do not pose a threat to coworkers are protected by the ADA's requirement for reasonable accommodation.

➤   Additional information on pandemics and preparedness plans can be
      found at *www.pandemicflu.gov and www.who.int/en*.

Health and Wellness Programs

Many organizations provide employee wellness programs, including nutrition and weight control, smoking cessation, stress reduction, and fitness. These programs yield healthier and more productive employees, which translates into savings on health insurance for the employer and employee. Motivating employees and their family members through information and incentives that are tied to wellness program participation and behavioral change also pays off. Although well-designed programs can benefit the organization and its employees, employers should assure that they comply with federal laws including the Employee Retirement Income Security Act (ERISA), Health Insurance Portability and Accountability Act (HIPAA), Americans With Disabilities Act (ADA), and Genetic Information Nondiscrimination Act (GINA), as well as any state or local laws.

SECTION 5

> ### ROI of Wellness Programs[4]
>
> Johnson & Johnson, a leader in wellness programs, offers a $150 benefits bonus to overweight employees who reduce their body mass index by 10 percent. It found that its wellness program slowed the rate of increase of its healthcare costs by $565 per employee.

Substance Abuse and Drug Testing

Substance abuse costs employers through reduced productivity, increased errors and accidents, and increased costs related to healthcare, workers compensation, tardiness, and absenteeism. Many organizations offer substance abuse programs that can include any and all of the following:

- A written policy.

    → See Chapter 27 (Employee and Labor Relations).

- Management training to understand all related policies, to recognize signs of substance abuse, to understand the importance of documenting performance and conduct issues, and to advise of the steps to take to deal with substance abuse in the workplace.
- Education programs for employees.
- Drug testing programs.
- Interventions and referrals to Employee Assistance Programs.

> ### The Drug-Free Workplace Act, 1988
>
> The Drug-Free Workplace Act requires federal contractors with contracts of $100,000 or more and recipients of grants to:
> - Develop a policy that maintains a drug-free workplace.
> - Specify penalties for policy violations.
> - Provide a copy of the policy to employees.
> - Establish a drug-awareness program

Types of drug testing include:
- Pre-employment, which must occur after an offer of employment has been made.
- Reasonable suspicion or for cause based on behavioral indicators.
- Post-accident or when an employee is involved in an unsafe practice.
- Post-treatment following rehabilitation.
- Random or unannounced testing, usually for specific employees for security or safety reasons.

Before implementing any type of drug-testing programs, organizations should seek advice from legal counselors as well as healthcare professionals, including EAP professionals.

Intervention strategies include:

◆ Constructive confrontation by management focusing on job performance.

◆ Counseling by Employee Assistance and other healthcare professionals, focusing on the cause and treatment of the problem.

> ➜   Appendix: Indicators of a Troubled Employee.

Access to EAP services are generally through a referral. Common types of referrals include:

◆ **Self-referrals**, in which an employee voluntarily seeks assistance for an issue affecting his or her life, either at work or away from work.

◆ **Management referrals**, which are voluntary referrals based on tangible, observed, and documented indicators of deteriorating job performance or behavior. If an employee fails to take advantage of the EAP, no direct management action should be taken, but the organization should continue to hold the employee accountable for performance and conduct, and take appropriate action if there is further deterioration.

◆ **Mandatory referrals** generally occur as the result of a positive drug test or when violent or potentially violent behavior is exhibited. Unlike management referrals, employees can be subject to management action, including termination, for failure to contact the EAP. Employees are often placed on leave until they contact the EAP, comply with a course of treatment, and receive an appropriate fitness for duty.

In developing policies and programs regarding EAPs, it is wise to seek professional advice. Making referrals to the EAP, whether management or mandatory, can be uncomfortable and difficult for managers, and they should receive appropriate training. Professional advisors can assist with the design and delivery of training.

> ➜   Employee Assistance Programs are also discussed in Chapter 21 (Employee Benefits).

Workplace Security

Workplace security covers a broad range of topics designed to protect an organization from a variety of threats including natural disasters, manmade threats, computer hackers, loss or theft of property and proprietary information, and workplace violence. Security programs require an integrated approach involving organizational entities such as human resources, facilities, security, finance, legal and public relations, as well as outside consultants specializing in risk management and Employee Assistance Programs.

A risk analysis and assessment should be conducted to identify the external forces or threats and internal weaknesses or vulnerabilities that the organization faces. This will determine how likely it is a loss will occur, the severity or impact of the loss on the organization, and the costs should a loss occur. Identifying and ranking risk (fatal, very serious, moderately serious, or negligible) provide the opportunity to be proactive and implement programs and controls to prevent damage to business assets.

Protecting physical assets generally includes the use of security guards, identification and external control systems (fingerprints or magnetic cards), structural barriers (gates or fences), and security hardware such as alarms, sensors, or video surveillance. Organizations also have practices to protect assets, including financial assets, against theft and fraud. These practices include sound auditing procedures, inventory and internal controls, fraud hotlines, and video surveillance.

Protecting confidential information is often accomplished with non-disclosure agreements and intellectual property agreements. These agreements should identify what information the organization considers confidential, how its use is limited, and for how long it will remain confidential. Such agreements are specific to every organization and legal advice should be sought in developing them. Additional protections that employers can take include:

- Developing a policy prohibiting inappropriate use/disclosure of proprietary information.
- Restricting the discussion or display of sensitive information.
- Restricting access to computer information and employee data.

Cybersecurity, or information technology security, focuses on the need for organizations to protect computers, networks, programs, and data from unintended or unauthorized access, change, or destruction from hackers or cyber criminals. Sensitive business information, as well as personal information about employees, is confidential, yet that data is often transmitted within the organization or across networks to other firms. Mobile computing devices are increasingly used for reviewing payroll information, performing shift-scheduling duties, processing approvals, and/ or handling back-end HR tasks, and public networks are often used to connect to corporate networks to access and transmit data. Cyber risk assessments should be performed to determine what information needs to be protected, to identify threats to this data, and to forecast the consequences of successful cyber-attacks.

> ➔ For additional information, The National Cyber Security Alliance has information about conducting a cyber risk assessment at *staysafeonline.org*.

Identity theft, the nation's number-one consumer fraud issue, occurs when someone fraudulently obtains and uses another person's personal information, such as name, Social Security number, or credit card number, without authorization, consent, or knowledge. Employers must understand the risks and implement the necessary systems and precautions to protect the security of their employees' personal and confidential information so that employees do not become the victims of identity theft and employers are at minimal risk of liability for unauthorized access, breach, or theft of such information.

> ➔ The Federal Trade Commission has issued guidance, which can be found at *business.ftc.gov/documents/bus59-information-compromise-and-risk-id-theft-guidance-your-business*.

Protecting human assets involves not only the protections in place for physical assets and safety training, but also guidelines for protecting employees who travel or work outside the United States where issues of political stability and animosity toward American companies may exist. Another security issue involves special needs for preventing the kidnapping of executives.

Workplace violence presents the largest threat to workers and employers. Some of the leading causes of violence include stress, domestic violence, and mental illness. Perpetrators can include strangers, coworkers, and former employees. Violence can take the form of homicide, stalking, verbal and physical threats and harassment, inappropriate communication, and defacing of property.

Organizations can take a proactive approach to reduce the risk of workplace violence by:

- Checking references and monitoring employee behavior.
- Giving employees a vehicle to express concerns, such as an EAP.
- Maintaining a zero-tolerance policy for violence.

> → See Chapter 27 (Employee and Labor Relations).

- Educating and training managers and staff.
- Conducting threat assessments that include identifying early warning signs, reporting all threats, developing a threat assessment team and management plan, and documenting all threat incidents, responses, and outcomes.

Troubled employees exhibit similar signs and symptoms regardless of the root cause of their problem (substance abuse, mental illness, stress). It is important to work with EAP or other healthcare professionals in addressing these issues.

> → Additional resources can be found at the National Institute of Occupational Safety and Health website: *www.cdc.gov/niosh/topics/violence*; and the OSHA website: *www.osha.gov*.

Emergency Preparedness and Response

Emergency preparedness and response programs should include procedures that define the steps an employer will take during and immediately after a violent incident occurs in the workplace. Senior management should be involved to set priorities, identify resources including team members, and communicate the program.

A crisis management plan should be tested, be kept up-to-date, and include the following elements:

- Emergency notification procedures (police, fire, ambulance, internal security, employee assistance program);
- Initiation of an internal crisis management team;
- Assessment of the immediate safety of the workplace;
- Proper notification to those in danger;
- Counseling for those involved;
- Employer investigation of the incident; and
- Public relations concerns.

Finally, organizations should have continuity plans that in addition to identifying threats and impacts, provides a framework for ensuring that the organization is able to withstand disruption, interruption, or loss of normal business functions/operations.

> → Information on emergency preparedness and response can be found at NIOSH'S website: *www.cdc.gov/niosh*; and at the National Institute of Environmental Health Sciences website: *tools.niehs.nih.gov/wetp*.

Disaster Recovery[5]

Cantor Fitzgerald suffered the most devastating corporate casualties on September 11, 2001, losing 658 of its 960 New York–based employees. One key recovery element was the mirror site that Cantor had established at its data center in Rochelle Park, New Jersey, which replicated all of the machines, connections, and functionality inside the company's WTC headquarters. Another key element was Cantor's surviving headquarters employees. With the company's three-shift, around-the-clock schedule, some Cantor employees weren't scheduled to work at the time of the 9/11's attacks.

The Legal Landscape Continues

In addition to the laws discussed earlier, the following affect risk management:

- **Sarbanes-Oxley Act** has substantially impacted the procedures for financial reporting, internal controls, and accountability. There are also provisions for whistleblower protections and prohibitions for destroying, altering, or falsifying any document or record relative to a federal investigation.

  → See Chapter 20 (The Legal Landscape of Employee Benefits).

- **Health Insurance Portability and Accountability Act** includes standards to protect the privacy of individually identifiable information that include the authorization and required use and disclosure of information. It applies to group health plans, healthcare providers, and healthcare clearing houses.

  → See Chapter 20 (The Legal Landscape of Employee Benefits).

- **The Electronic Communications Privacy Act, 1986** is comprised of the Wiretap Act, 1968, and its amendments, which prohibit interception of emails in transmission, and the Stored Communications Act, 1986, which protects email in storage.

Discussion Questions

1. What are some of the current risk management issues facing your organization today?
2. What has your organization done to address emerging risk management issues?
3. If an organization makes a strategic decision to stress employee health and wellness, what can it do to assure that employees participate in the programs and that the programs are compliant with all the relevant legal requirements?
4. Safety programs are often associated with industrial environments. Why are they important for all employers? If you were to design an employee health and safety program for your organization, what would it include?
5. In designing management briefings and employee training regarding risk management, what topics would you include for each audience? How would you deploy the training?

SECTION 5

30

Ending the Employment Relationship

"Is it ever appropriate to advise someone via text or email that their employment is being terminated?" was the question posed to a career advice column. The response was "This is not the best approach. Pick up the phone. If the circumstances are extraordinary and the employee cannot be reached, send a registered letter."

Whether people leave voluntarily or involuntarily, it is important that they leave with dignity and respect. They will feel positively about their experience and perhaps refer others to your organization or even return to work for you again in the future.

Types of Terminations

A voluntary termination is one that an employee initiates, such as retirement or resignation. Reasons that employees resign include a new job, relocation, and returning to school.

It is advisable to request a letter of resignation to document the reason the employee is leaving. When the employee puts his or her reason in writing, it shows that it was the employee's decision and helps the employer if an unemployment claim or other legal challenge is filed.

If you're an at-will employer, however, beware of putting any condition on a voluntary termination. It could violate your at-will policy. Legal advice should always be obtained.

Avoid putting statements such as the following in an employee handbook, for instance. They could be interpreted as conditions on voluntary terminations:

- Any employee who voluntarily resigns is required to provide advance written notice of no less than two weeks. Failure to provide such notice may result in the employee not being eligible for rehire.
- If you want to end your employment, we ask that you notify us at least two weeks before your intended last day. Notice should be given in writing to your supervisor. The two-week notification period should be used for transition of work assignments.

Rather than compel the employee to provide notice, request it. Consider the following:

- If you voluntarily terminate your employment, you may choose to provide a notification period to allow for the transition of work assignments and to help us prepare the necessary documents for your termination.
- Retirement is a type of voluntary termination. To assure that there is ample time to prepare for any necessary benefits, you may choose to provide a notification period prior to your retirement.

An involuntary termination is one that the organization initiates, such as termination for cause, which can be a step in a corrective action process, or layoff, which is generally a reduction in the workforce resulting from a loss of business or a merger/acquisition.

Other circumstances can also result in an involuntary termination, such as the end of a temporary assignment, the expiration of a leave of absence in accordance with company policy and/or legal requirements, or other administrative actions. The company is technically initiating these actions, but they are not for cause or a reduction in force.

Sometimes organizations will allow an employee to resign in lieu of a termination for cause, or will categorize a termination as a resignation by mutual agreement. Negotiating what would otherwise be a for-cause negotiation has some risk, and you'd be wise to get legal guidance. For example, if men are allowed to resign in lieu of termination because they ask to do so more frequently than women ask, it could be a practice that results in adverse impact for women; it might appear that women are being terminated more frequently than men. Offer it to everyone or don't offer it at all. If you have a sound reason for terminating someone for cause, do so.

When an employer finds that it is necessary to reduce its workforce, it should take the following actions into consideration:

- Conduct an adverse impact analysis under attorney-client privilege to ensure that there is no indication of potential discrimination. This is important if some employees are being chosen for layoff and others in the same department or unit are being retained.
- Offer either a severance package or pay in lieu of notice, depending on industry and geographic standards. The practice of pay in lieu of notice occurs when an organization finds it necessary to release employees without providing advance notice of the layoff.
- Offer outplacement.

Sample Layoff Script

[Name], changing economic conditions have resulted in a loss of revenue and have caused us to restructure in order to reduce costs. This will result in the elimination of a number of positions, including your position.

[Today] will be your last day of work with us and we have information to provide regarding your final paycheck, severance package, COBRA, unemployment insurance and the outplacement services available to you. I know this is a great deal of information to absorb at once, and I'm sorry to have to communicate this to you. I want to take a minute to see how you're doing. Are you okay?

Just so you're aware: About 35 positions are being eliminated throughout the day. While I can't share any other names, I can share that this decision was made after a long and careful review of many options. The hardest thing for a manager to do is selecting positions for elimination realizing that the people attached to those positions will be affected.

Finally, I just want to thank you for all your hard work and dedication for the past [two years]. I'm personally going to miss working with you. Thank you for all you have done for us.

Legal Landscape

In addition to the antidiscrimination laws discussed in Chapter 3 (The Legal Landscape of Employee Rights), there are additional laws to consider when terminating employees.

Worker Adjustment and Retraining Notification Act (WARN), 1988

The Worker Adjustment and Retraining Notification Act (WARN) protects workers, their families, and communities by requiring most employers with 100 or more employees to provide notification 60 calendar days in advance of plant closings and mass layoffs.

- A plant closing is a temporary or permanent shutdown of a single employment site that results in an employment loss during any 30-day period for 50 or more full-time employees.
- A mass-layoff is a reduction in force during any 30-day period that results in the employment loss at a single employment site for either 50 or more employees if they compose 33 percent of the workforce, or 500 or more full-time employees.

WARN requires that notice also be given to employees' representatives, the local chief elected official, and the state dislocated worker unit.

Generally, WARN covers employers with 100 or more employees, not counting those who have worked less than six months in the last 12 months and those who work an average of less than 20 hours a week.

The Department of Labor's (DOL) Employment and Training Administration (ETA) administers WARN at the federal level, and some states have plant closure laws of their own. A State Dislocated Worker Unit Coordinator can provide more information on notice requirements in a specific area.

SECTION 5

➤   For additional information and to find a link to the States Dislocated Worker Unit Coordinator, visit *www.doleta.gov/layoff/rapid_coord.cfm*.

Employee Retirement Income Security Act of 1974 (ERISA)

The organization should consider whether to address severance pay in exchange for a release of claims on an ad hoc basis or by means of an established severance plan subject to the Employee Retirement Income Security Act (ERISA) of 1974.

➤   See Chapter 20 (The Legal Landscape of Employee Benefits) for more about ERISA.

➤   For additional information, visit *www.dol.gov/dol/topic/retirement/ erisa.htm*.

Older Workers Benefit Protection Act of 1900 (OWBPA)

The Older Workers Benefit Protection Act of 1990 (OWBPA) amended the Age Discrimination in Employment Act (ADEA) to specifically prohibit employers from denying benefits to older employees. An employer may ask an employee to waive his or her rights or claims in connection with an exit incentive program or other employment termination program. However, the ADEA, as amended by OWBPA, sets out specific minimum standards that must be met in order for a waiver to be considered knowing and voluntary and, therefore, valid. Among other requirements, a valid ADEA waiver must:

1. Be in writing and be understandable.
2. Specifically refer to ADEA rights or claims.
3. Not waive rights or claims that may arise in the future.
4. Be in exchange for valuable consideration.
5. Advise the individual in writing to consult an attorney before signing the waiver.
6. Provide the individual at least 21 days to consider the agreement and at least seven days to revoke the agreement after signing it.

If an employer requests an ADEA waiver in connection with an exit incentive program or other employment termination program that impacts two or more employees, the minimum requirements for a valid waiver are more extensive. It is important to seek legal advice.

➤   For additional information on Waivers and Claims under the ADEA, visit *www.eeoc.gov/federal/digest/xi-6-3.cfm*.

➤   The OWBPA is also discussed in Chapter 20 (The Legal Landscape of Employee Benefits).

Consolidated Omnibus Budget Reconciliation Act (COBRA), 1985

The Consolidated Omnibus Budget Reconciliation Act (COBRA) gives workers and their families (qualified beneficiaries) who lose their health benefits the right to choose to continue group health benefits provided by their group health plan for limited periods of time under certain circumstances (qualifying events). Individuals who elect to continue their benefits under COBRA may be required to pay the actual cost of the plan (employer and employee contributions) plus a 2-percent administration fee.

A qualified beneficiary generally is an individual, covered by a group health plan on the day before a qualifying event, who is an employee, an employee's spouse, or an employee's dependent child. In certain cases, retirees may be qualified beneficiaries. In addition, any child born to or placed for adoption with a covered employee during the period of COBRA coverage is considered a qualified beneficiary.

The length of time an employee can continue coverage under COBRA depends on the type of qualifying event.

Qualifying Events for Employees, Spouses, and Dependent Children	Length of Continuation
Termination of employment for gross misconduct	0
Voluntary or involuntary termination of employment for reasons other than gross misconduct	18 months
Reduction in the number of hours of employment	18 months
Employee is disabled when terminated or when hours are reduced	29 months
Divorce or legal separation from, or death of the covered employee	36 months
Loss of dependent child status	36 months

COBRA coverage ends when:

+ The employee or dependent fails to pay premiums on a timely basis.
+ Medical insurance is obtained from a new employer, or coverage is gained under Medicare.
+ The employer goes out of business or ceases to maintain a group health plan.

When employees become eligible for coverage under COBRA, they must be notified of their rights under COBRA and the provisions of the law. COBRA information must also be contained in the plan's summary plan description. Employers have a responsibility to notify the plan administrator of the employee's death, termination of employment or reduction in hours, or Medicare entitlement.

When the plan administrator is notified that a qualifying event has happened, it must in turn notify each qualified beneficiary of the right to choose continuation coverage.

COBRA allows at least 60 days from the date the election notice is provided to inform the plan administrator that the qualified beneficiary wants to elect continuation coverage.

The covered employee or a family member has the responsibility to inform the plan administrator of a divorce, legal separation, disability, or a child losing dependent status under the plan. If covered individuals change their marital status, or their spouses have changed addresses, they should notify the plan administrator.

> ➤ For additional information, visit *www.dol.gov/dol/topic/health-plans/ cobra.htm#doltopics* and *www.dol.gov/ebsa/newsroom/fscobra.html.*

SECTION 5

Terminations for Cause

If it is necessary to terminate an employee for cause, consider the following:

- Have there been violations of policies, practices, or guidelines? Are they serious?
- How has the company dealt with similar violations in the past?
- Have the parties in question been involved with policy violations in the past?
- How long have these employees been employed by the company?
- What is their performance history?
- Are there federal, state, or local laws that require specific action in this particular case?
- Are there any other mitigating circumstances?
- If claims have been made, such as claims of harassment or discrimination, have they been thoroughly investigated and has the evidence been examined?

Corroborating evidence, such as statements from witnesses who can confirm or deny facts based on firsthand experience or observation, directly confirms a disputed allegation.

Circumstantial evidence consists of things an individual has said or done in other situations, which make it more likely than not that the fact(s) in the dispute actually happened. It is not necessarily about the specific allegations. In reviewing evidence, keep in mind that:

- A fact is information that has been seen, heard, read, or otherwise directly observed.
- An inference is an opinion or conclusion drawn from a fact or facts.

Documentary evidence provides background information which will help you verify facts and identify additional individuals who may have information. Documentary evidence includes, but is not necessarily limited to:

- Letters.
- Payroll records.
- Computer/system records.
- Memos.
- Security tapes.
- Calendars/planners.
- Expense reports.
- Emails.
- Voice mails.
- Time records.

Consider the alternatives, such as:

- Disciplinary or corrective action in accordance with your company's policy, such as a counseling, warning, or suspension.
- Performance improvement, including training, education, or reassignment.
- Intervention, including EAP referrals, coaching, or counseling.

Will the employee be a willing participant if performance improvement or intervention is recommended?

➙   Appendix: Manager's Termination Checklist.

Employers should be prepared in advance to[1]:

- Block computer system access.
- Change passwords.
- Remove the employee's name as a signatory to any business-related document.
- Collect keys, identification badges, and company property.
- Obtain adequate personal security if the situation becomes hostile.

Termination Notifications

Notification of the termination decision should be planned with care. The employee's direct supervisor and a human resources representative should attend a termination meeting to avoid disagreements about what was communicated. Hold the meeting in a neutral, private setting. Select seats so that an angry or violent employee will not be able to block the exit.

Plan in advance what to say in a termination meeting. Essential topics to cover are:

- That a decision has been made to terminate employment.
- The reason(s) and key facts supporting the decision.
- The effective date of separation.
- Separation package and benefits.
- A review of the policy and procedures for giving references.
- A review of applicable post-termination restrictions, such as non-compete or non-disclosure agreements.
- What will happen immediately following the meeting (for example, cleaning out the employee's office, returning company property, escort from the building).
- Other exit activities such as an exit interview survey or outplacement meetings.
- Whom to contact about post-termination issues.

Layoffs

Layoffs are, unfortunately, a fact of corporate life. Companies get acquired and positions become redundant. Business softens and the organization must find ways to reduce costs, including making reductions in staff. Affected employees are not at fault. They are just in an unfortunate situation. Here are some pointers to assure that when layoff decisions must be made, the employees losing their jobs are treated fairly and respectfully:

- Overcommunicate and be open and honest. Let all employees know the timing of the layoffs. Affected employees should be advised of any severance benefits they will receive.
- Treat everyone equitably. Use objective criteria to determine which positions will be eliminated. Avoid using subjective criteria (such as constructing a negative performance review prior to the layoff) to justify including someone in the layoff.
- Help people find jobs. Outplacement assistance goes a long way, not just in aiding the employees find new jobs, but in maintaining a positive culture and reputation.

Give as much notice as possible. Time is the best asset for an employee losing a job. Don't hide behind confidentiality concerns as an excuse for little or no notice. If you have legitimate concerns regarding a particular employee, address that concern separately, but don't let others who will be affected suffer.[2]

SECTION 5

When considering layoffs, remember that positions are being eliminated, not people. Don't be tempted to call a termination for cause a layoff. If the person's position is vital to your organization, you can't leave it unfilled. You may also be vulnerable to outside challenges. Follow your performance management or corrective discipline processes if you have to deal with an employee having performance or workplace behavior issues.

Outprocessing and Exit Interviews

It is important that the employment relationship end with the same degree of care as when it began. Processes should be in place to ensure a smooth transition out of the organization. Appropriate administrative functions, such as security, IT, accounting, and so forth, should be notified in order to make arrangements for the return of company property and cancellation of access to the organization's systems (telephone, computer, security).

Outprocessing meetings with the employee usually include:

◆ Review of eligibility for benefits continuation and conversion including all necessary forms to ensure they are properly completed.

◆ Return of all property, such as credit cards, identification and building access cards, keys, computers, and other electronic equipment.

◆ An opportunity to review and comment on the employee's job-related experiences.

Many employers provide an exit interview assessment form that gives the employee an opportunity to share opinions and ideas about their employment experience. Some organizations conduct post-termination surveys three to six months after termination as a way to follow up and gain additional insights.

> ➔ See Chapter 13 (Strategic Retention) for more information on using exit interview data to develop employee retention strategies.

Any data gathered from exit interviews should be summarized with the intent of looking for trends, not individual complaints. For example, looking at exit interviews quarterly—to determine if there is turnover in a particular location or to evaluate if a significant percentage of exiting employees mention they would have liked to have had more training—will give your organization something to improve. It is sometimes tempting to take one person's comments and run with them, but it is advisable to wait until you have more data before making changes.

Sample Outprocessing Instructions

This package contains information about your benefits upon termination, as well as forms that you need to complete.

Prior to your last day, you will need to turn in:

- ◆ All keys (desk keys, door keys, etc.).
- ◆ Computers and computer equipment.
- ◆ Cell phones.
- ◆ Facility access cards.
- ◆ Company/client-issued badges.
- ◆ Any other company property.
- ◆ Any other client property.

If you have any open or outstanding accounting items, such as travel reimbursement, you will be notified by the accounting department and will have to arrange to close out these items.

If you have any questions concerning completion of the termination forms or your benefits, please contact: _____ .

→ Appendix: Sample Exit Interview Questions.

Maintaining a Relationship With Former Employees

Employee terminations may be the end of the formal employment relationship, but they need not be the end of all contact with the employees. It is beneficial for employers to keep the lines of communication open with employees who leave. Valued former employees can be a source of recruitment and referrals, and they may choose to return. Retired employees and those considering retirement might be retained if provided with the right incentives. Flexible scheduling arrangements that have been particularly successful for older workers include[3]:

- ◆ Part-time.
- ◆ Casual or on-call programs.
- ◆ Phased retirement, which features reduced hours over a period of time.
- ◆ Rehearsal retirement, which provides the opportunity to work part-time and offering non-paid hours to volunteer organizations.
- ◆ Job sharing. This can be beneficial to the organization if it partners an older adult with a younger trainee and allows for the transfer of knowledge.

SECTION 5

Staying in Touch With Former Employees[4]

The welcome mat is out for former employees at Chevron, one of the world's leading integrated energy companies. Chevron has an online alumni network to keep up with its former employees and provide opportunities for them to come back as contract workers if they are interested. The Chevron Alumni Community website is a wonderful tool that enables former Chevron employees to consider career opportunities, refer associates, and keep abreast of corporate activities at Chevron.

In addition, former employees can use the Alumni site to sign up for Chevron's Bridges Program, which allows them be considered for specific contract assignments in technical disciplines for Chevron and its subsidiaries. "The value they bring back and the knowledge they bring back is what we're really interested in," said D'Renda Syzdek, human resources counselor and former Alumni Bridges program manager.

Bringing former employees back sends the message to current employees that Chevron values their individual skills and expertise. "Many retirees and former employees have 20 to 30 years' experience. They have spent their professional lives doing just what we are expecting new hires to do. You can't beat that level of experience," stated Beth Hutton, training and competency program manager. The former employees return to Chevron comes complete with a familiarity of the corporate culture and a history of proven success within the corporation.

Reduced recruiting costs are also a motivator for Chevron management to use and support the Chevron Alumni Community website. The system has its own applicant tracking system, complete with resumes, performance reviews and commendations. But the best asset of the system is that all of the applicants have "been there, done that" at Chevron.

Turnover

Some turnover can be positive for an organization—for example, when an employee realizes that your culture isn't a good fit for him/her and makes the choice to resign. This provides you with the opportunity to fill this position with someone who does fit and who will, hopefully, stay a little bit longer. Turnover provides your organization with the opportunity to bring in people with different talents, ideas, and strengths that are needed to move you ahead in your marketplace. However, turnover can have a negative impact on your organization, so it needs to be carefully managed.

→   See Chapter 13 (Strategic Retention).

When looking at turnover data, consider evaluating more than just the percentages. You may want to look at:

- How many high-potential employees left who you wanted to keep?
- How many employees left whose departure didn't hurt your organization?
- How many employees left for reasons that, if you'd known about them, you could have been able to address and perhaps keep them? (This is controllable turnover.)
- How many employees left for reasons you couldn't do anything about? (This is uncontrollable turnover.)
- How many employees left within the first six months of employment? (This may indicate something is wrong with your selection process.)

The better you understand your turnover, the better chance your organization will have to make changes that are necessary to retrain the talented people you've worked so hard to hire and develop.

Discussion Questions

1. What steps does your organization take to stay in touch with valued employees who have left the organization?

2. What type of outplacement services do you offer? Under what circumstances are they offered? Do you offer different levels of service for various circumstances or types of employees?

3. What types of monetary compensation, such as severance, do you offer employees who are involuntarily terminated? If you offer a severance package, do you do so on an ad hoc basis or by means of an established severance plan subject ERISA?

4. What processes does your organization have in place to ensure a smooth transition out of the organization? What steps do you take to make sure there is a transition of any work assignments? As part of the process, do any face-to-face interviews take place with the employee to discuss their experiences?

5. If your organization conducts exit interviews (either in person or as a written survey) and/or post-termination surveys, how do you use the information obtained?

CONCLUSION

Emerging Trends and Challenges

We are experiencing an explosion of change: the influences of continually fluctuating laws and regulations, economic factors, technology, and globalization. Nothing is static. Throughout the chapters in this book, we've talked about the impact of these changes not only on the human resources professional, but in the organizations they support. These changes affect organizations of all sizes and in all industries, and innovative ways of managing work are evolving in response to these changes. Social media usage impacts a great deal more than just how organizations recruit new talent. We're also using social media platforms for employee development, and for facilitating the management of and communication with workforces spread around the globe.

The increased availability of good data means that organizations can now make decisions based on data and not on antidotal information. This is having a deep impact on the human resources field in particular; however, it also impacts everything an organization does.

The ways in which organizations are rewarding their employees are changing dramatically. Variable pay, a type of incentive compensation, is on the rise as we see a decrease in merit pay adjustments tied to performance ratings. A contributing factor to this trend is the re-engineering of performance management systems within many of these organizations.

Total reward systems, which go beyond how employees are paid, are also evolving. Responding to employees' desires for more flexibility and work-life integration, companies such as the Virgin Group are doing away with formal vacation policies and providing unlimited vacation. CEO Richard Branson has said, "Treat people as human beings, give them that flexibility and I don't think they'll abuse it. And they'll get the job done."[1] Netflix's offer of unlimited parental leave and full pay to employees in the first year after the birth or adoption of a child is one of the most generous parental leave policies in the United States to date, particularly among large employers.[2] Following Netflix's example, other companies in the technology industry—Adobe, Amazon, and Google, to name a few—began adjusting their parental leave policies.

Though these changes may reflect the needs of the knowledge workers in higher-paying jobs looking for more flexibility and even willing to forego more pay in exchange for more balance, employees in other industries, such as service or manufacturing, are at the lower end of the labor market. These workers are having opposite experiences with low wages and limited benefits, raising concerns about inequities and gaps. Such gaps give rise to concerns and discussions about raising the minimum wage and mandatory paid sick and parental leave.

Enter the so-called "gig economy." More and more individuals are becoming part of the contingent workforce, working as independent contractors, freelancers, or temporary workers. They work on single projects or tasks. They work on demand. Whether by choice (the desire to be independent) or by need (the inability to find full-time employment or the need to supplement income), the number of workers in the gig economy is growing. Although the data are unreliable, current estimates of the number of independent contractors range between 3 million and 50 million.[3] Disruptive and innovative technology are spawning new companies, such as Uber and Lyft, which provide ride services, that are contributing to the rise of such workers. The advantages of such a working arrangement includes providing flexibility and variety of work. The disadvantages include a lack of consistency in the hours, pay, and work itself, along with a lack of benefits. The concern about the lack of benefits for such workers is raising interesting questions and suggestions about changing the current social contract with workers that was designed for an industrial workforce.

According to Virginia senator Mark R. Warner, an entrepreneur himself before entering public life, there is a safety net missing for freelancers and contractors working in this new economy, and he wants to re-engineer the American economy to provide a system of portable benefits. People still need access to healthcare and retirement benefits, as well as protection from injury and loss of income. Warner is calling for innovation and creativity to provide such benefits, suggesting one scenario in which freelancers and contractors would partially fund their own benefits and carry them from job to job, with employers making contributions as well.[4]

The movement to re-engineer the social contract with workers has begun. In order to attract and retain workers, some organizations are moving to offer a version of traditional benefits for part-time or independent contractors. There has been a re-purposing of the 11th-century guild model, with Uber agreeing to create a guild that could negotiate discounts on life insurance and disability benefits for New York drivers. Etsy, an online craft marketplace, is proposing regulatory changes that would allow its sellers to set aside money to pay their taxes and create a federal government-run portal that would be in charge of certain benefits.[5] Another model has existed within the building-trades unions in which members were sent by the union to a job site. They essentially did work as contractors for a variety of organizations throughout the course of their working years, but received benefits from the union.

It is not just the American economy and workplace that are being impacted by change. In the United Kingdom, an employment tribunal has rejected Uber's argument that it is a technology company that links self-employed drivers with people who need rides, and not an employer.[6]

What is clear is that the way work is being performed is changing, and these changes are presenting both challenges and opportunities for organizations. We are no longer rooted in time and place to get work accomplished. Rules crafted during the industrial era no longer have relevance in many industries. Employers need to be aware of such changes and the impact they are having on their organizations, and take responsibility to ensure that workers' protections are not eroded in the process. If they do not, their freedom to implement new policies and benefits may be usurped by legislative mandates or the emergence of unions.

This is certainly not a call to rapidly abandon all that is old, but it is an appeal to examine what is and is not working in your organization. If it is time for new initiatives, those initiatives need to be carefully thought through before being implemented. There needs to be a strategic alignment with your organization's mission and values. Unlimited vacation or parental leave may sound interesting, but is it right for your organization? The business case for any new initiative has to be made, it has to be relevant, and it has to have an economic benefit for the organization and the worker. Organizations have to consider various options and the cost and benefit of each of those options.

We once heard historian and author David McCullough speak at a conference. During his speech, he said that you have to know where you've been to know where you're going. While writing this book, we often looked to the past—workers' lives without the protections that laws and regulations now provide—to understand the present. Understanding the past explains how we've evolved to where we are today with respect to human resources and management practices. The human resources profession is, and should be, a dynamic force that shapes organizations and public policy. It's time for innovation and creativity to take hold and leverage the technology that is giving rise to change and to new industries in the new economy that we are in today.

APPENDIX

Additional Resources

Note: All forms included in this appendix are *samples* only. In light of changing legal requirements and state law variations, employers should always consult with employment counsel before using them.

Definitions Under the ADA

- An individual with a disability is specifically defined as a person who:
  - ▷ Has a physical or mental impairment that substantially limits one or more major life activities.
  - ▷ Has a record of such an impairment (for example, an individual with a history of heart attacks, or an individual with a history of cancer which is in remission); has a history of or has been misclassified as having a mental or physical impairment.
  - ▷ Is regarded as having such an impairment (for example, someone whose controlled, high blood pressure does not limit work activities, but the employer has an unsubstantiated fear that the individual will suffer a heart attack if given certain duties). An individual is "regarded as" having a disability if the employee established that he/she has been discriminated against because of an actual or perceived physical or mental impairment. This ensures that people who suffer adverse actions because they are perceived as disabled can prevail if they prove that they were discriminated against. However, the "regarded as" requirement does not apply to transitory and minor impairments expected to last less than six months.
- A qualified individual can perform a position's essential functions with or without a reasonable accommodation.

- Essential functions are those duties and responsibilities fundamental to the position. For example:
    - ▷ Receptionist: Answer telephones.
    - ▷ Warehouse worker: Lift up to 50 pounds.
    - ▷ Accounts Receivable specialist: Maintain accounting ledger and prepare reports.
- Disability refers to a physical or mental impairment substantially limiting a major life activity.
    - ▷ Physical or mental impairment means any physiological disorder or condition, cosmetic disfigurement, or anatomical loss affecting one or more body systems, or any mental or psychological disorder, such as an intellectual disability, organic brain syndrome, emotional or mental illness, and specific learning disabilities.
    - ▷ An impairment is a disability if it substantially limits the ability of an individual to perform a major life activity as compared to most people in the general population.
    - ▷ An impairment that is episodic or in remission is a disability if it would substantially limit a major life activity when active.
    - ▷ Mitigating measures cannot be considered in determining whether an individual has a disability, with the exception of ordinary eyeglasses and contact lenses. In other words, employees will be evaluated without regard to the hearing aids, medication, prosthetic devices, and other measures they use to manage their impairments.
- Major life activities are activities that an average person can perform with little or no difficulty, such as caring for oneself, performing manual tasks, seeing, hearing, eating, sleeping, walking, standing, sitting, reaching, lifting, bending, speaking, breathing, learning, reading, concentrating, thinking, communicating, interacting with others, and working; **and** the operation of a major bodily function.
- A reasonable accommodation is a modification or adjustment to a job, the work environment, or the way things usually are done. Absent undue hardship, a reasonable accommodation must be made to an otherwise qualified individual who has an actual disability or who has a record of a disability. There is no obligation to make an accommodation for an individual who is regarded as having an impairment.

Guidelines for Avoiding Retaliation

Background

- Employees have the legal right to workplace issues resolved, including bringing them management's attention for internal resolution, filing charges of discrimination with government agencies, and initiating lawsuits.
- Violation of an employee's right may result in substantial penalties.
- Illegal retaliation can occur when action is taken against the employee **because of** the complaint of discrimination, or complaint about workplace practices, even if the complaint has no merit.
- Companies have been successful in winning lawsuits based on alleged discrimination. However, because of subsequent actions taken against the employee by management, the lawsuit has been amended to include charges of retaliation, and the same employer was not successful in defending the retaliation claim.
- Charges of unlawful retaliation continue to increase.

Management Guidance

- Retaliation is a serious issue. If an employee files a charge of discrimination, or otherwise complains about workplace practices, treat the person as if the charge had not been filed.
- Avoid taking any action that could be interpreted as retaliatory, such as:
  - ▷ Firing, demoting, disciplining, or otherwise treating the employee differently.
  - ▷ Threatening action or criticizing the employee for filing a charge.
  - ▷ Discussing the charge with the employee. This could be viewed as coercion.
  - ▷ Discussing the charge with anyone inside the company, other than those individuals with a business need to know—generally immediate management, human resources, and the legal department (including outside lawyers).
  - ▷ Discussing the charge with anyone outside the company, such as customers, vendors, suppliers, or other colleagues.
  - ▷ Allowing coworkers to tease or harass the employee about the charge, without regard as to how they gained knowledge of the issue.
- If the employee who filed the charge has performance or workplace conduct issues, the following guiding principles should be followed:
  - ▷ Proceed with caution. Involve appropriate company resources, such as human resources, legal, or your immediate management.
  - ▷ Set clear performance and conduct expectations to everyone you manage.
  - ▷ Communicate those expectations to all individuals.
  - ▷ Consistently apply those expectations to all individuals.
  - ▷ Document any incidents of performance or conduct issues, discussions with the employee about those issues and any management actions taken.
  - ▷ Communicate to employees the company policies on complaint resolution and encourage their use.

APPENDIX

Guidelines for Preventing Workplace Discrimination

Unlawful discrimination occurs when an employment decision is made or someone is treated differently (either treated less favorably or received preferential treatment) because of a characteristic (protection) covered by law, such as race, color, national origin, religion, or gender. For example, consider the following statements:

- "Women are not dependable because they always take time off when their kids are sick. I'd rather hire a man for the job."
- "Joe is getting on in years and may be retiring soon. He wouldn't be a good candidate for the promotion."

Subtle behavior is often not intentional, but can be discriminatory. For example, referring to a woman as "young lady" may not be blatantly discriminatory, but it could send an inadvertent message that females are not as mature as men and thus not as qualified.

Harassment is also a form of discrimination. It is illegal to harass someone because of his or her race, color, religion, national origin, gender, age, disability status, ethnic background, or citizenship. Some examples of harassment include:

- Disparaging or disrespectful remarks and comments.
- Slurs and epithets.
- Threatening or intimidating communications, whether written, verbal, or electronic.
- Jokes, teasing, remarks, drawings, cartoons, or photos that poke fun at any religion, national origin, gender, age, disability, or any other protection.
- Behavior that ridicules someone because of his or her religious beliefs, gender, age, ethnic background, disability, or any other protection.
- Work assignments based on sex or race or religion. For example, not assigning a woman to a project to satisfy a client's request.

Employers are required to provide reasonable accommodation for an employee's religious beliefs, so long as it does not impose a serious hardship or otherwise interfere with business operations. A serious hardship can include anything that is more than minimally expensive, anything that violates the rights of others, anything that might conflict with a collective bargaining agreement, or anything that would compromise health or safety requirements.

Any deeply held belief of a moral, ethical, or spiritual nature is considered to be a religious belief. The employee does not have to belong to a conventional, recognized religion.

Some examples of reasonable accommodation include:

- Time off for religious observances. This can include allowing the use of paid or unpaid leave or shift reassignments.
- Exceptions to dress codes and appearances, as long as they don't compromise health or safety requirements.
- Allowing time and space to pray during work hours.

Guiding principles to maintaining a work environment that fosters respect and inclusion are:

- Make objective employment decisions without regard to race, sex, other protected category, or anything that is not job-related. For example, failing to hire someone because he/she has expressed the need to take time off for religious observances.

- Avoid assumptions and stereotypes. They can give rise to disrespectful behavior and lead to unlawful practices.
- Communicate company policies to your staff, particularly policies on anti-discrimination, harassment, and problem resolution.
- Be aware of your staff's actions. Don't tolerate offensive or disrespectful behavior.
- Communicate any concerns to management or human resources, as appropriate under your policies and practices. If discriminatory behavior is taking place, you have the responsibility to take action.
- Be consistent in your treatment of the staff.
- Take appropriate management action when necessary. Remember that preferential treatment of members of racial/ethnic minority groups and females is equally unlawful as it is with respect to white males.
- Take requests for religious accommodation and disability accommodation seriously, and seek guidance and review on all requests for accommodation with management.
- Assure that all workers, regardless of protected status, are given the same considerations and opportunities.
- Don't inquire about retirement plans or assume someone is planning to retire.
- Avoid documenting statements that refer to age in someone's performance appraisal (for example, "He's slowing down, but does well for his age.").

Preventing Harassment: Managers' Initiatives

Follow your organization's policy and enforce the policy and the rules.

- ◆ Immediately document observed or reported incidents of harassment.
- ◆ Notify human resources immediately.

If an employee says that he or she will handle the incident and does not want you to disclose it, you must advise that this is not an option. (The company is obligated to investigate once it has knowledge of alleged discrimination/harassment.)

- ◆ Remain neutral. Do not take sides.
- ◆ Maintain confidentiality.

Set a positive tone and example through your own actions and behaviors.

- ◆ Be mindful of behavior, language, and social interactions.
- ◆ Be respectful of others' personal space.

Be open to discussing the issue of harassment.

- ◆ Distribute copies of the policy when requested by management.
- ◆ Remind employees that discriminatory/harassing behaviors or remarks, or any other disrespectful behaviors or remarks do not belong in the workplace.

Be actively alert for inappropriate workplace behavior. Treat it seriously.

- ◆ Act quickly. Don't put it off.
- ◆ Address improper conduct if you see it happening.
- ◆ Don't ignore it; it won't go away.
- ◆ Remember that, as a supervisor, if you knew or should have known of conduct that potentially could be harassment or discrimination, the company is liable to show that immediate and appropriate corrective action was taken.

APPENDIX

Sample Non-Competition/Non-Solicitation/Successors and Assigns/Severability Provisions

NON-COMPETITION PROVISION

1. The Employee specifically agrees that for a period of_____ [months/years] after the Employee is no longer employed by the Company, the Employee will not engage, directly or indirectly, either as proprietor, stockholder, partner, officer, employee, or otherwise, in the same or similar activities as were performed for the Company in any business [within a ____-mile radius of the Company] [within ____ miles of an office of the Company] [within a State where the Company has offices] [within the State of _____] that distributes or sells products or provides services similar to those distributed, sold, or provided by the Company at any time during the ____ [months/years] preceding the Employee's termination of employment.

2. For a period of ____ [months/years] after the Employee is no longer employed by the Company, the Employee will not, directly or indirectly, either as proprietor, stockholder, partner, officer, employee, or otherwise, distribute, sell, offer to sell, or solicit any orders for the purchase or distribution of any products or services that are similar to those distributed, sold or provided by the Company during the ____ [months/years] preceding the Employee's termination of employment with the Company, to or from any person, firm, or entity that was a customer of the Company during the ___ [months/years] preceding such termination of employment.

NON-SOLICITATION OF CUSTOMERS/CLIENTS PROVISION

Employee agrees that for _____ [months/years] after Employee is no longer employed by the Company, Employee will not directly or indirectly solicit, agree to perform, or perform services of any type that the Company can render ("Services") for any person or entity who paid or engaged the Company for Services, or who received the benefit of the Company's Services, or with whom Employee had any substantial dealing while employed by the Company. However, this restriction with respect to Services applies only to those Services rendered by Employee or an office or unit of the Company in which Employee worked or over which Employee had supervisory authority. This restriction also applies to assisting any employer or other third party.

NON-SOLICITATION OF EMPLOYEES PROVISION

For a period of _____ [months/years] from the date that Employee is no longer employed by the Company, Employee shall not take any actions to assist Employee's successor employer or any other entity in recruiting any other employee who works for or is affiliated with the Company. This includes, but is not limited to: (a) identifying to such successor employer or its agents or such other entity the person or persons who have special knowledge concerning the Company's processes, methods or confidential affairs; and (b) commenting to the successor employer or its agents or such other entity about the quantity of work, quality of work, special knowledge, or personal characteristics of any person who is still employed at the Company. Employee also agrees that Employee will not provide such information set forth in (a) and (b) above to a prospective employer during interviews preceding possible employment.

SAMPLE SUCCESSORS AND ASSIGNS PROVISION

This Agreement may be assigned by the Company in the event of a merger or consolidation of the Company or in connection with the sale of all or substantially all of the Company's business.

SAMPLE SEVERABILITY PROVISION

The covenants of this Agreement shall be severable, and if any of them is held invalid because of its duration, scope of area or activity, or any other reason, the parties agree that such covenant shall be adjusted or modified by the court to the extent necessary to cure that invalidity, and the modified covenant shall thereafter be enforceable as if originally made in this Agreement. Employee agrees that the violation of any covenant contained in this Agreement may cause immediate and irreparable harm to the Company, the amount of which may be difficult or impossible to estimate or determine. If Employee violates any covenant contained in this Agreement, the Company shall have the right to equitable relief by injunction or otherwise, in addition to all other rights and remedies afforded by law.

Signed:

_____

Employee Name   Date

Sample Non-Disclosure Agreement

NON-DISCLOSURE AGREEMENT

This Agreement is made as of the _____ day of _____ 20XX, by and between (client) and (consultant). The Parties intend to disclose to each other proprietary/confidential information (the "Confidential Information") as further described in Paragraph 1 below, and in consideration of the receipt thereof, each Party hereby agrees to protect that information as required hereunder.

The purpose for the disclosure of Confidential Information to be disclosed by each Party is described as follows: (short description of nature of consulting engagement).

The Parties further agree as follows:

1. The Parties may exchange Confidential Information under this Agreement in oral, visual, or written form, which may include, but not be limited to, documentation, specifications, drawings, models, sketches, computer programs, reports, data techniques, designs, codes, and financial, statistical, or technical information. Where possible, each Party shall identify its Confidential Information with an appropriate, conspicuous legend ("Proprietary" or "Company Confidential"). All other non-tangible (discussions, briefings, etc.) disclosures shall be identified as Confidential Information at the time of disclosure and will be summarized in writing, identified with a legend as described above, and forwarded to the other Party within thirty (30) days of disclosure. Each Party's duty to protect such information shall commence from initial disclosure.

2. Each Party shall hold each other's Confidential Information in strict confidence and shall use it only for the purpose described above. Each Party shall limit distribution of the other's Confidential Information only to those individuals within its organization who have a need to know such information in order to accomplish the Purpose. Neither Party shall disclose any of the other's Confidential Information to any other person, organization, or corporation without the other Party's prior written approval.

3. Each Party shall protect the other's Confidential Information with at least the same degree of care that it uses to protect its own Confidential Information; provided, however, that this obligation shall not apply to any portion of the information that:

   a. is or becomes publicly available, other than through the fault or negligence of the receiving Party;

   b. was known to the receiving Party, without restriction, at the time of receipt from the Disclosing Party;

   c. is rightfully and lawfully obtained by the receiving Party from a third Party rightfully and lawfully possessing the same without restriction;

   d. is independently developed by the receiving Party without having had access to the information disclosed hereunder, as evidenced by appropriate documents;

   e. is obligated to be produced under an order of a court of competent jurisdiction, providing that the Disclosing Party is immediately notified by the Recipient Party; or

   f. is disclosed in any event, after the expiration of five (5) years from the date such information was delivered to Recipient Party.

     g.   The Receiving Party shall not use the Disclosing Party's Confidential Information under any of these exceptions without advance notification to and concurrence from the Disclosing Party of the appropriateness of the exception.

8.   All Confidential information obtained by either Party hereunder shall remain the property of the Disclosing Party and shall be returned to it, or destroyed, promptly upon request, together with all copies made thereof by the Receiving Party. Upon request, the Receiving Party shall promptly submit to the Disclosing Party a certificate of destruction.

9.   Except as specifically provided for herein, neither Party shall make use of the other Party's Confidential Information for its own benefit or the benefit of any third party. Each Party agrees to notify the other as soon as possible if it becomes aware of any misappropriation, misuse, or disclosure of the other's Confidential Information.

10.   Neither the Confidential Information nor the act of disclosure thereof by either Party shall constitute a grant of any license of any kind either under any trademark, patent, or copyright, or application for same, or otherwise, nor shall they constitute any representation, warranty, assurance, guarantee, or inducement by either Party with respect to the infringement of any trademark, patent, copyright, any right of privacy, or any right of third persons.

11.   EACH PARTY IS PROVIDING THIS CONFIDENTIAL INFORMATION "AS IS" AND MAKES NO WARRANTY, EXPRESS OR IMPLIED, AS TO THE ACCURACY, CAPABILITY, EFFICIENCY, MERCHANTABILITY, OR FUNCTIONING OF THIS INFORMATION. IN NO EVENT WILL EITHER PARTY BE LIABLE FOR ANY GENERAL, CONSEQUENTIAL, INDIRECT, INCIDENTAL, EXEMPLARY, OR SPECIAL DAMAGES, EVEN IF THE OTHER PARTY HAS BEEN ADVISED OF THE POSSIBILITY OF SUCH DAMAGES.

12.   Each Party accepts the other's Confidential Information on the condition that it indemnifies and holds harmless each other Party, its Board of Directors/Trustees, officers, agents, and employees, from any and all liability or damages, including attorneys' fees, court costs, and other related costs and expenses, arising out of its use of this information irrespective of the cause of said liability.

13.   In compliance with U.S. Department of Commerce Export Administration Regulations and the U.S. Department of State International Traffic in Arms Regulations as they exist during the applicability of this Agreement, and notwithstanding any other provision of this Agreement, neither Party shall attempt to, nor knowingly export or re-export to any country prohibited from obtaining such data, either directly, or indirectly through affiliates, licensees, or subsidiaries, any U.S. source technical data acquired from each other, any products utilizing such data or any proprietary/confidential information provided under this or any ancillary agreements, to any countries outside the U.S. that export may be in violation of U.S. Export Laws or Regulations. Nothing in this provision shall relieve either Party from any other obligation stated elsewhere in this Agreement not to disclose such information.

14.   This Agreement shall be effective as of the date first written above and shall terminate one (1) year thereafter, provided, however, that this Agreement may be terminated by either Party at any time via written notice of termination to the other Party. A Party's obligations herein shall survive the termination of this Agreement. Notwithstanding the termination or expiration of any other Agreement executed in conjunction with

this Agreement, the obligations of the Parties with respect to Confidential Information shall continue to be governed by the Nondisclosure Agreement.

15. Points of Contact for all communication pertaining to this agreement, and subject to change upon written notice:

For (client):
Company Name
Address
City, State Zip
ATTN: _____
For (consultant):
Company Name
Address
City, State Zip
ATTN: _____

16. In the event that any of the provisions of this Agreement shall be held by a court or other tribunal of competent jurisdiction to be unenforceable, that portion shall be severed and a new enforceable provision shall be negotiated by the Parties and substituted to accomplish the intent of the severed provision as nearly as practicable. The remaining provision s of the Agreement shall remain in full force and effect.

17. No waiver or modification of this Agreement will be binding upon either Party unless made in writing and signed by a duly authorized representative of such Party, and no failure or delay in enforcing any right will be deemed a waiver.

18. All documentation, correspondence, and communications relating to this Agreement shall be in the English language.

19. Each Party shall bear all costs and expenses incurred by it under or in connection with this Agreement. Nothing in this Agreement shall be construed as an obligation by either Party to enter into a contract, subcontract, or other business relationship with the other Party.

20. Neither Party may assign or transfer this Agreement or any of its rights and obligations hereunder to any third party (except to a legally recognized successor in interest to all or substantially all of the Party's assets) without the prior consent in writing from the other Party, which consent shall not be unreasonably withheld.

21. This Agreement, which shall be governed by the laws of (state), represents the complete and exclusive understanding of the Parties pertaining to the disclosure of this proprietary/company-confidential information. It may be amended only by a mutually executed writing.

The Parties agree to the above as signified by executing below:

For: (Client)   For: (Consultant

Signature: Signature:

Name:`   Name:

Title: Title:

APPENDIX

Sample Statement of Work

A. Statement of Work:

(Name of consultant or consulting firm) agrees to (describe type of work) for (your organization).

B. Scope of Work (Steps to be taken; following is a representative scope for information purposes only):

Consultant proposes the following to complete this project:

1. Gather appropriate informational data.
2. Consultant to meet with appropriate managers, in particular, VP Human Resources and Manager, Human Resources, to glean any other relevant information (List titles to be included).
3. Consultant will submit a written draft of material and present to client for their review.
4. Consultant may recommend that client present this written draft to an internal Focus Group to determine if each individual can readily understand the content of this document.
5. Client will review the written draft, modify as needed, and return to Consultant.
6. Consultant will review the modified information from client and adjust the written document.
7. Consultant will provide completed document to client no later than (agreed to due date).

C. Efforts and Service Fee:

Describe the time proposed to do the work and the cost (can be a project fee, daily rate or hourly rate.

D. Consultant:

Show credentials of person (s) who will do the work.

E. Non-Disclosure:

Consultant agrees to keep confidential any and all material submitted by the Client.

Signed:

_____

Consultant   Date

_____

Client   Date

Sample Job Description

JOB TITLE: Administrative Assistant II
FLSA STATUS: Non-Exempt
REPORTS TO: VP Marketing
LOCATION: Corporate
POSITION SUMMARY:

Under the direct supervision of the Vice President of Marketing, this position provides administrative and secretarial support for the Vice President and the Marketing Department. In addition to typing, filing, and scheduling, performs duties such as financial record-keeping, payroll, coordination of meetings and conferences, obtaining supplies, coordinating direct mailings, and working on special projects. Also, answers non-routine correspondence and assembles highly confidential and sensitive information. Deals with a diverse group of important external callers and visitors as well as internal contacts at all levels of the organization. Independent judgment is required to plan, prioritize, and organize diversified workload, recommends changes in office practices or procedures.

Summary: Administrative/Secretarial: Provides administrative support to the Vice President of Marketing and the Marketing Department including high-level secretarial support.

1. Schedules and organizes complex activities such as meetings, travel, conferences, and department activities for all members of the department.
2. Performs desktop publishing. Creating and developing visual presentations for the Vice President.
3. Establishes, develops, maintains, and updates filing system for the Vice President and the department. Retrieves information from files when needed. Establishes, develops, maintains, and updates library of trade journals and magazines.
4. Organizes and prioritizes large volumes of information and calls.
   a. Sorts and distributes mail. Opens mail for the Vice President. Drafts written responses or replies by phone or email when necessary. Responds to regularly occurring requests for information.
   b. Answers phones for Vice President and Marketing Department. Takes messages or fields/answers all routine and non-routine questions. Works in cooperation with other System Development Assistants to cover phones.
3. Acts as a liaison with other departments and outside agencies, including high-level staff such as CEOs, Presidents, Senior Vice Presidents, and Chiefs. Handles confidential and non-routine information and explains policies when necessary.
4. Works independently and within a team on special nonrecurring and ongoing projects. Acts as project manager for special projects, at the request of the Vice President, which may include: planning and coordinating multiple presentations, disseminating information, coordinating direct mailings, creating brochures.
5. Coordinates division of workload with the administrative assistant in Community Relations.
6. Types and designs general correspondences, memos, charts, tables, graphs, business plans, etc. Proofreads copy for spelling, grammar, and layout, making appropriate changes. Responsible for accuracy and clarity of final copy.

APPENDIX

7. Supports Market Data Analyst in maintenance of the department finances. Activities include: copying check requests & sending to Accounts Payable Travel reimbursement, documenting corporate credit card expenses to corporate finance.

QUALIFICATIONS/SKILLS & KNOWLEDGE REQUIREMENTS

♦   Work requires an extensive knowledge of business and an excellent command of the English language.

♦   Must have knowledge of secretarial, office administrative procedures, and knowledge of use and operation of standard office equipment, at a level generally acquired through 1+ years related experience.

♦   Must have knowledge of a variety of computer software applications in word processing, spreadsheets, database and presentation software.

♦   Must have high level of interpersonal skills to handle sensitive and confidential situations. Position continually requires demonstrated poise, tact, and diplomacy.

♦   Some analytical ability is required in order to gather and summarize data for reports, find solutions to various administrative problems, and prioritize work.

♦   Work requires continual attention to detail in composing, typing, and proofing materials, establishing priorities, and meeting deadlines.

APPROVALS:

Supervisor Name _____

Title _____

Date _____

GENERAL INFORMATION

The above statements are intended to describe the general nature and level of work being performed by individuals assigned to this position. They are not intended to be an exhaustive list of all duties, responsibilities, and skills required of personnel so classified.

The incumbent must be able to work in a fast-paced environment with demonstrated ability to juggle and prioritize multiple, competing tasks and demands, and to seek supervisory assistance as appropriate.

Incumbents within this position may be required to assist or find appropriate assistance to make accommodations for disabled individuals in order to ensure access to the organization's services (may include: visitors, patients, employees, or others).

Sample Job Application

[Company] is an equal opportunity employer and does not discriminate against otherwise qualified applicants on the basis of race, color, creed, religion, ancestry, age, sex, marital status, national origin, disability or handicap, or veteran status.

PERSONAL

Name: _____ Date: _____

       Last   First   Middle

Address: _____

      Number & Street City   State   Zip code

Driver's License Number: _____ State: _____ Exp. Date: _____

Position Sought: _____ Full-Time ❑ Part-Time ❑

Date Available: _____ Salary Desired: _____ Phone Number: _____

Are you legally eligible for employment in the United States? ___ Yes ___ No
(If offered employment, you will be required to provide documentation to verify eligibility.)

Have you ever been employed in any facility of [Company]? ___ Yes ___ No
If yes, please state facility name, location and dates of employment: _____

EDUCATION

Please indicate education or training that you believe qualifies you for the position you are seeking.

High School:_____ Number of years completed (circle one): 1 2 3 4
Diploma: ___ Yes ___ No   G.E.D.: ___ Yes ___ No
School(s): _____ City/State: _____

College and/or Vocational School: _____

Number of years completed (circle one): 1 2 3 4

School(s): _____ City/State: _____
Major: _____ Degrees Earned: _____

Other Training or Degrees
School(s): _____ City/State: _____
Course: _____ Degree or Certificate Earned: _____

PROFESSIONAL LICENSE or MEMBERSHIP
Type of License(s) Held: _____
Other Professional Memberships: _____

(You need not disclose membership in professional organizations that may reveal information regarding race, color, creed, sex, religion, national origin, ancestry, age, disability, marital status, veteran status, or any other protected status.)

This application for employment is good for 30 days only. Consideration for employment after 30 days requires a new application.

SKILLS

Word Processing: ___ MS Word ___ WordPerfect ___ Other Typing speed ___ wpm
Data Entry: ___ Excel ___ Lotus 123 ___ CRT ___ Other
Other Software Skills: _____

RECORD OF CONVICTION

During the last ten years, have you ever been convicted of a crime other than a minor traffic offense?   ___ Yes   ___ No

If yes, explain:

(A conviction will not necessarily automatically disqualify you for employment. Rather, such factors as age, date of conviction, seriousness and nature of the crime, and rehabilitation will be considered.)

EMPLOYMENT: List last employer first, including U.S. Military Service.

May we contact your present employer?   ___ Yes   ___ No

If any employment was under a different name, indicate name: _____

Employer: _____ Telephone: _____

Address: _____

Dates of Employment: From _____ (mm/dd)   To _____ (mm/dd)

Position: _____ Salary: _____

Supervisor: _____ Department: _____

Duties: _____   FT ___ PT ___ No. of Hours

Reason for Leaving _____

Employer: _____ Telephone: _____

Address: _____

Dates of Employment: From _____ (mm/dd)   To _____ (mm/dd)

Position: _____ Salary: _____

Supervisor: _____ Department: _____

Duties: _____   FT ___ PT ___ No. of Hours

Reason for Leaving _____

REFERENCES

Professional		Personal	
Name	_____	Name	_____
Address	_____	Address	_____
	_____		_____
Phone	( ) _____	Phone	( ) _____
Name	_____	Name	_____
Address	_____	Address	_____
	_____		_____
Phone	( ) _____	Phone	( ) _____

APPLICANT'S CERTIFICATIONAND AGREEMENT

I hereby certify that the facts set forth in the above employment application are true and complete to the best of my knowledge and authorize [Company] to verify their accuracy and to obtain reference information on my work performance. I hereby release [Company] from any/all liability of whatever kind and nature that, at any time, could result from obtaining and having an employment decision based on such information.

I understand that, if employed, falsified statements of any kind or omissions of facts called for on this application shall be considered sufficient basis for dismissal.

I understand that should an employment offer be extended to me and accepted that I will fully adhere to the policies, rules, and regulations of employment of the Employer. However, I further understand that neither the policies, rules, regulations of employment or anything said during the interview process shall be deemed to constitute the terms of an implied employment contract. I understand that any employment offered is for an indefinite duration and at will and that either I or the Employer may terminate my employment at any time with or without notice or cause.

_____

Signature of Applicant   Date

Sample Release Information to Include on Employment Applications

Reference Checks. I authorize [Company] to communicate with references and former employers to verify information related to this application in order to make an employment decision. I agree to hold such persons harmless with respect to any information they may give about me.

Background Investigations. In making this application for employment an investigative consumer report may be obtained from a consumer reporting agency for the purpose of evaluating employment history. This report may contain information regarding my past education, past employment, and general reputation from public record sources. I understand that I have a right to request additional disclosures regarding the nature and scope of the investigation.

Consumer Report Disclosure Notice & Authorization.

Thank you for your application. This Consumer Report Disclosure Notice and Authorization is to inform you that [the organization] may obtain or cause to be obtained a consumer report as part of its pre-employment background check. Such a report, which may contain information bearing on your credit worthiness, credit standing, credit capacity, character, general reputation, personal characteristics, or mode of living, will be used for employment purposes only. The fact that [the organization] may obtain a consumer report does not mean that [the organization] has otherwise decided to offer you employment.

By signing this form below, you authorize [the organization] to obtain or cause to be obtained a consumer credit report.

If hired, this authorization shall remain in effect and serve as continuing authorization for [the organization] to obtain consumer reports at any time during your employment with [the organization].

Applicant's Name: _____

Signature: _____

Sample Internal Transfer Policy

Purpose: This policy exists to offer employees of the XYZ Company the opportunity for skill development and career development through executing a transfer/promotion to a position outside their department/division but within the organization. This policy applies to all employees whether part or full-time below the level of Senior Vice President.

1. All positions below the level of Senior VP will be posted internally on the organization's job posting site. Positions will be posted internally for five business days prior to going to outside sources for candidates.

2. Employees who have been in their current position for at least one year and are not currently on a performance improvement plan are eligible to apply for the open position by completing the Internal Job Transfer/Promotion Form available on the organization's intranet and attaching a current resume.

3. Employees must obtain the approval of their current manager prior to submitting the form to Human Resources.

4. HR will evaluate the internal candidate's qualifications against the job specifications and qualified candidates will be shared with the hiring manager. Candidates will be notified at that time whether or not they are being considered.

5. The Hiring manager, with support from HR, will determine which candidates to interview and select based on skills, abilities, and qualifications. All decisions will be made without regard to age, color, race, national origin, religion, gender, disabilities, veteran status, or sexual orientation.

6. If an internal candidate is selected, HR and the hiring manager will work with the releasing manager on a timeframe for the employee to transfer to the new position.

The hiring manager and/or HR will meet with internal candidates who were not selected to discuss where they need to improve their skills in order to move forward in the company.

Sources for Minority Applicants

African-American Career World magazine: *www.eop.com/aacw.html*

American Jewish World Service: *www.ajws.org/index.cfm*

The Black Collegian: *black-collegian.com*

Black Enterprise: *blackenterprise.com*

National Black MBA Association: *www.nbmba.org*

Black MBA Magazine: *www.blackmbamagazine.net*

National Hispanic Business Association: *nhba.org*

Hispanic Career World: *eop.com*

Careers & the DISabled: *eop.com*

LATPRO Hispanic Jobs: *www.latpro.com*

Project Hired *kings.projecthired.org/public*

HireDiversity.com: *www.hirediversity.com*

Indian Country Today: *indiancountry.com*

Native American Employment Opportunities: *hanksville.org/NAresources/indices/NAjobs.html*

Veterans Enterprise: *www.veteransenterprise.com*

Veterans' Vision: *www.vetsvision.org/vetsvision.html*

Women's Business Enterprise National Council: *www.wbenc.org*

HispanicOnline: *www.hispaniconline.com*

AfricanAmericanJobsite.com: *www.africanamericanjobsite.com*

DiversityLink.com: *www.diversitylink.com*

Diversity Search: *www.diversitysearch.com*

iHispano.com: *ihispano.com*

Saludos.com: *saludos.com*

Workforce50: *Workforce50.com*

Quintessential Careers: Job and Career Resources for Mature and Older Job-Seekers: *quintcareers.com/mature_jobseekers.html*

Legal and Illegal Interview Questions

	Legal Questions	Illegal Questions
Gender/ Family Issues	If applicant has relative employed with your organization	Gender of applicant Number of children Marital status Spouse's occupation Childcare arrangements Healthcare coverage through spouse
Race	None	Applicant's race/skin color Photos attached to resumes/applications
National Origin or Ancestry	Whether applicant has legal right to be employed in the U.S. Ability to write/speak English fluently (if job-related) Other languages spoken (if job-related)	Ethnic association of surname Birthplace of applicant or applicant's parents Nationality, lineage, national origin Nationality of applicant's spouse Whether applicant is a citizen of another country Applicant's native tongue Maiden name (of married woman) Note: State clearance requirements in your position description and in all recruitment ads.
Religion	None	Religious affiliation Religious holidays observed
Age	If applicant is over age 18 If applicant is over age 21 (if job related)	Date of birth Date of high school graduation Age
Disability	Whether applicant can perform certain job related functions	If applicant has a disability Nature or severity of disability Whether applicant has ever filed a workers' compensation claim Recent or past surgeries and dates Past medical problems
Other	Convictions*	Number and kinds of arrests Specific years of school attendance or graduation date Height or weight unless bona fide occupational qualification** Veteran status, discharge status, branch of service Contact in case of emergency (at application or interview stage)

* Disclosure of criminal record does not automatically disqualify an applicant from employment consideration. Each case must be judged on its own merits.

** Bona Fide Occupational Qualifications (BFOQ) are legitimate reasons why an employer can exclude persons on otherwise-illegal bases of consideration (for example, gender or age).

APPENDIX

Phone and Video Screening Template

Applicant Name: _____

Phone Number or Video Link: _____

Date of Interview: _____

1. What was it about our position that caused you to apply?
2. Why are you looking for a new position?
3. What salary range are you looking for?
4. What are the top five duties you have in your current (last) job?
5. What are some examples of decisions you make on a daily basis?
6. [Insert one or two job-related questions here using the recommended questioning format in Chapter 9 (The Interview).]
7. Describe your ideal organizational culture.
8. If we were to come to an agreement and you would be offered this position, when are you available to start?

Questions Applicants May Ask Employers in Interviews[1]

- Why do you enjoy working for this company?
- What attracted you to this organization?
- Can you describe the work environment here?
- How soon are you likely to fill this position?
- What sets this organization apart from your competition?
- Who are your top three competitors?
- What is the next step in the interview process?
- How do my skills match up with your job requirements?
- How do I compare with other candidates you've interviewed for this position?
- How does this position relate to the bottom line?
- Could you explain the management structure here?
- What advice would you give someone in my position?
- If I am hired for this position, what would be my first responsibility?
- What challenges might I face if I am selected for this position?
- What are the three main goals this year for this organization?
- How do you see this position impacting the achievement of those goals?
- What development opportunities will I have here to advance my skill development?
- What personal or professional qualities do you admire most in people who work for you?
- What types of people do really well here and why?
- Is there a succession plan in place?
- What happened to the person who held this job previously?
- What is the organization's customer service philosophy?
- What is the organization's employee retention strategy?
- If I am selected for this position, will I manage anyone who applied for this position? If yes, why were they not considered for the job?
- I understand there were layoffs in the past two years. Can you review the reasons why this decision was made and what was done to ensure those who stayed felt positively about the company?
- What rewards and recognition programs have been successful here?
- How does this organization deal with mistakes?
- What are the greatest challenges I will face in this position?
- Is there anything personally or professionally that you believe would prevent me from being successful here?
- Can you give me some examples of the best and worst aspects of the organization's culture?
- What makes this a great place to work?
- When top performers leave, why do they leave and where do they go?
- How will my performance be evaluated?

APPENDIX

Sample Behavioral Interviewing Questions

Communications Skills

Tell me about a time when you felt you had to overcome resistance to your ideas in your organization. How did you communicate this? Describe how you felt. How did you get buy-in for your idea? If you didn't get buy-in, what did you learn from this experience?

How would you describe your communication style?

Tell me about a time when you had to make an unplanned presentation. How did you organize your thoughts? How did you feel about this?

Describe a situation in which effective interpersonal communications skills contributed to your success?

Initiative

Give me an example of a time when you worked on a project with little supervision. How did you get started? Describe the results.

Describe a situation in which your initiative made little difference in the outcome of a project or job. What was the result? What did you learn from this experience?

Integrity and Trust

Describe a situation where someone has put trust in you. How did you feel? How did you earn that person's trust?

How would your last employer describe your work habits and ethics?

Describe a time when you made a mistake. How did you handle the situation? What did you learn from it?

Leadership/Coaching

As a leader, what do you do when people on your team aren't pulling their weight?

What is one of the greatest leadership challenges you have ever faced? What did you do? What was the result?

Teamwork/Collaboration

How do you promote teamwork? How effective are you in making this happen and why?

Describe a time when you worked with someone who was difficult to work with. What was the outcome?

How do you handle situations with people who don't agree with you?

Sample Reference Checking Template

Applicant Name: _____

Position being considered for: _____

Date conducted: _____

Reference name and title: _____

Reference phone or email contact: _____

Process

- Introduce yourself and explain that the applicant has listed them as a reference for (fill in position title) and your organization.
- Ask if this is a convenient time to talk and if not, when to reschedule.
- Assure the reference that the information he or she shares will be confidential.
- Briefly describe the job duties and then ask the following questions:
  1. What was your working relationship to the candidate? Supervisor? Peer?
  2. How long have you been acquainted with the candidate?
  3. How long did you and the candidate work together?
  4. Confirm dates of employment shown on the resume/application.
  5. What were the job duties of the candidate when you worked together?
  6. Is the candidate eligible for rehire and if not, why?
  7. Please comment on how well you think the candidate would handle the job I described.
  8. Does the candidate have any developmental needs?
  9. End with, "Is there anything else you can tell me to help us make a good hiring decision?"

Thank the reference for his or her time and help!

Template for a Telecommuting Agreement

I have read, understand, and agree to the duties, obligations, responsibilities, and conditions for telecommuters described in this document. Specifically:

I agree that I am responsible for:

- Establishing specific telecommuting work hours,
- Furnishing and maintaining my remote work space in a safe manner, and
- Employing appropriate security measures and protecting company assets, information, trade secrets, and systems in my remote work location.

I understand that:

- Telecommuting is voluntary and I may stop telecommuting at any time.
- THE COMPANY may at any time change any or all of the conditions under which I am permitted to telecommute, or withdraw permission to telecommute.

Remote work location: Please specify either employee residence or other remote work location. Please describe the work space at the remote work location:

- I understand that I am responsible for establishing an appropriate work environment within my home for work purposes. THE COMPANY will not be responsible for costs associated with initial set-up (e.g., remodeling, furniture, or lighting), nor for repairs or modifications to the home office space. I understand that THE COMPANY will offer appropriate assistance in setting up a work station designed for safe, comfortable work.

Telecommuting schedule:

- I agree to the following work schedule: (Select and complete one of the three options below)
  1. On a weekly basis as follows (Specify regular telecommuting work hours):
  2. On a monthly basis as follows (Specify regular telecommuting work hours):
  3. No regular schedule (Separate permission for each telecommuting day)
- I understand that I must be accessible by phone within a reasonable time period during the agreed-upon work schedule, and if I am telecommuting on a regular basis. Further, my manager and I will discuss the frequency of regular communication and I agree to abide by that agreement.
- I understand that I am responsible for maintaining time records in accordance with THE COMPANY's policies.

The following applies to those employees who are not exempt from the overtime requirements of the Fair Labor Standards Act.

- I understand that as a non-exempt employee, I will be required to record in a manner designated by the organization all hours worked. Hours worked in excess of those specified per day and per work week, in accordance with state and federal requirements, will require the advance approval of the supervisor. Failure to comply with this requirement can result in the immediate cessation of the telecommuting agreement.

Company assets to be used at remote work location: (Specify/describe the equipment with appropriate ID numbers, and any other assets that will be assigned to the employee. This should include hardware and software, as appropriate. IT and/or facilities management should be consulted.)

- I understand that any and all equipment (hardware/software/other) supplied by THE COMPANY will be maintained by THE COMPANY. Equipment supplied by THE COMPANY is to be used for business purposes only. I agree to sign an inventory of all office property and agree to take appropriate action to protect the items from damage or theft. Upon termination of employment all company property will be returned to THE COMPANY, unless other arrangements have been made.

If the employer has Asset Management Guidelines, they should be included or referenced. Consider the following for developing policies, guidelines and agreements:

- *Does a policy or guideline exist that defines who is responsible in case of theft of hardware, software or data at remote sites? In case of damage?*
- *Does a policy or guideline exist for "appropriate" personal use of company equipment?*

Asset and information security:

- I understand that consistent with THE COMPANY's expectations of information asset security for employees working at the office, as a telecommuting employee I will be expected to ensure the protection of proprietary company and customer information accessible from my home office. Steps include, but are not limited to, securing any storage media (such as portable drives), use of locked file cabinets and desks, regular password maintenance, and any other steps appropriate for the job and the environment.

Consider the following for developing policies, guidelines and agreements: (This list is not meant to be all-inclusive. There may be other considerations after consulting with IT and security professionals.)

- *Are the remote sites physically secure?*
- *Is a full physical inventory of remote site equipment and user systems maintained and periodically verified?*
- *Are backup media available and secured on-site for remote site equipment?*
- *Is all paper data (proprietary, confidential, etc.) physically secure at the remote site?*
- *Is there a process for the return of equipment and proprietary data upon termination of employment or necessary company access?*
- *Does a policy exist for repair of equipment that contains proprietary information?*
- *Is there insurance for liability and personal injury at the remote site?*
- *If equipment is stolen, can proprietary information be accessed by the perpetrator?*
- *Is all media destruction (proprietary, confidential, etc.) at the remote site consistent with THE COMPANY's security policies?*
- *Does a policy exist to obtain access to important proprietary information at remote sites?*
- *Is there a formal, complete, and tested disaster recovery plan in place for the remote sites?*
- *Are there virus scanning capabilities required on remote sites? How often are they updated?*

APPENDIX

- *Are measures in place to ensure the proper disposal of confidential data (paper, fax, digital, etc.) at remote sites?*
- *Are users aware of the signs of a virus or worm?*
- *Are users familiar with the use of virus scanners?*
- *Are users aware of the remote access security policies?*
- *Do remote access users and their managers receive security training prior to using remote access? Do they receive annual security training?*

Non-company equipment, software, and data to be used at remote work location: Specify/describe the personal or other non-company equipment that will be used by employee. This should be approved by management.

- I understand that I am responsible for any equipment that I may supply, if deemed appropriate by THE COMPANY, including maintenance. THE COMPANY accepts no responsibility for damage or repairs to equipment I supply. I further understand that THE COMPANY reserves the right to make determinations as to appropriate equipment, subject to change at any time.

Other business-related expenses:

- THE COMPANY agrees to supply the telecommuting employee with appropriate office supplies (pens, paper, etc.) for successful completion of job responsibilities. THE COMPANY will also reimburse the employee for all other business-related expenses such as phone calls, shipping costs, etc. that are reasonably incurred in accordance with job responsibilities.

APPENDIX

The FLSA Duties Test Checklist

Highly Compensated Employee

In addition to the salary requirement discussed in Chapter 17:

- ❑ Performs office or non-manual work, and

- ❑ Customarily and regularly performs at least one of the duties of an exempt executive, administrative, or professional employee identified in the standard tests for exemption as exempt from overtime requirements.

Executive Duties Test

- ❑ Primary duty is managing the enterprise, or managing a customarily recognized department or subdivision of the enterprise;

- ❑ Customarily and regularly directs the work of at least two or more full-time employees or their equivalent; and

- ❑ Has the authority to hire or fire other employees, or the employee's suggestions and recommendations as to the hiring, firing, advancement, promotion, or any other change of status of other employees must be given particular weight.

Administrative Duties Test

- ❑ Primary duty is the performance of office or non-manual work directly related to the management or general business operations of the employer or the employer's customers.

- ❑ Primary duty includes the exercise of discretion and independent judgment with respect to matters of significance.

- ❑ Is paid on a salary basis (meets the requirements of the salary-basis test) or on a fee basis (i.e., an agreed sum for a single job so long as it is at a rate that equals the salary threshold for the salary-basis test)..

Professional Duties Test

Learned professional

- ❑ Primary duty is the performance of work requiring advanced knowledge, (in a field of science or learning customarily acquired by a prolonged course of specialized intellectual instruction) defined as work that is predominantly intellectual in character and that includes work requiring the consistent exercise of discretion and judgment.

Creative professional

- ❑ Primary duty is the performance of work requiring invention, imagination, originality, or talent in a recognized field of artistic or creative endeavor.

   Both learned and creative professionals can be paid on a salary basis (meets the requirements of the salary-basis test) or on a fee basis (i.e., an agreed sum for a single job so long as it is at a rate that equals the salary threshold for the salary-basis test).

APPENDIX

Computer Employee Exemption	Outside Sales Exemption
Employed as a computer systems analyst, computer programmer, software engineer or other similarly skilled worker in the computer field (generally not "help desk" employees). Primary duty consists of any of or a combination of the following duties, the performance of which requires the same level of skills:	☐ Primary duty is making sales or obtaining orders or contracts for services or for the use of facilities for which a consideration will be paid by the client or customer. ☐ Is customarily and regularly engaged away from the employer's place or places of business (does not include internet, telephone or mail sales). ☐ If a driver, primary duty is making sales.
☐ The application of systems analysis techniques and procedures, including consulting with users, to determine hardware, software, or system functional specifications;	
☐ The design, development, documentation, analysis, creation, testing, or modification of computer systems or programs, including prototypes, based on and related to user or system design specifications;	
☐ The design, documentation, testing, creation or modification of computer programs related to machine operating systems; or	
☐ Is paid on a salary basis (meets the requirements of the salary-basis test) or on a fee basis, on an hourly basis at a rate not less than $27.63 per hour.	

Job Analysis Interview Questions

Employee Information
- Name of Employee: _____
- Job Title: _____
- Department: _____
- Date: _____

Job Introduction
- Describe the nature, purpose, and location of the job.

Job Duties
- What are the main duties and responsibilities of your job?
- Describe your duties in terms of daily duties, periodic duties, and duties performed at irregular intervals
- How long does each of your duties take to accomplish?
- How do you do each of these duties?
- Are you performing any duties that are not part of your current job description? Describe.
- Do you use any special tools, equipment, or other sources of assistance in performing your job? If so, please list them and the frequency with which they are used.
- Describe the frequency and degree to which you are engaged in such activities as pushing, throwing, pulling, carrying, sitting, running, kneeling, crawling, reaching, climbing....

Job Criteria/Results
- How would you describe success in your job?
- Have work standards been established (errors allowed, time taken for a particular task, etc.)? If so, what are they?
- Describe the successful completion and/or end results of your job.

Records and Reports
- What records or reports do you prepare as part of your job?
- Who do you send these reports/records to?

Supervisor
- Who is your supervisor?
- What kinds of questions or problems would you ordinarily refer to your supervisor?
- Are the instructions you receive clear and consistent with your job description?

Authority
- What is the level of authority you have in your job?
- What is your level of accountability, and to whom are you accountable?
- What kinds of independent action are you permitted to take?

Responsibilities

- Are you responsible for any confidential material? If so, please describe how you handle it.
- Are you responsible for any money or things of monetary value? If so, please describe how you handle it.

Compensation

- Considering your level of productivity, and the skill required to fulfill your responsibilities, do you think you are underpaid? Equitably paid? Overpaid?

Knowledge

- What special knowledge or specific work aids are needed in this job?
- Describe the level, degree, and breadth of knowledge required in these areas.
- What are the educational requirements for this job?
- What type of licensing or certification is needed for this job?
- Can you indicate what training time is needed to arrive at competency in this job?
- What sort of job training is needed for this job?

Skills/Experience

- What activities of this job must you perform with ease and precision?
- What manual skills are required to operate machines, vehicles, equipment, or tools?
- What level of experience and skills are required for your job?

Abilities

- What mathematical ability do you need in this job?
- What reasoning or problem-solving ability must you have in this job?
- What interpersonal abilities are required?
- What supervisory abilities are needed?
- What physical abilities such as strength, coordination, or visual acuity must you have?

Working Instruments

- Please describe briefly what machines, tools, equipment, or work aids you work with on a regular basis.

Health and Safety

- What safety equipment or procedures are needed in this job?
- How frequently are these safety procedures or equipment used in this job?
- Does your work present any type of hazardous or unusual working conditions? How frequent are they?

Working Conditions

- Describe your working conditions.
- Describe the frequency and degree to which you are exposed to such conditions as cramped quarters, moving objects, inadequate ventilation, temperature extremes, etc.

Management Scope (for management positions only)
- How many staff do you supervise directly? Indirectly?
- How many trainees do you supervise directly? Indirectly?

Professional Functions
- Human Resources. What is your authority for:
  ▷ Recruitment and selection?
  ▷ Training and development?
  ▷ Performance appraisal?
  ▷ Compensation and benefits?
- Accounting
  ▷ What financial responsibilities do you have?
  ▷ What budget level do you manage? $ _____
- Administration
  ▷ List assets/facilities you manage.
  ▷ Identify value of each.
- Document Authority
  ▷ What documents are you allowed to sign alone?
  ▷ What documents do you sign with another level of signature?

Management Activities
- Describe your involvement in the following activities:
  ▷ Work assignments.
  ▷ Instruction and training.
  ▷ Performance appraisal.
  ▷ Discipline.
  ▷ Grievance handling.
  ▷ Placement.
  ▷ Workflow.
  ▷ Program improvements.
  ▷ Developing new programs.
  ▷ Troubleshooting.
  ▷ Reports.
  ▷ Follow-through.
  ▷ Other supervisory duties.

Sample Salary Structure

Nonexempt
40% Range, 12% Grade Increases

Grade	Minimum	Mid-Point	Maximum	
15	14.10	16.92	19.74	Hourly
	29,325	35,190	41,056	Annual
14	12.59	15.11	17.62	Hourly
	26,183	31,420	36,657	Annual
13	11.24	13.49	15.74	Hourly
	23,378	28,054	32,729	Annual
12	10.04	12.04	14.05	Hourly
	20,873	25,048	29,223	Annual
11	8.96	10.75	12.54	Hourly
	18,637	22,364	26,092	Annual
10	8.00	9.60	11.20	Hourly
	16,640	19,968	23,296	Annual

Key Definitions Under the FMLA

"Employee Eligibility" means that, though an employee must have worked at least 12 months and 1,250 hours during the prior 12 months, the 12-month period need not be consecutive. However, the employer need only look back for seven years prior to the date the leave begins.

"Compliance year" can be specified using one of four methods:

- The calendar year;
- Any fixed 12-month period, such as a fiscal year;
- A rolling 12-month period measured forward from the date an employee's first FMLA leave begins; or
- A rolling 12-month period measured backward from the date an employee uses any FMLA leave.

The first two methods allow the employee to stack leave, or take leave back to back (for example, the last 12 weeks of the current calendar year and then the first 12 weeks of the subsequent year). The 12-month service threshold is met as of the date the leave begins, not the date of the request for leave.

"Needed to care for" means providing physical and/or psychological care. The employee does not need to be the only individual or family member available to provide the care, nor is the employee required to provide actual care (in other words, someone else is providing in-patient or home care) as long as the employee is providing at least psychological comfort and reassurance.

"A serious health condition" under the FMLA means an illness, injury, impairment, or physical or mental condition that involves a period of incapacity, and treatment (either inpatient care or continuing treatment) by a healthcare provider.

"Key employees" are defined as salaried, FMLA-eligible employees who are among the highest paid 10 percent of all employees within 75 miles of a covered work site. Key employees may be excluded from the job restoration requirement of the FMLA provided that they are so notified by management.

"A family member" (for purposes of Family & Medical Leave) is:

a. A spouse—a husband or wife, as defined or recognized under state law for purposes of marriage, including common law marriages. The regulatory definition of spouse under the FMLA was amended in 2015 so that eligible employees in legal, same-sex marriages will be able to take FMLA leave to care for their spouse or family member, regardless of where they live. This will ensure that the FMLA will give spouses in same-sex marriages the same ability as all spouses to fully exercise their FMLA rights. The definition of a spouse expressly includes individuals in lawfully recognized same-sex and common law marriages and marriages that were validly entered into outside of the United States if they could have been entered into in at least one state.

b. A parent—a biological parent or individual who stands or stood "in loco parentis" to the employee when the employee was a child. (*This does not include in-laws.*)

c. A daughter or son—a biological, adopted, or foster care child, a stepchild, a legal ward, or a child of a person who is or was standing "in loco parentis."

   An eligible child is under the age of 18, or age 18 or older and "incapable of self-care" because of a mental or physical disability. Disability is defined to mean that the individual requires assistance or supervision in three or more activities of daily living (for example, grooming, dressing, eating, cooking, cleaning).

"A family member" (for purposes of Military Caregiver Leave) is:

a. Next of kin of a covered service member means the nearest blood relative other than the covered service member's spouse, parent, son, or daughter (such as: brothers and sisters, grandparents, aunts and uncles, and first cousins).

b. Son or daughter on active duty or call to active duty status means the employee's biological, adopted, or foster child, stepchild, legal ward, or a child for whom the employee stood "in loco parentis," who is on active duty or call to active duty status, and who is of any age.

c. Son or daughter of a covered service member means the service member's biological, adopted, or foster child, stepchild, legal ward, or a child for whom the service member stood "in loco parentis," and who is of any age.

d. Parent of a covered service member means a covered service member's biological, adoptive, step or foster father or mother, or any other individual who stood "in loco parentis" to the covered service member. This term does not include parents-in-law.'

"A healthcare provider" is defined in the regulations to be fairly extensive, including, but not limited to doctors, clinical psychologists, dentists, chiropractors, and all medical para-professionals who fall within the definition of "healthcare provider" (nurse practitioner, nurse-midwives, clinical social workers and physicians assistants, performing within the scope of their practice as defined under state law).

In addition to reinstating the employee at the end of the leave, and providing continued benefits, there are other obligations and provisions that are important to understand.

"Intermittent Leave" is defined as FMLA leave taken in separate blocks of time due to a single qualifying reason.

♦ Employees **must** be allowed to take leave intermittently or on a reduced leave schedule when **medically necessary** for treatment (or recovery from treatment) related to a serious health condition, for recovery from a serious health condition or to care for a seriously ill family member.

♦ When leave is needed for planned medical treatment or to care for a family member, the employee must try to schedule treatment so as to not unduly disrupt the employer's operation.

"An equivalent position" is one that is virtually identical in terms of pay, benefits, and working conditions, including privileges, perquisites, and status. It must involve the same or substantially similar duties and responsibilities that must entail substantially equivalent skill, effort, responsibility, and authority.

"Alternative positions to accommodate intermittent leave." An employee may be required to temporarily transfer to an alternative position during the period that the intermittent or reduced leave schedule is required only if the leave is foreseeable based on planned medical treatment. The alternative position must have equivalent pay and benefits, but does not have to have equivalent duties. If the employee accepts light duty assignment while still eligible for FMLA leave, the employee must be reinstated to his/her original or equivalent position.

Guidelines for Choosing a Benefits Broker

- Determine your needs (for example, plan design and implementation, cost-effective benefit strategies, educating employees, management reports, etc.).
- Determine the scope of coverage, such as health, wellness, dental, life, disability, long-term care, voluntary benefits, etc.
- Determine the type of partner.
  - ▷ Agents, who represent insurance companies and typically sell only one product or for only one company.
  - ▷ Brokers, who are independent and can sell multiple products for multiple companies.
- Research potential candidates. Look to colleagues and industry groups for referrals:
  - ▷ National Association of Health Underwriters
  - ▷ Council of Insurance Agents & Brokers
  - ▷ Independent Insurance Agents & Brokers of America
  - ▷ United Benefit Advisors
  - ▷ International Foundation of Employee Benefit Plans
- Interview potential candidates.
  - ▷ *Where do you think the employee benefits market is heading?*
  - ▷ *Will we have a dedicated account manager?*
  - ▷ *What is your understanding of our needs?*
  - ▷ *How will you approach this project?*
  - ▷ *What differentiates you from others?*
- Evaluate potential candidates.
  - ▷ Check an agent's or broker's disciplinary record. Your state's insurance commissioner's office consumer hotline will provide the information.
  - ▷ Pay attention to licenses and certifications:
    - ◆ CEBS (Certified Employee Benefits Specialist)
    - ◆ CFP (Certified Financial Planner)
    - ◆ CHC (Certified in Healthcare Compliance)
    - ◆ CLU (Certified Life Underwriter)
    - ◆ REBC (Registered Employee Benefits Consultant)
    - ◆ RHU (Registered Health Underwriter)
- Check references.
  - ▷ How did you like working with this consultant?
  - ▷ What was the scope of the project?
  - ▷ Did you get the results you wanted on time and within budget?
  - ▷ Did you feel the consultant understood your business and your needs?
  - ▷ Did you receive an individualized solution for your organization?
  - ▷ What are this provider's strengths and weaknesses?
  - ▷ How does this provider compare with others you've used?
  - ▷ Would you use this provider again?

APPENDIX

Sample Training Evaluation Form

Training Evaluation Form
Course Title

Facilitator: _____

Date: _____

Location: _____

We are constantly striving to improve our workshops. You can help us by completing this Workshop Evaluation.

Please rate the following, using a scale of 1 (disagree strongly) to 5 (agree strongly):

Overall I found this session helpful.	1	2	3	4	5
The trainer was effective.	1	2	3	4	5
The materials were useful.	1	2	3	4	5
The discussions were informative.	1	2	3	4	5
Exercises will help me apply content.	1	2	3	4	5
I learned something new.	1	2	3	4	5

What is one thing you will commit to trying *tomorrow*?	
What worked well?	
What did not work well?	
What would you like us to do differently in the future?	
Is there anything else you would like to tell us about this workshop?	

Plan for Performance Improvement

Performance Improvement Plan Period: From _____ to _____

Employee Information

Name:
Job Title:
Department:
Supervisor Name:
Supervisor Title:

Identify 3–5 tasks that need to be achieved during the performance improvement period.

Task Definition: Describe what needs to be completed.

Action Plan: Describe how the task will be completed and how the results will be measured.

Target Date: State the expected date when the task needs to be completed.

Task Definition: Describe what needs to be completed.

Action Plan: Describe how the task will be completed and how the results will be measured.

Target Date: State the expected date when the task needs to be completed.

Task Definition: Describe what needs to be completed.

Action Plan: Describe how the task will be completed and how the results will be measured.

Target Date: State the expected date when the task needs to be completed.

APPENDIX

Task Definition: Describe what needs to be completed.

Action Plan: Describe how the task will be completed and how the results will be measured.

Target Date: State the expected date when the task needs to be completed.

Task Definition: Describe what needs to be completed.

Action Plan: Describe how the task will be completed and how the results will be measured.

Target Date: State the expected date when the task needs to be completed.

Signatures

                                                                                            Date

Employee: _____

Reviewing Manager: _____

Next Level Manager: _____

Human Resources: _____

Sample Performance Evaluation

Performance Period: From _____ to _____

Employee Information

Name: _____
Job Title: _____
Department: _____
Supervisor Name: _____
Supervisor Title: _____

Performance Evaluation Steps

a. Reviewing Manager provides employee with a copy of the appropriate Performance Evaluation Form and any written documentation of the employee's job responsibilities. Employee completes the self-evaluation portions (Section I, Part A and Part B; and Section II, Part B) and returns it to the Reviewing Manager within a two-week period. The rating sections will be completed by the Reviewing Manager.

b. Reviewing Manager reviews employee's self-evaluation, completes comments and examples as well as Section IV, Summary and Development Plan, and prepares comments for discussion. Reviews with next level of management and Human Resources.

c. Reviewing Manager sets a time for the evaluation feedback session to discuss and finalize the evaluation. This date should be no more than two weeks after the employee has provided the self-evaluation.

d. During the feedback session, ratings are discussed and entered on the form. Signature and comments of the employee are obtained. The employee may have further time to provide comments.

e. After all management approvals have been obtained, the Performance Evaluation Form is reviewed with Human Resources and placed in the employee's personnel file.

Performance Ratings and Definitions

a. **Outstanding:** Performance consistently far exceeds expectations and job requirements. Accomplishments were made in unexpected areas as well. Results obtained all exceeded those expected. Always understood the overall objectives of the department. Showed initiative, and thought beyond the details.

b. **Exceeds Standard:** Performance consistently exceeds expectations and job requirements. Quality and quantity of work standards were met and objectives were achieved above the standards established. Took on extra projects and tasks, while principal responsibilities were done well.

c. **Fully Satisfactory:** Performance consistently meets expectations and job requirements. May exceed expectations from time to time. There were no critical areas where accomplishments were less than planned.

d. **Below Standard:** Performance does not consistently meet expectations, rarely exceeds expectations, but may usually meet minimum requirements for the job. Not all planned objectives were accomplished within the established standards, and some position responsibilities were not completely met. Development activities will be implemented to assure that performance improves to "fully satisfactory" within stated time frame in PIP.

   e. **Unsatisfactory:** Performance is below the minimum acceptable level. Position responsibilities not being met, and important objectives have not been accomplished, even with close supervision and guidance. PIP must be implemented.

Section I. Employee completes Part A from position description. Employee completes Part B stating factual, quantifiable accomplishments. Reviewing Manager may add or modify Part B. Part C will be completed by Reviewing Manager during Feedback Session.

A. Duties & Responsibilities	B. Performance Comments	C. Rating				
		1	2	3	4	5

Section II. **How results were accomplished—skill/ability levels:** Employee completes Part B, providing specific examples that will be used to support the Performance Rating. Reviewing Manager may add or modify Part B. Part C will be completed by Reviewing Manager during Feedback Session.

A. Factors	B. Examples	C. Rating				
		1	2	3	4	5
Quality—Exhibits conformance to standards in work performed; committed to quality concept; strives to meet expectations of management and clients.						
Drive & Commitment—Undertakes tough assignments; strives for personal improvement and success; is reliable and conscientious; supports company goals.						
Initiative—Is self-starting/ enthusiastic; searches for new ideas; has a sense of urgency about next step.						

Adaptability—Adjusts in a changing environment; adapts to new people, ideas, policies, and procedures; is flexible; is resourceful; is open-minded.					
Technical Competence & Knowledge—Degree to which the person is technically competent, up to date; respected and sought as a resource; externally recognized through honors, presentations, as appropriate.					
Teamwork—Works effectively as a team member; contributes to overall company goals; is cooperative; assists others; applies tact and courtesy in dealing with others; has a positive impact and encouraging influence on others.					
Planning & Organization—Budgets time effectively; follows through; completes work on a timely and cost effective basis; schedules resources to meet goals.					
Communication—Has effective written and oral skills; successfully communicates with others; clearly expresses ideas and thoughts; effectively informs others; listens effectively.					
Business Development—Supports BD plans; effectively interfaces with clients.					
Project Management—Demonstrates ability in adhering to budget, resource planning, scheduling, and tracking projects; delivers quality work product within budget in timely manner.					

Section III. **Summary.** Reviewing Manager completes this Section.

1.   Overall performance rating of Sections I & II
     ❑ Outstanding
     ❑ Exceeds Standard
     ❑ Fully Satisfactory
     ❑ Below Standard
     ❑ Unsatisfactory

2.   Identify major areas of strength:

3.   Identify development needs for improvement in present job and/or to prepare for future responsibilities:

4.   Identify action steps for specific areas that will be taken, such as commitments to enable employee to perform at a higher level. Specify development activities and timetables.

Section IV. **Employee Review & Comments**

I have had an opportunity to review and discuss this performance evaluation. My signature does not necessarily indicate that I am in agreement with its contents.
Comments:

                                                                                          Date

Employee Signature   _____

Section V. **Approval Signatures:**

                                                                                          Date

Reviewing Manager   _____

Next Level Manager _____

Human Resources   _____

Sample Performance Factors

Adaptability: Adjusts in a changing environment; adapts to new people, ideas, policies, and procedures; is flexible; is resourceful; is open-minded; responds to changing requirements on a timely basis.

Client Service: Understands and is responsive to customers' goals, mission, and needs; builds enduring customer relationships and maintains good will; gains trust and respect of customers; always does what's best for the client.

Communication: Actively listens; accepts feedback; has effective written and oral skills and clearly expresses ideas and thoughts; communicates all information necessary for effective action on a timely basis; establishes communication links with internal and external stakeholders based on trust and respect; is effective and persuasive and is able to define position/problem areas.

Company Spirit: Contributes to an environment that supports the delivery of quality, value, and outstanding service to our clients.

Consequences of Outcomes: Meets prescribed schedules while adhering to cost constraints and quality standards.

Dealing With Ambiguity: Effectively copes with change and isn't upset with vague situations; comfortably shifts focus and handles risk and uncertainty.

Delivers Results: Focuses on key issues, tasks, and priorities; makes timely decisions; takes action and follows through on decisions.

Drive and Commitment: Undertakes tough assignments; strives for personal improvement and success; is reliable and conscientious; supports company goals.

Effectiveness of Coworker Relations: Coordinates activities with others to meet business objectives; is able to work effectively on a team.

Effectiveness of Customer Relations: Communicates, understands, and responds to internal and external customers consistent with sound business practices.

Independent Judgment: Analyzes problems and makes sound decisions; works independently on a continuing basis.

Initiative: Works with limited direction and a sense of urgency; searches for new ideas.

Integrity and Ethics: Exercises high standards of business conduct; is trustworthy, is intellectually honest; lives the values of the organization.

Interpersonal Savvy: Relates well to all people at all levels, inside and outside the organization; builds appropriate rapport and constructive relationships; uses diplomacy and tact; diffuses high-tension situations comfortably.

Knowledge: Possesses a high degree of technical knowledge and competence and applies it; stays abreast of new developments.

Planning and Organization: Budgets time and schedules resources effectively; completes work on a timely and cost effective basis; delivers quality work products within budget.

APPENDIX

Problem-Solving and Creativity: Defines and solves complex problems with innovation; responds to changing requirements on a timely basis; plans objectives; develops effective work schedules.

Project Management: Adheres to budget, resource planning, scheduling, and tracking projects; delivers quality work product on time and within budget.

Quality: Meets expectations of management and clients while adhering to standards of quality; is committed to continuous improvement.

Strategic Agility: Anticipates future consequences and trends accurately; has broad knowledge and perspective; articulates visions of possibilities and likelihoods; creates competitive and breakthrough strategies and plans.

Supervisor Responsibility: Inspires confidence; directs activities; utilizes expertise; and organizes activities to meet stated goals.

Teamwork: Works effectively as a team member; contributes to overall organizational goals; is cooperative; builds trusting relationships with peers and client staff; fosters collaboration by applying tact and courtesy in dealing with others; has a positive impact and encouraging influence on others.

Technical Competence and Knowledge: Understands and applies state-of-the-art knowledge and methods in his/her relevant field; is respected and sought as a resource; enables, promotes and practices continuous learning; actively promotes, dissemination of knowledge to potential users and beneficiaries.

Sample Performance Ratings and Definitions

1. **Outstanding:** Performance consistently far exceeds expectations and job requirements. Accomplishments were made in unexpected areas as well. All results obtained exceeded those expected. Always understood the overall objectives of the department. Showed initiative, and thought beyond the details.

2. **Exceeds Expectations:** Performance consistently exceeds expectations and job requirements. Quality and quantity of work standards were met, and objectives were achieved above the standards established. Took on extra projects and tasks, while principal responsibilities were done well.

3. **Meets Expectations:** Performance consistently meets expectations and job requirements. May exceed expectations from time to time. There were no critical areas where accomplishments were less than planned.

4. **Below Expectations:** Performance does not consistently meet expectations, rarely exceeds expectations, but may usually meet minimum requirements for the job. Not all planned objectives were accomplished within the established standards, and some position responsibilities were not completely met. Development activities will be implemented to assure that performance improves to "fully satisfactory" within stated time frame in a performance improvement plan.

5. **Unacceptable:** Performance is below the minimum acceptable level. Position responsibilities are not being met and important objectives have not been accomplished, even with close supervision and guidance.

Setting Performance Objectives

Performance Period: From _____ to _____

Employee Information:

Name: _____

Job Title: _____

Department: _____

Supervisor Name: _____

Supervisor Title: _____

Performance Planning: Identify 3–5 performance objectives to be achieved during the performance period that align with business/unit objectives. Goals should be SMART (Specific, Measurable, Attainable, Relevant, and Trackable)

---

1. Overall goal and objective #1 (what is the expectation?):

2. Specific performance objectives (action steps—how the overall objective will be met):

3. Outcome measures (results and how the results will be measured):

4. Time of goal (target completion date):

---

1. Overall goal and objective #1 (what is the expectation?):

2. Specific performance objectives (action steps—how the overall objective will be met):

3. Outcome measures (results and how the results will be measured):

4. Time of goal (target completion date):

---

1. Overall goal and objective #1 (what is the expectation?):

2. Specific performance objectives (action steps—how the overall objective will be met):

3. Outcome measures (results and how the results will be measured):

4. Time of goal (target completion date):

Employee Signature/Date _____

Manager Signature/Date _____

APPENDIX

Checklist for Effective Investigation Interviews

☐ **Start with "broad" questions.** Move to "narrow" questions after the interviewee has sketched the parameters of the events.

☐ **Ask open-ended, non-leading questions** (for example, who, what, when, where, how, and why type questions). Probe for specifics. Ask only one question at a time.

☐ **Ask questions that will enable the interviewee to relate events chronologically.** This will help resolve credibility issues. Ask questions that are designed to give you relevant facts.

☐ **Keep the interview on track.** Individuals who are nervous or emotional tend to ramble. Control the interview by asking specific questions aimed at determining the facts, not speculations or opinions.

☐ **Ask follow-up questions to be sure that the information you are given is accurate.**

☐ **Ask the "tough" questions.** Don't let the interviewee's discomfort stop you from getting to the truth. Don't ask only preplanned questions. Continue questioning until you are satisfied with the clarity and level of detail of the responses. You may want to save particularly difficult or embarrassing questions until the end of the interview.

☐ **Avoid leading questions.** Don't put words in the person's mouth. Don't lead the person or suggest the answer you want the interviewee to give.

☐ **Review your understanding of the information discussed.** Repeat the interviewee's responses and ask for clarification. Don't make assumptions.

☐ **Don't form conclusions prematurely or test them with interviewees.** Although this can be a way to get information, you want avoid suggesting the wrong conclusion.

☐ **Encourage dialogue by:**
   ▷ Putting the interviewee at ease.
   ▷ Stressing that no conclusions have been reached.
   ▷ Using listening skills.

Checklist for Gathering the Facts

❏   Obtain all relevant facts from the employee. Be specific and avoid speculation.

❏   What happened (e.g., ask: "Exactly what went on?")

❏   Who was involved?

❏   When did the incident take place (date, time)?

❏   Where did the incident take place (e.g., ask: "Were you in an office? Whose? Was the door open or shut?")?

❏   What was said? By whom (e.g., ask: "Exactly what did she say? How did you respond?")?

❏   Was the employee's ability to work affected? If so, how? Ask for examples.

❏   Were there any observers/witnesses? If so, who (e.g., ask: "Was anyone else present or did anyone else overhear anything?")?

❏   Was the incident isolated or was it part of a pattern (e.g., ask: "Has something similar happened before? If so, when, how frequently?")?

❏   Get details of any prior occurrences.

❏   Have other employees been affected?

❏   Has the employee talked to anyone else within the company about this issue? If so, who?

❏   Has the employee talked to anyone else outside the company about this issue? If so, who?

❏   Are there any written documents relevant to the issue that the employee knows about?

❏   Has the employee kept any written records or diaries that are relevant to the issue? Any expense reports, personnel file memos, other notes?

❏   Does the person raising the issue know if any other employees have the same or similar concern?

❏   Are there any other issues this employee wants to discuss?

❏   Does the employee have any additional facts or information that would be helpful in an investigation, if one is merited?]

Employee Handbook Table of Contents

APPENDIX

Guidelines for Documenting Workplace Issues

When faced with charges of discrimination, proper documentation of all employment activities may be necessary to explain the activity in question. Some guidelines to follow include:

1. **Maintain written records on an ongoing basis, as incidents occur.** Do not wait until a serious problem develops and then begin to make written records.
2. **Document all disciplinary incidents**, even informal warnings and counseling regarding minor issues and problems.
3. **Document any discussion in which an employee is informed of applicable rules of conduct or standards of performance.** If the employee raises objections or seems to have difficulty understanding what is expected, make a written note of it. Your documentation should include any assistance or solutions you discussed with the employee. Your discussions should include next steps that may be taken if the situation does not improve.
4. **Document positive accomplishments.** You may wish to rely on such instances to justify selection of one employee over another for a promotion or favorable assignment. Documentation of positive efforts is just as important as documentation of problems.
5. **Keep records in a consistent manner for all employees.** Any aspect of performance or behavior that you put into writing should be done for all employees under your supervision.

Maintain written records.

*   Keep an incident log.
*   Include the date, time, and place of each occurrence.
*   Include first and last names of individuals involved.
*   Create short, specific entries that focus on behavior—what the employee has done or failed to do.
*   Include explanations so a third party (or a jury) can understand it. (For example, explain acronyms or company-specific terminology.)
*   Be sure they are legible if they are handwritten.
*   Stick to job-related facts only. Be specific and objective. Stick to the facts and don't draw conclusions. Indicate the sources of your information, such as your own observations or the name of the person who reported the incident to you. Leave out any speculation. In preparing to write up the incident, use the following questions as guidance:
    ▷ What specifically occurred?
    ▷ When and where did it happen?
    ▷ Who was involved?
    ▷ Is there sufficient detail to support a future decision to take management action?
    ▷ Have you described the results of the behavior?
    ▷ What circumstances, if any, may have influenced the behavior? For example:
        *   Was there an emergency situation?
        *   Did unusual or adverse conditions exist?
*   Sign and date your notes, or otherwise identify who prepared them.

- Keep documentation in a secure place, where it will be accessible if needed by someone else in management in your absence, but not in a place where it will be open to review by employees.

Document the results of any meeting with employees.

- Indicate that the documentation you prepared was shared with the employee, if applicable.
- Indicate any prior applicable discipline or counseling.
- Discuss the employee's response.
- Document that you discussed with the employee the consequences of further occurrences.

Remember: Defensible documentation will include:

Facts. The conduct or behavior will be described in accurate, factual terms.

Objectives. Those performance and behavior expectations that the employee failed to meet should be explained in a constructive way.

Solutions. Forms of assistance, coaching, or guidance provided to the employee must be described. Explain what specific suggestions you provided to help the employee reach established objectives.

Actions. The steps you are taking now, and those that you will take if objectives are not met or behavior does not improve, need to be clearly articulated.

APPENDIX

Guidelines to Address Union Activity

General Guidelines: Do's

The following is what supervisors should do if union organizing occurs:

- Do answer questions asked by an employee or employees.
- Do give straightforward information concerning the company's policies. (Do not guess.) If you do not know an answer, it is appropriate to tell the employee that you will find the answer for him or her.
- Do state the company's position on unionization.
- Do be a good listener and observer. You can and should listen to employees as long as the information is volunteered.
- Do tell employees that signing a union card is the first step to joining a union.
- Do respond immediately to any potentially violent situation. Violence or the threat of violence by employees is a serious rules violation and should be dealt with through the disciplinary process.
- Do inform senior management of any union activities or rumors of such activity.

General Guidelines: Do Not's

The following is what supervisors should *not* do if union organizing occurs:

- Do not question employees about their union membership preferences or activities or those of other employees. (It is acceptable to listen if the information is volunteered.)
- Do not spy on union activities or create the impression of doing so.
- Do not use threats of reprisal, retaliation, or force (actual or implied).
- Do not promise any incentives to any employee, including those who refrain from joining the union or who may oppose organizing activities.
- Do not make statements alleging that unionization will take away current vacation benefits or other benefits and privileges.
- Do not look at or accept union cards. If approached by a union representative, inform the union representative that you are not authorized to handle such matters.
- Do not discuss complaints or petitions with groups of employees. Ask the group to return to work immediately.
- Do not start or sign an anti-union petition.
- Do not treat union sympathizers unequally (overtime, desirable assignments, favoritism, etc.).
- Do not ask employees how they intend to vote.
- Do not encourage employees to withdraw their authorization cards from the union.
- Do not prohibit employees from wearing union insignia at work.

Sample Categories of Unacceptable Conduct

The following categories include, but are not limited to, those types of conduct considered unacceptable and may be the basis of a disciplinary action, including termination.

a. **Failure to Work Harmoniously With Others, including coworkers, customers, subordinates, or superiors.** Examples of unacceptable conduct in this category include, but are not necessarily limited to, malicious gossip and/or spreading rumors or otherwise creating discord; interfering with another employee on the job; harassment or any type of discriminatory behavior.

b. **Insubordination.** Failing or refusing to follow directions of a supervisor or any other individual authorized to direct the employee.

c. **Violation of Safety and/or Security Regulations.** Willfully or negligently disregarding or violating any published safety, security, or risk management policy or procedure.

d. **Unauthorized Removal or Use of Property.** Removing any property (the employer's or client's, or property of another) from the workplace without prior written approval. This includes unauthorized removal/use of the employer's equipment or property for personal use or profit.

e. **Gambling.** Gambling of any kind during work hours on the employer's or client's property, including online gambling.

f. **Drugs.** Engaging in prohibited conduct, possessing, using, distributing, manufacturing, purchasing, dispensing, or selling illegal drugs, as described in the Substance Abuse Policy.

g. **Intoxicants.** Being under the influence of alcohol or other intoxicants, unless authorized by an appropriate official, while working or on the employer's premises. A supervisor may refer an employee exhibiting signs and symptoms of alcohol abuse to the employee assistance program.

h. **Possession of Firearms.** Unauthorized possession of dangerous or illegal firearms, weapons or explosives on the employer's property.

i. **Harm or Threat of Harm.** Examples of unacceptable conduct in this category include, but are not necessarily limited to, physically harming or threatening to harm any persons or property, including intimidation, physical altercations, threats of harm (whether verbal or written), and vandalism. A supervisor may refer an employee exhibiting signs and symptoms of violent tendencies to the employee assistance program for the purpose of verifying fitness for duty.

j. **Unexcused Absences or Tardiness.** Failure to report to work, report to work on time, report back to work from a scheduled break or appointment; or leaving the work assignment or premises during the employee's scheduled working time for that day unless prior authorization has been received from the supervisor; sleeping on working time, wasting time, or loitering.

k. **Failure to Protect the Organization's Business Interests.** Examples of unacceptable conduct in this category include failing to protect or otherwise acting in willful or wanton disregard of the employer's interests, failing to protect (disclosing or misusing information about) the confidentiality of projects, documents, or other information pertaining to company business. This can also include falsifying or misrepresenting

APPENDIX

data and material information relevant to the employer's business, such as making or causing to be made false entries in the organization's books or records, verbally or in writing misrepresenting data in reports, an employment application, time records, benefits, accounting of time records, travel records, and other work records and receipts.

l.   **Violating the Nondisclosure Agreement.** Giving confidential or proprietary information to competitors or other organizations or to unauthorized employees; working for a competing business while working for the employer; breach of confidentiality of personnel information.

m. **Soliciting and Distributing Literature.** Examples of unacceptable conduct in this category include soliciting, collecting, or selling for any purpose during working time and in the workplace, except as specifically authorized by management. Individuals not employed by the organization are not permitted to solicit, collect, sell, or distribute literature, pamphlets, or any other documents for any purpose on the employer's premises, unless specifically invited to do so.

n.   **Outrageous Behavior.** Any conduct, whether verbal, physical, or both, that is immoral, indecent, or so disruptive of the work environment that it has no place in a professional setting.

o.   **Criminal Conduct.** Any act, or failure to act, that would be considered criminal in nature.

Sample Disciplinary Notice

DATE: June 1, 2011

EMPLOYEE NAME: Employee Smith

DISCIPLINARY ACTION: Letter of Caution

ISSUE: Absenteeism and Tardiness

EXPLANATION (specific behaviors observed and the dates they occurred):

Over the past three months, you have been absent on the following days:
March 2, March 18, April 4, April 21, May 9, and May 27.
In addition, you arrived late on the following days:
March 7, March 23, March 30, April 8, April 18, April 28, May 2, May 13, and May 23.

IMPACT:

It is important in your position of customer service representative that you be at work and arrive on time in order to be available to meet with customers both on the phone and in person. Your absenteeism and tardiness have caused an increased workload for your coworkers and have impacted the level of service that the department provides.

CORRECTIVE ACTION:

You are expected to be at work during your regularly scheduled shifts. If you know in advance that you need time off, you are to notify me so that arrangements can be made for coverage. You are expected to arrive at work on time and if there are unforeseen delays, you must call and advise me so coverage can be arranged.

The company has an Employee Assistance Program (EAP) available to assist its employees with personal issues, including work-life balance issues. You may take advantage of this program at any time. All contact with the EAP is confidential.

EXPECTATIONS:

Unless there is a marked improvement in your attendance over the next thirty days, further disciplinary action will be taken, up to and including termination.

SIGNATURES:

| Manager | Manager Jones | _____ | June 1, 2011 |
| Employee | Employee Smith | _____ | June 1, 2011 |

APPENDIX

Managing Conflict Through Open Communication

Use dialogue and listening skills to create an environment for open communication.

Separate the people from the problem.

Determine if the parties:

- Are ready to talk and listen.
- Can suspend judgment long enough to hear each other's perceptions and feelings.
- Can think in terms of "I" statements rather than "you" statements.
- Want to resolve rather than blame.

Focus on interests not positions.

Determine what:

- The perceived loss or threat of loss that has led each party to perceive a problem.
- What each party thinks about the problem.
- What each party thinks about the other.
- Assumptions and cultural differences underlie each party's behavior.
- The nature of the differences—facts, goals, methods, values.

Create options.

Determine:

- How each party is approaching the situation—collaborating, sharing, avoiding, competing, or accommodating.
- What each party feels is an acceptable outcome. More than two alternatives are a must.
- What both parties can agree on.
- What will prevent the resolution from taking shape.
- If there are follow-up issues that need to be taken care of later and if a date needs to be set for follow-up.

Insist on using objective criteria.

Depending on the issue, determine fair standards such as:

- Precedent.
- Professional standards.
- Industry standards.
- Moral/ethical standards.
- Efficiency and costs.
- Equal treatment.

Indicators of a Troubled Employee

Physical Signs and Changes

Poor personal hygiene.

Sleepiness.

Walking difficulty.

Coordination difficulty.

Tremors.

Red eyes, pupil changes, jerky eye movements.

Less interest in appearance.

Restlessness.

Speech impairment.

Constant runny nose.

Performance and Behavior Changes

Increased Absenteeism

Unexcused absences.

Excessive sick leave.

Improbable reasons for absences.

Higher rate of absence (cold, flu, etc.).

Excessive tardiness.

Monday/Friday absence pattern.

On-The-Job Absenteeism

Frequent workstation absences.

Numerous restroom visits.

Frequent breaks (coffee, smoking, etc.).

Long lunches.

Physical illness on the job.

Difficulties in Concentration/Confusion

Work requires greater time and effort.

Frequent daydreaming.

Easily distracted.

Job/projects take longer.

Missed deadlines.

Inability to maintain work demands.

Difficulty with complex assignments.

Difficulty recalling instructions.

Lowered Job Quality/Efficiency

Decreased interest in job tasks.

Increased errors.

Increased carelessness.

Poor decision quality.

Decreased output.

Wasted time and materials.

Sporadic Work Patterns

Wide swings in productivity.

Variation of work quality.

Increased Accidents

On the job.

Off the job.

Diminished Interpersonal Skills

Overreacts to criticism (real or imagined).

Wide swings in mood.

Irritability.

Customer/peer complaints.

Avoids coworkers/others.

Unusual Behavior

Bizarre actions on the job.

Temper tantrums.

Emotional outbursts.

Physical violence.

Coming/returning to work in a "changed" condition.

APPENDIX

Safety Checklist

Safety is everybody's business and should be given primary importance in every aspect of planning and performing all activities. We care about the welfare of our employees, and we want to protect you against industrial injury and illness. Therefore, it is important that all injuries (no matter how slight), as well as any potential safety hazard, be reported to your manager immediately.

The following are common sense, general safety rules.

- ❒ Avoid overloading electrical outlets with too many appliances or machines.

- ❒ Use flammable items, such as cleaning fluids, with caution.

- ❒ Walk—don't run.

- ❒ Use stairs one at a time.

- ❒ Report to your manager if you or a coworker becomes ill or is injured.

- ❒ Ask for assistance when lifting heavy objects or moving heavy furniture.

- ❒ Smoke only in designated smoking areas.

- ❒ Keep cabinet doors and file and desk drawers closed when not in use.

- ❒ Sit firmly and squarely in chairs that roll or tilt.

- ❒ Avoid "horseplay" or practical jokes.

- ❒ Keep your work area clean and orderly, and the aisles clear.

- ❒ Stack materials only to safe heights.

Watch out for the safety of fellow employees.

Manager's Termination Checklist

Before you take action against an employee, especially termination, ask yourself the following:

- ☐   Am I comfortable with the facts?

- ☐   Am I comfortable with the evidence supporting the facts?

- ☐   Have I communicated performance and conduct expectations to the employee?

- ☐   Have I discussed the problem with the employee?

- ☐   Have I followed company policies (i.e., progressive discipline and/or performance improvement)?

- ☐   Have I clearly documented the problem?

- ☐   Have I considered the employee's tenure and employment history? Would termination prevent vesting in benefits in the near future?

- ☐   Am I treating the employee like others in the same situation?

- ☐   Am I potentially violating public policy, state laws, or federal laws?

- ☐   Have I explored alternatives (for example, transfer, training)?

- ☐   Can I defend my decision?

- ☐   Have I discussed the issue with HR or other appropriate resources in the organization?

- ☐   Am I treating the employee with respect?

No employee should be summarily discharged.

Be sure you have gathered and reviewed all of the relevant information and facts before taking action.

Sample Exit Interview Questions

The following are sample exit interview questions that you can incorporate into your process:

- What is your primary reason for leaving?
- If you are leaving to join another organization:
  - ▷ Why did you start looking for another job?
  - ▷ Did anything specific trigger your decision to leave?
  - ▷ Did you consider another position in this organization? Why or why not?
- What was most satisfying about your job?
- What was least satisfying about your job?
- What would you change about your job?
- Did your job duties turn out to be as you expected?
- Did you receive enough training to do your job effectively?
- Did you receive adequate support to do your job?
- Did you receive sufficient feedback about your performance?
- How frequently did you receive feedback?
  - ▷ Ongoing feedback?
  - ▷ Annual feedback only?
- Were you satisfied with this organization's merit review process?
- Did this organization help you to fulfill your career goals?
- What would you improve to make our workplace better?
- Were you happy with your pay, benefits, and other incentives?
- Overall how would you describe management?
  - ▷ The organization-wide management?
  - ▷ Your immediate management?
- What feedback can you provide regarding the management, both organization-wide and your immediate management?
- Based on your experience with us, what do you think it takes to succeed at this organization?
- Did any organization policies or procedures (or any other obstacles) make your job more difficult?
- Would you consider working again for this organization in the future?
  - ▷ If so, under what circumstances and in what type of position?
- Would you recommend working for this organization to your family and friends?
- What did you like most about this organization?
- What did you like least about this organization?
- If you are leaving to join another organization, what does your new organization offer that this organization doesn't?
- Do you have any other comments?

Notes

Chapter 1

1. Lipkin, *Y in the Workplace*, p. 18.
2. Armstrong and Mitchell, *The Essential*, pp. 163–8.
3. Meister and Willyerd, "Mentoring," p. 69.
4. Tulgan, *Not Everyone*, p. 39.
5. Schell and Solomon, *Managing*, p. 7.
6. Covey, *The 7 Habits*, pp. 236–60.
7. Tyler, "Global Ease."

Chapter 2

1. Collins, *Good to Great*, p. 41.
2. Day, "Developing," p. 16.
3. John Berry, PriceWaterhouseCoopers website, *www.pwc.com*.
4. Mulcahy, "How I Did It," p. 124.

Chapter 3

1. Muhl, "The Employment-at-Will," p. 1.

Chapter 4

1. Buckingham and Coffman, *First, Break*, p. 105.

Chapter 5

1. Adapted from Cornell University Cooperative Extension Diversity website, *www.staff.cce.cornell.edu*.
2. Adapted from Gupta, *A Practical Guide*.

Chapter 6

1. Mornell, *Hiring Smart*, p. 4.
2. Freiberg and Freiberg, *Nuts* p. 66.
3. Share, "150 Funniest."

Chapter 7

1. Welsh, *Jack*, p. 383.
2. Thompson and Greif, *No More*, p. 121.
3. Grensing-Pophal, "How You Treat," p. 74.

Chapter 8

1. Collins, *Good to Great*, p. 54.
2. Personal conversation with Lance Richards.
3. Personal conversation with Mary Walter Arthur.
4. Madia and Borgese, *The Social*, p. 207.

Chapter 9

1. Mornell, *Hiring Smart*, p. 228.
2. Haneberg, "High Impact."
3. Sims, *The 30-Minute*, p. 21.
4. 42 U.S.C. paragraph 2003-2(e).
5. Ibid.
6. Ibid.

Chapter 10

1. These percentages are from Paul and Fox's presentation at the 7th Annual Labor and Employment Law Advanced Practices Symposium, Las Vegas, Nevada, March 30–April 1, 2011.
2. Fatemi, "The True."

Chapter 11

1. Mornell, *Hiring Smart*, p. 120.

Chapter 12

1. Finnegan, "The Race," p. 22.
2. Lee, "For Onboarding.

Chapter 13

1. Girard, *The Google*, p. 63.
2. "Cost of Turnover."
3. "Raise the Employee Engagement Ante," SHRM 2011 Talent & Staffing Management Conference Exposition, San Diego, California, April 12, 2011.
4. Ibid.
5. Ibid.
6. Buckingham and Coffman, *First, Break*, p. 28.
7. Finnegan, *Rethinking*.

Chapter 14

1. Kruse, *Employee*, p. 5.
2. Morgan, "Driving."
3. Hastings, "Full Engagement."
4. "Creating a New."
5. Georgia Sherrill, "Long View of Employee Engagement," 2010 SHRM Conference, San Diego, California, June 29, 2010.

Chapter 15

1. Couch, "This Memo."
2. Shipman and Kay, *Womenomics*, p. 36.
3. "Trends."
4. Families, *2011 Guide*, p. 49.
5. Shipman and Kay, *Womenomics*, p. 38.
6. Families, p. 71.
7. Cornelia Gamlem, "Impact of Economy on Older Workers," Equal Employment Opportunity Commission meeting, November 17, 2010
8. Families, p. 74.
9. Schulte, "At Some."
10. "Latest Telecommuting."
11. Morgan, "Five Things."
12. Fallon, "4 Issues."

Chapter 16

1. Nelson, *1001 Ways*, Preface.
2. Shepherd, "Getting Personal," p. 24.
3. Lallande, "Recognize," p. 54.

Chapter 17

1. *Franklin D. Roosevelt*, pp. 624–25.

Chapter 18

1. "Salary Budgets."
2. Lawler, *Strategic Pay*, p. 154.
3. Greene, "Effectively Managing."
4. Green and Clough, "GE."
5. Miller, "Bonus."
6. Henderson, *Compensation*, p. 58.
7. Allender, Elkins, and Larson, "Sales Compensation."
8. Grossman, "Are You?"

Chapter 20

1. "Employee Retirement."
2. Grossman, "Are You?"

Chapter 21

1. Cadbury, *The Chocolate Wars*, p. 164.
2. This report was an addendum to Met Life's *8th Annual Employee Benefits Trends Study*, conducted in 2010. It can be found on MetLife's website at *http://bit.ly/2mXAjmF*.
3. Drew, "Benefits Choices," p. 29.
4. Roberts, "Open Enrollment," p. 52.

Chapter 22

1. This material is paraphrased from Gupta, *A Practical Guide*.

Chapter 23

1. LeadershipQuotes.com.
2. Plumb, "'Corp-U'," p. 18.
3. Ibid., p. 19.
4. Ibid.
5. Ibid.
6. This is paraphrased from Shea, *The Mentoring*.
7. Jefferson, Pollock, and Wick, *Getting*, p. 6.

Chapter 24

1. Argyris, "Teaching."

Chapter 25

1. Zander and Zander, *The Art*, p. 26.
2. Mirza, "'Creative'," p. 34.
3. Buckingham and Goodall, "Reinventing," p.4.
4. Bianco-Mathis, "The Reinvented."
5. Cunningham, "In Big Move."
6. Buckingham and Goodall, "Reinventing," pp. 9–10.
7. Ibid., pp. 7–8.
8. Walker, *Human Resources*, p. 274.
9. Pulakos, *Performance*, p. 7.
10. McGregor, "This Big."
11. "Getting the Most."
12. Green and Clough, "GE Considers."
13. Cunningham and McGregor, "Why Big."
14. Deblieux, "The Deblieux Report."
15. Tyler, "The Tethered."

Chapter 26

1. Gregerman, *Surrounded*, p. 82.
2. Ibid., p. 80.
3. Booher, *Communicate*, p. 42.
4. Ibid., p. 18.
5. Ibid., p. 41.
6. Ibid., p.25.
7. Buckingham and Goodall, "Reinventing," p. 11.
8. Bianco-Mathis, "The Reinvented."

Chapter 27

1. Zander and Zander, *The Art*, p. 79.
2. From *The Autobiography of Mother Jones* (1925). Mother Jones was an organizer for the United Mine Workers, 1900–1920.
3. "Reorganized Labor."

Chapter 28

1. Albright, *Read*, p. 65.
2. Patterson, Grenny, McMillan, and Switzler, *Crucial Conversations*, p. 11.
3. Eisaguirre, *The Power*, p. 20.
4. Watkins, *The Essentials*, p. 65.
5. Thomas and Kilmann, "Thomas-Kilmann."
6. Fisher and Ury, *Getting to Yes*, p. 15.
7. Watkins, *The Essentials*, p. 71.
8. Fisher and Ury, *Getting to Yes*, p. 157.
9. Ursiny, *The Coward's*, p. 136.
10. Ibid., p. 137.
11. Fisher and Ury, *Getting to Yes*, p. 85.
12. Gamlem and Mitchell, *The Essential*, pp. 134–5.
13. Watkins, *The Essentials*, p. 116.

Chapter 29

1. Meyerson, "A Fire."
2. "Performance and Reporting."
3. "OSHA at 40."
4. Bernstein, "Keeping."
5. Cantor Fitzgerald website (*www.cantor.com.*).

Chapter 30

1. "Involuntary Termination."
2. Jon Hyman, "A Humane," August 2016, p.20.
3. Gamlem, Cornelia. "Impact of Economy on Older Workers," Equal Employment Opportunity Commission meeting, Washington, D.C., November 17, 2010.
4. Chevron Alumni Community website (*alumni.chevron.com*).

Conclusion

1. Petroff, "Branson."
2. Madell, "Neflix."
3. Medici, "U.S. Sen."
4. Portnoy, "Saving Capitalism."
5. Ibid.
6. Adam, "In Landmark."

Appendix

1. From Kador, *200 Best*.

55

Bibliography

Adam, Karla. "In Landmark Decision, British Court Rules Uber Drivers Should Get Minimum Wage," *Washington Post*, October 28, 2016, *http://wapo.st/2nvK9O3*.

Albright, Madeleine. *Read My Pins*. New York: Melcher Media, 2009.

Allender, Therese, Rebecca Elkins, and Elizabeth Larson, "Sales Compensation Planning for HR Professionals," Alexandria, Va.: SHRM On-Line, 2007, *http://bit.ly/2mAGn0G*.

Argyris, Chris, "Teaching Smart People How to Learn," *Harvard Business Review*, Volume 69, 1991, pp. 99–109.

Armstrong, Sharon. *The Essential Performance Review Handbook*. Franklin Lakes, N.J.: Career Press, 2010.

Armstrong, Sharon, and Barbara Mitchell. *The Essential HR Handbook*. Franklin Lakes, N.J.: Career Press, 2008.

Bernstein, Larry. "Keeping Employees, Bottom Lines in Shape," *Washington Post*, July 5, 2011.

Bianco-Mathis, Virginia. "The Reinvented Performance Appraisal: Performance Coaching" Marymount University website, Marymount's HRM Blog, September 28, 2016, *http://bit.ly/2maO2aA*.

Booher, Dianna. *Communicate With Confidence*. New York: McGraw Hill, 1994.

Buckingham, Marcus, and Curt Coffman. *First, Break All the Rules: What the World's Greatest Managers Do Differently*. New York: Simon and Shuster, 1999.

Buckingham, Marcus, and Ashley Goodall. "Reinventing Performance Management," *Harvard Business Review*, April 2015, *http://bit.ly/18AceYm*.

Cadbury, Deborah. The Chocolate Wars. New York: Public Affairs Books, 2010.

Coens, Tom, and Mary Jenkins. *Abolishing Performance Appraisals*. San Francisco, Calif.: Berret-Koehler Publishers, Inc., 2000.

Collins, Jim. *Good to Great*. New York: HarperCollins, 2001.

"Cost of Turnover Tool Kit," SHRM website (*www.shrm.org*).

Couch, Robbie. "This Memo Joe Biden Sent His Staffers on Work Life Balance Is a Must-Read." Upworthy website, *http://u.pw/2n6q5AR*.

Covey, Stephen R. *The 7 Habits of Highly Effective People*. New York: Free Press, a Simon and Schuster imprint, 1989.

"Creating a New Deal for Middle Managers," Boston Consulting Group website, July 2010, *www.bcg.com*.

Cunningham, Lillian. "In Big Move, Accenture Will Get Rid of Annual Performance Reviews and Rankings," *Washington Post*, July 21, 215, *http://wapo.st/2mXznyz*.

Cunningham, Lillian, and Jena McGregor. "Why Big Business Is Falling out of Love With Annual Performance Reviews," Washington Post, August 17, 2015, *http://wapo.st/2mDxZOK*.

Day, David V. "Developing Leadership Talent." In *Effective Practice Guidelines Series*. Alexandria, Va.: SHRM Foundation, 2007, p. 16.

Deblieux, Mike, "The Deblieux Report: Performance as a Systems Issue," November 2010, *www.deblieux.com*.

Downey, Diane, Tom March, and Adena Berkman. "Assimilating New Leaders: The Key to Executive Retention," AMA, 2001.

Drew, Robb. "Benefits Choices: Educating the Consumer," *HR Magazine*, March 2011.

Eisaguirre, Lynne. *The Power of a Good Fight*. Indianapolis, Ind.: Alpha Books, 2002.

"Employee Retirement Income Security Act." Wikipedia website, *http://bit.ly/2maJEZu*.

Fallon, Nicole. "4 Issues Your Company's Telecommuting Policy Should Address," *Business News Daily*, *http://bit.ly/1Aj02VE*.

Families and Work Institute. *2011 Guide to Bold New Ideas for Making Work Work*, 2011.

Fatemi, Falcon. "The True Cost of a Bad Hire—It's More Than You Think," *Forbes*, September 28, 2016.

Finnegan, Frank, "The Race for Talent: Retaining and Engaging Workers in the 21st Century," *The Journal of the Human Resources Planning Society*, Volume 27, Issue 3, 2004, p. 22.

Finnegan, Richard P. *Rethinking Retention in Good Times and Bad*. Boston, Mass.: Davies-Black, 2009.

Fisher, Roger, and William Ury. *Getting to Yes*. New York: Penguin Books, 1991.

Franklin D. Roosevelt, Public Papers and Addresses, Vol. V New York: Random House, 1936, *http://bit.ly/2nvXZj8*.

Freiberg, Kevin, and Jackie Freiberg. *Nuts: Southwest Airlines' Crazy Recipe for Business and Personal Success*. New York: Broadway Book, 1997.

Gamlem, Cornelia, and Barbara Mitchell. *The Essential Workplace Conflict Handbook*. Pompton Plains, NJ: Career Press, 2015.

"Getting the Most out of Performance Appraisal Systems." SuccessFactors website, *http://bit.ly/2mXz9r0*.

Girard, Bernard. *The Google Way: How One Company Is Revolutionizing Management as We Know It*. San Francisco, Calif.: No Starch Press, 2009.

Green, Jeff, and Rick Clough. "GE Considers Scrapping Annual Raise," *http://bloom.bg/1tceobJ*.

Greene, Robert J., "Effectively Managing Base Pay: Strategies and Programs for Success," Alexandria, Va.: SHRM On-Line, 2010, *http://bit.ly/2mAOTNb*.

Gregerman, Alan S. *Surrounded by Geniuses*. Naperville, Ill.: Sourcebooks, Inc., 2007.

Grensing-Pophal, Liz. "How You Treat Internal Applicants Can Affect Morale," *HR Magazine*, December 1, 2006.

Grossman, Robert J., "Are You Clear?" Alexandria, Va.: SHRM On-Line, October 1, 2005, *http://bit.ly/2mXuXI3*: accessed May 9, 2011.

Gupta, Kavita. *A Practical Guide to Needs Assessment*. San Francisco, Calif.: Pfeiffer, a John Wiley & Sons, Inc. imprint, 1999.

Haneberg, Lisa, "High Impact Middle Management," ERE website, July 10, 2009, *www.ere.com*. Accessed July 30, 2011.

Hastings, SPHR, Rebecca, "Full Engagement Around the World," SHRM website, January 3, 2011, *www.shrm.org* .

Henderson, Richard I. *Compensation Management*. Englewood Cliffs, N.J.: Prentice Hall, 1994.

Hyman, Jon. "A Humane Approach to Layoffs," *Workforce*, August 2016.

"Involuntary Termination of Employment in the United States," SHRM website, December 1, 2008, *http://bit.ly/2mDsD6l*.

Jefferson, Andrew, Roy Pollock, and Calhoun Wick. *Getting Your Money's Worth From Training & Development: A Guide to Breakthrough Learning for Managers*. San Francisco, Calif.: Pfeiffer, a Wiley imprint, 2009.

Kador, John. *200 Best Questions to Ask on Your Interview*. McGraw Hill Companies, Inc., 2002.

Kruse, Kevin E. *Employee Engagement 2.0: How to Motivate Your Team for High Performance*. Richboro, Penna.: The Kruse Group, 2012.

Lallande, Ann, "Recognize Your Investments," *HR Magazine*, April 2008, p. 54.

Lancaster, Lynne C., and David Stillman. *When Generations Collide—Who They Are, Why They Clash, How to Solve the Generational Puzzle at Work*. New York: HarperCollins, 2002.

"Latest Telecommuting Statistics," *http://bit.ly/1I3jNaZ*.

Lawler III, Edward E. *Strategic Pay*. San Francisco, Calif.: Jossey-Bass, 1990.

Lee, David, "For Onboarding Success, Remember This Mantra," HumanNature@Work website, November 20, 2009, *http://bit.ly/2nzPrER*. Accessed July 27, 2011.

Lipkin, Nicole. *Y in the Workplace: Managing the "Me First" Generation*. Franklin Lakes, N.J.: Career Press, 2009.

Madell, Robin. "Neflix Provides Breakthrough for Working Parents in America," *http://bit.ly/1gZOqCi*.

Madia, Sherrie A., and Paul Borgese. *The Social Media Guide: Everything You Need to Know to Grow Your Business Exponentially With Social Media*. Buffalo, N.Y.: Full Court Press, an FCPressLLC imprint, 2010.

McGregor, Jena. "This Big Change Was Supposed to Make Performance Reviews Better. Could it Be Making Them Worse?," *Washington Post*, June 6, 2007, *http://wapo.st/2mR486C*.

Medici, Andy, "U.S. Sen. Mark Warner: Here's Why We Must Rethink Employment, Benefits in the Uber 'Gig' Economy," *http://bit.ly/1Sx5I6y*.

Meister, Jeanne C., and Katie Willyerd, "Mentoring Millennials," *Harvard Business Review*, May 2010, p. 69.

Meyerson, Harold, "A Fire That Still Burns Bright," *Washington Post*, March 23, 2011.

Miller, Stephen, "Bonus Binge: Variable Pay Outpaces Salary," *http://bit.ly/2maXSJP*.

———., "Executive Comp Plans Target Stronger Performance Ties," SHRM website, 2011, *http://bit.ly/2nNnVTE*. Accessed May 9, 2011.

Mirza, Beth. "'Creative Endeavors': An Interview With Lori McAdams, Vice President of Human Resources, Pixar Animation Studios," *HR Magazine* (April 2011), p. 34.

Morgan, Jacob. "Five Things You Need to Know About Telecommuting," Forbes, May 4, 2016, *http://bit.ly/2mR4Cts*.

Morgan, Lloyd, "Driving Performance and Retention Through Employee Engagement 2010," Corporate Leadership Council website, *www.clc.executiveboard.com* .

Mornell, Pierre. *Hiring Smart: How to Predict Winners & Losers in the Incredibly Expensive People Reading Game*. Berkeley, Calif.: Ten Speed Press, 1997.

Muhl, Charles J., "The Employment-at-Will Doctrine—Three Major Exceptions," U.S. Bureau of Labor & Statistics website, *http://bit.ly/2mDlItU*.

Mulcahy, Anne. "How I Did It: Xerox's Former CEO on Why Succession Shouldn't Be a Horse Race," *Harvard Business Review*, October 2010, *http://bit.ly/2n6xaBs*.

Nelson, Bob. *1001 Ways to Reward Employees*. New York: Workman Publishing Company, 2005.

"OSHA at 40." SHRM website, *http://bit.ly/2mXEE9i*.

"Our Mission, Management Principles and Values," CSC website, *http://bit.ly/2maTxGs*.

Patterson, Kerry, Joseph Grenny, Ron McMillian, and Al Switzler. *Crucial Conversations*. New York: McGraw Hill, 2002.

"Performance and Reporting: The DuPont Commitment." Dupont website, *http://bit.ly/2nA3Dh2.*.

Petroff, Alanna. "Branson: Take as Much Vacation as You Want!," *http://cnnmon.ie/1rnssdU.*

Pink, Daniel H. *Drive: The Surprising Truth About What Motivates Us*. New York: Riverhead Hardcover, a Penguin Group imprint, 2009.

Plumb, Tierney, "'Corp-U' Turn: Boardroom to Lecture Hall," *Washington Business Journal*, July 9, 2011, p. 18.

Portnoy, Jenna. "Saving Capitalism: A Restless Senator's New Obsession," *Washington Post*, October 10, 2016, *http://wapo.st/2mR6fas.*

Pulakos, Elaine D. *Performance Management*. Alexandria, Va.: The SHRM Foundation, 2004.

"Reorganized Labor." SHRM website, *http://bit.ly/2nA3nPd.*

Roberts, Bill. "Open Enrollment Tools Evolve," *HR Magazine*, July 2011.

Rothwell, William J. "Beyond Rules of Engagement: How Can Organization Leaders Build a Culture that Supports High Engagement." *A Dale Carnegie® White Paper*. Hauppauge, N.Y.: Dale Carnegie & Associates, Inc., 2007.

"Salary Budgets Increase Stalled at 3 Percent for Third Year in a Row," A Report by WorldatWork, August 2, 2016, *http://bit.ly/2nhPacv*

Schell, Michael S., and Charlene M. Solomon. *Managing Across Cultures: The Seven Keys to Doing Business with a Global Mindset*. New York: McGraw Hill, 2009.

Schulte, Brigid, "At Some Start-Ups, Fridays Are So Casual That it's Not Even a Workday," *Washington Post*, February, 6, 2015, *http://wapo.st/1AFQF4R.*

Share, Jacob. "150 Funniest Resume Mistakes, Bloopers and Blunders Ever," JobMob, *Laugh Out Loud Funny*, November 25, 2007, *http://bit.ly/2mXtBNs.* Accessed July 26, 2011.

Shea, Gordon. *The Mentoring Organization*. Menlo Park, Calif.: Crisp Publications, Inc., 2003.

Shepherd, Leah, "Getting Personal," *Workforce*, May 2010, p. 24.

Shipman, Claire, and Katty Kay. *Womenomics*. HarperCollins, 2009.

Sims, Doris. *The 30-Minute Guide to Talent and Succession Management: A Quick Reference Guide for Business Leaders*. Bloomington, Ind.: AuthorHouse, 2009.

Smith, W. Standon. *Decoding Generational Differences: Fact, Fiction...or Should We Just Get Back to Work?* New York: Deloitte LLP, 2008.

Thomas, Kenneth W., and Ralph H. Kilmann, "Thomas-Kilmann Conflict Mode Instrument." Ralph H. Kilmann website, *www.kilmann.com/conflict.html.*.

Thompson, Debra, and Bill Greif. *No More Rotten Eggs: A Dozen Steps to Grade-AA Talent Management*. New York: McGraw Hill, 2010.

"Trends in Workplace Flexibility," A Report by WorldatWork, *http://bit.ly/2mANCWr.*

Tulgan, Bruce, *Not Everyone Gets a Trophy: How to Manage Generation Y*. San Francisco, Calif.: Jossey-Bass, a Wiley imprint, 2009.

Tyler, Kathryn, "Global Ease." *HR Magazine*, May 2011.

———. "The Tethered Generation." *HR Magazine*, May 2007.

Ursiny, Tim. *The Coward's Guide to Conflict*. Naperville, Ill.: Sourcebooks, Inc., 2003.

Walker, James W. *Human Resources Strategy*. New York: McGraw Hill, 1992.

Watkins, Michael, Subject Advisor. *The Essentials of Negotiations*. Boston, Mass.: Harvard Business School Press, 2005, p. 65.

Welsh, Jack. *Jack: Straight From the Gut*. New York: Business Plus, a Grand Central Publishing imprint, 2001.

Zander, Rosamund Stone, and Benjamin Zander. *The Art of Possibility*. New York: Penguin Group, 2000.

55

Index

About the Authors

Barbara Mitchell

Barbara Mitchell, managing partner of The Mitchell Group, is a human resources and organization development consultant. Barbara served in senior human resources leadership positions with Marriott International and Human Genome Sciences, and co-founded The Millennium Group International, LLC in 1998.

Barbara's book *The Essential Workplace Conflict Handbook*, coauthored with Cornelia Gamlem, was published in September 2015 by Career Press. *The Essential Human Resources Handbook*, coauthored with Sharon Armstrong, was published in July 2008 by Career Press. She also contributed to *On Staffing—Advice and Perspective from HR Leaders* and *Cover Letters for Dummies*. She served on the Society of Human Resource Management's Special Expert Panel on Consulting and Outsourcing in recognition of her expertise and long service to the HR profession.

Barbara is a past president of the Employment Management Association, which was a professional emphasis group of the Society for Human Resource Management (SHRM). She is a past president of the Personnel and Industrial Relations Association (PIRA) of Los Angeles, the Leesburg/Greater Loudoun (VA) SHRM chapter, and WTPF, the Forum for HR Professionals.

Barbara is a graduate of North Park University (Chicago, Illinois) and has taken graduate-level classes at UCLA and the University of Denver. She is a frequent speaker on topics relating to recruitment, retention, generations at work, and many other topics, and has presented at many trade associations nationally. Barbara is a docent at the Smithsonian American Art Museum and a past board member of Habitat for Humanity Northern Virginia.

Cornelia Gamlem

Cornelia Gamlem, SPHR, is president and founder of the GEMS Group Ltd., a management consulting firm that helps a wide range of clients with issues related to HR initiatives, business effectiveness, and compliance. Prior to starting this practice, she worked for CSC, where she held senior HR positions and was responsible for managing policies, programs, and initiatives supporting best human resources and employment practices. Cornelia's book *The Essential Workplace Conflict Handbook*, also co-authored with Barbara Mitchell, was published in September 2015. In addition, she is co-author of a book about affirmative action: *Roadmap to Success: 5 Steps to Putting Action Into Your Affirmative Action Program*. Cornelia has also authored white papers and articles for industry publications.

An active volunteer, Cornelia served on a number of task forces with national employers' groups that influenced public policy and in several volunteer leadership positions for the Society of Human Resource Management (SHRM), including its National Board of Directors, its Global Forum Board of Directors, and its National Workplace Diversity Committee.

She has testified before the Equal Employment Opportunity Commission on three occasions and is often called upon for interviews. She has been quoted in the *Wall Street Journal, New York Times, Financial Times, Newsday, Boston Globe*, and *Fortune*, and she frequently speaks to business groups. A graduate of Marymount University, where she received a master's degree in human resource management, Cornelia is also certified as Senior Professional in Human Resources (SPHR). She has taught HR courses at a number of colleges and universities in the Washington, D.C. metropolitan area.

Stay Connected With Barbara and Cornelia

Visit our websites:
www.bigbookofhr.com
www.essentialworkplaceconflicthandbook.com

Read our weekly blog:
makingpeoplematter.blogspot.com

Follow us on Twitter:
@bigbookofhr
@gotworkconflict